DEMOCRATIC

EDUCATIONAL THEORY

HARPER'S SERIES ON TEACHING

Under the Editorship of

ERNEST E. BAYLES

Democratic

Educational Theory

ERNEST E. BAYLES

The University of Kansas

HARPER & BROTHERS · PUBLISHERS
NEW YORK

DEMOCRATIC EDUCATIONAL THEORY
Copyright © 1960 by Ernest E. Bayles
Printed in the United States of America
All rights in this book are reserved.
No part of the book may be used or reproduced
in any manner whatsoever without written permission except in the case of brief quotations
embodied in critical articles and reviews. For
information address Harper & Brothers
49 East 33rd Street, New York 16, N.Y.

B-K

Library of Congress catalog card number: 60-5727

CONTENTS

Preface   vii

1. Experiments with Reflective Teaching   1
2. How We Behave   34
3. Learning and Transfer   45
4. Idealism, Realism, and Pragmatism   63
5. Is Modern Science Inductive?   83
6. Existence, Causation, and Intelligence   93
7. Relativistic Value-Theory   103
8. The Meaning of Appreciation   120
9. Religion and Character Education   132
10. A Definition of Democracy   147
11. Democracy and Keeping School   166
12. Reflective Teaching   188
13. American Educational Purpose and Program   203
14. Appraisal of Pupil Progress   217
15. John Dewey and Progressivism   236
16. Present Status of Educational Theory in the United States   252

Index   261

PREFACE

THIS book represents an accumulation of more than thirty years of my thought on what ought to be the major tenets of a genuinely democratic educational program, one which is comprehensive and consistent and at the same time practical. To be comprehensive, it must take into account the psychological nature of learners and of learning as well as the nature of the social-political matrix in which education is to be conducted, and it must formulate a competent statement of educational purpose. To be consistent, all parts must be harmoniously related to one another, thereby making the overall treatment distinctly philosophical. To be practical, there must be clearly stated principles of what is to be taught and of how it is to be taught, of content and of procedure. Hence, the book is essentially educational philosophy but with clear and open treatment both of curriculum and of method.

Although the scientific-psychological-philosophical orientation of the book is admittedly and unapologetically relativistic, my purpose has not been to write a relativistic or pragmatic philosophy of education. Rather, my purpose has been to work out the logical consequences of our assumed national democratic commitment in terms of an educational program. I certainly do not consider democratic education to be the only kind possible. But, as long as our nation is democratically committed, it would seem that a thoroughly democratic educational program is, ideally, the only kind for us. That what we now have falls much short of such an ideal is not only admitted, but averred.

Long before the recent rash of undiscerning and irresponsible criticisms of American education, I was actively concerned about apparent shortcomings both in our theory and in our practice, and was pointing to what seemingly should be done about them. A glance at the dates of the reports described in the first chapter of this book will show that most of those studies were performed approximately twenty years ago. What is distressing about the much publicized criticisms of today is that they are almost wholly based on the premise that we have departed from time-proven ways and should *return* to them. As painstaking and enlightened investigation will show, we have not departed enough from time-honored ways. High-school teachers have adhered too closely to the ways their liberal-arts-college teachers have taught them, to enable them to provide their students much help for democratic living in an atomic age. To repeat a cliché, we cannot make progress by going backwards. We would not think of returning to 1920 automobile design to improve automotive travel today; yet to do so would be far less of a national catastrophe than to return to 1920 educational design or to any before that. To make progress, we must *know* the past so as to avoid repeating old errors. But it is highly improbable that we should *return* to the past.

This is my fourth textbook designed specifically to promote improvement in educational theory. However, since my concern has always been for a theory which is intensely practical, in the earlier books the practical has been predominant. The first two were high-school textbooks[1] which it was hoped would assist teachers in reflective teaching. The third[2] was a college text in professional education, about two-thirds of which was devoted to theory and the remainder to illustrative units chosen from a very wide variety of subject matters and of school levels and designed to exemplify the theory. This fourth book deals almost wholly with the theoretical, with only as much of exemplification as seems necessary to make the practical outworkings of theory clear. In consequence, whereas the third book may have impressed the profession generally as a general-methods text, the present one should show itself to be on educational theory or philosophy.

Another aspect of my concern with practicality is a conscious attempt to write simply, straightforwardly, and understandably. I have tried to avoid "pedagoguese" and pedanticism. Moreover, I have definitely rejected the tendency to try to bolster the argument by recourse to supportive statements or quotations from the writings of others. At the close of most chapters is a carefully chosen bibliography, made up of two kinds of selections: (1) ones which tend to support or supplement the ideas presented and (2) ones which present contrasting, oppositional, or alternative views. In this way I hope to give credit to writers who have been of major influence on my own thinking, as well as to give readers some suggestions as to where they might look for further pertinent discussions.

It will be noted that certain parts of this book have appeared previously as articles in various professional magazines. It should be recognized, however, that in each case the part was used only if and when it carried forward the argument of the book, saying seemingly what I still had to say and doing so satisfactorily. In no case, I believe, was the previous publication exactly reproduced in its entirety; changes were made as and when they appeared desirable. Actually, as these articles were originally written and published, it was with the expectation that they would eventually be gathered together to form the nucleus of a book which

---

[1] Ernest E. Bayles and R. Will Burnett, *Biology for Better Living,* New York: The Silver Burdett Company, 1942, 754 pp.; Ernest E. Bayles and Arthur L. Mills, *Basic Chemistry,* New York: Macmillan, 1947, 718 pp.

[2] Ernest E. Bayles, *The Theory and Practice of Teaching,* New York: Harper and Brothers, 1950, 354 pp.

would represent a systematic and sequential line of thought on public education in this country. Other articles were considered but were not included because they did not fit closely into the thought-line. Consequently, for those portions of the book which are essentially based upon previous publication, I wish to give the following credit and to express my thanks to the respective publishers for written permission to republish:

To *The Science Teacher,* for use of the article, "Is Modern Science Inductive?" Vol. 21, No. 3 (1954) pp. 1–5. This article represents virtually the whole of our Chapter 5.

To *Educational Theory,* for use of the article, "Existence, Causation, and Intelligence," Vol. 7, No. 1 (1957) pp. 38–44. This article, a bit expanded and with a few minor changes, represents our Chapter 6.

To *Progressive Education,* for use of the article, "The Meaning of Appreciation," Vol. 33, No. 3 (1956) pp. 65–70. This article, practically unchanged, is our Chapter 8.

To *The Phi Delta Kappan,* for use of the article, "A Relativistic Religion," Vol. xxxx, No. 1 (1958) pp. 33–36. The A-section of our Chapter 9 is the expanded form which was cut down for publication in the magazine.

To *Progressive Education,* for use of the article, "A Basic Issue in Democratic Education: Thought Guidance Without Thought Control," Vol. 34, No. 3 (1957) pp. 65–69. This article represents about half of our Chapter 11 and is incorporated in the middle part of the chapter.

To *The School and Society,* for use of the article, "Present Status of Educational Theory in the United States," Vol. 87, No. 2145 (1959) pp. 5–8. This article represents virtually the whole of our Chapter 16.

To the committee on publications of the School of Education of the University of Kansas, I wish to express thanks for publication of the following and for permission to use them in this book:

"Experiments with Reflective Teaching," *Kansas Studies in Education,* Vol. 6, No. 3 (April, 1956) 32 pp. This report is reproduced essentially in its entirety in our Chapter 1.

"Education for Democracy," *Kansas Studies in Education,* Vol. 8, No. 2 (May, 1958) 32 pp. Part I of this study is considerably expanded to form our Chapter 10, and Part II is combined with the fifth article listed above and somewhat expanded to form our Chapter 11. A bit of Part II also appears in our Chapter 12.

"Relativism II," *University of Kansas Bulletin of Education,* Vol. 7, No. 3 (1953) pp. 77–82. This article might be said to form the core of our Chapter 7, but has been almost doubled in length, with parts rewritten, so that this chapter is quite different from the original article.

It may seem somewhat of a stage gesture for a teacher to acknowledge indebtedness to his students for assistance in both enhancement and clarification of his own professional outlook, but in this case such ac-knowledgement is not an empty one. Through the years of working *with* students—undergraduate and graduate, in regular classes, in seminars, as practice teachers, on special projects, on masters' theses and doctors' dissertations, in private conferences and conversations, and in ordinary "bull sessions"—the give-and-take of open human communication has been a major source of my own education. To my sons now grown to manhood, to my wife now a grandmother, and to my lovely daughters-in-law I am similarly indebted.

To name teachers from whom I have learned much—Charles Hub-bard Judd, Frank N. Freeman, Franklin Bobbitt, Henry C. Morrison, George S. Counts, H. Gordon Hullfish, H. B. Alberty, Orville G. Brim—is more of an honor to me than to them. But the influence of two must be acknowledged over and above all others—Raymond Holder Wheeler by whom in 1928–1929 I was introduced to Gestalt-Organismic psychology, and Boyd H. Bode by whom in 1931–1932 I was instructed in pragmatic thought and was brought to comprehend the untapped significance of harmony or consistency of life outlook as an American educational ob-jective. To all of these I am deeply grateful.

ERNEST E. BAYLES

Lawrence, Kansas
October, 1959

DEMOCRATIC

EDUCATIONAL THEORY

CHAPTER 1

Experiments with
Reflective Teaching

IN the course of educational history, and particularly within the past half-century, there has been much experimentation with teaching procedures. But there seems to have been very little dealing with genuinely reflective teaching. The term, *reflective teaching,* is herein taken to mean conducting classes in such manner as to promote reflective studies of student problems; studies which achieve the solid substance of Dewey's Complete Act of Thought. Since the content of this chapter is not only educationally significant but also likely to be highly interesting and immediately practical to both experienced and inexperienced school personnel, especially teachers, it has been thought desirable to present it at the very beginning of our study. Many comments and observations ought to be found usable, even before discussion of the theoretical considerations or the rationale which support them.

It is the purpose of this chapter to present the outcomes of a number of experimental investigations involving serious and rather competent attempts to employ reflective teaching. It is not claimed that the employed procedures were, in all cases or even in any case, fully reflective. In fact, since all but the Trefz and Reader studies represented only the first time that the teacher had attempted to teach in this way, it would be an absurdity to assume that the procedures actually followed were undeviatingly reflective. As the Trefz and Reader studies will show, it appears that a teacher can gain competence in such teaching as she or he gains experience in it. The change-over is gradual rather than abrupt. Much is learned and achieved the first year, but each subsequent year provides an increment, and a teacher is likely to be doing a much more thorough job the sixth year than the first.

Nor is it claimed that the measurement of results was, in all cases or even in any case, all that it should have been. All investigations were conducted with classes and students assigned to the teachers in the course of normal enrollments. The tests used as measuring instruments were those available to teachers in small and medium-size school systems of Kansas and Missouri. All studies were, in whole or in part, performed in connection with master's theses, prepared at the University of Kansas under the writer's advisement. The studies are scattered over the period from 1940 to 1953, most of them in the early part.

As shown in Chapter 12, reflective teaching is the name that we give to classroom procedures which follow general reflective form. A question is raised whose answer is unknown, study follows looking toward an answer, and finding the answer marks the culmination or conclusion of the study. The teacher is not giving silver-platter handouts. She or he is acting essentially as chairman of a group of investigators who are following suitable methods in carrying out their investigations. The classes, on which the following reports are made, were all conducted, in as far as each teacher was able under the circumstances to do so, in this manner.

A STUDY IN AMERICAN GOVERNMENT

The Droll Study

In 1940, Helen Andres Droll[1] reported an experiment with a high school class in United States government composed of about 20 students from grades 11 and 12, located in a small town in western Kansas. The class was taught during a spring semester. Two intelligence examinations showed the students to be not far from average; the median IQ on one test was 101 and on the other 102. In fact, when compared with the national average of high school juniors and seniors which is reported by the U.S. Office of Education to be about 107, this class would appear to have been a bit below average.[2]

The class was somewhat unusual in that a large portion was of foreign-born parentage. German or French was spoken in most of

[1] Helen Andres Droll, "A Study of a Semester's Work in Government at the High School Level, Presented in Accordance with the Dewey-Bode Point of View," unpublished Master's thesis, University of Kansas, 1940.

[2] Grayson N. Kefauver, Victor H. Noll, and C. Elwood Drake, *The Horizontal Organization of Secondary Education*, Washington, D.C.: U.S. Office of Education, Bulletin No. 17, Monograph No. 2, 1932, p. 138.

the homes. This situation might have established somewhat of a language handicap whereas, on the other hand, because of European parental background it might have established an unusual interest in problems relating to citizenship. The intelligence examinations were given, not to members of this class by themselves, but in connection with the regular high school testing program, and the scores were obtained from the regular file.

Five units were covered during the semester. They were as follows:

Unit   I: Our dependence on others and how group life has grown in meaning and obligations.
Unit II: What is government?
Unit III: How the will of the people is expressed.
Unit IV: What is citizenship?
Unit V: It is said that the United States is in position to exert the moral leadership of the world today. How can we best exercise that moral leadership?

No single textbook was followed. Information was gained from whatever sources were available—a not very voluminous school library, free materials obtained from state and federal governmental and other sources, visits to local points of interest which were related to the studies, and talks by a few local citizens. Class meetings were discussional in nature, reflective in general form, and classroom examinations were given occasionally, both essay and objective types. The essay-type examination items tended to be interpretational whereas some of the objective-type items were distinctly factual.

Mrs. Droll was a mature, experienced teacher; attractive, likable, and intelligent.

Results of the study, in terms of student achievement, were presented in two forms: informal measures and scores on standardized achievement tests. Some of the informally measured results were (1) active work in the classroom and keen interest in local, state, and national affairs; (2) an increase of 85 percent in the number of periodicals checked from the school library by students in this class over the number checked out to the same group in the previous semester and a much higher group average in reading of periodicals than any other class in school; (3) much voluntary reporting in class of radio programs on governmental matters; (4) active interest in the control of local public utilities; (5) voluntary comments on news from the local papers; (6) 121 percent more historical books and biographies read by members of this class-group than by pupils of English classes who were not enrolled in this government course; (7) an increased number of editorials and stories on governmental affairs in the monthly issues of the high school newspaper, all except one contributed by members of this group; and (8) inclusion, among points of interest which members of this class wrote the Chamber of Commerce that they wished especially to visit during a school trip to a city some distance away, of the mint, the federal building, the civic center, the state building, and the city police court.

Two standardized achievement tests were administered during the next-to-last week of the semester: the *Nation-wide Every-pupil Scholarship Contest Examination* sponsored by the Kansas State Teachers College, Emporia, and the *Brown-Woody Civics Test*. Norms for the Emporia test were based on a total of 3277 papers of students who took the examination and, for the Brown-Woody, on 3508 papers.

Since the Emporia examination was used in connection with a nationwide scholarship contest, it may have been that many of the students who took it were selected from their schools as among those most likely to make high scores and were coached for such an examination. Hence, an entire class taking the examination would normally be expected to make a median score somewhat below the standard median for the examination. How much difference this might make we have no way of knowing, so it is not taken into account in any of the following reports on results of Emporia scholarship-contest examinations. The reader, however, may well keep this point in mind.

The results for this class on the Emporia Scholarship Examination were as follows: of Mrs. Droll's group, two scores were in the high 1 percent, five more were in the high 5 percent, two more were in the high 10 percent, two more were in the high 15 percent, and the entire class was in the high 35 percent of all the more than 3000 students tested. The median for this class was within the high 15 percent of all students tested. Moreover, there was no special preparation for this examination.

On the *Brown-Woody Civics Test,* of the 3508 test results tabulated, all but one of the members of Mrs. Droll's class had scores within the upper 35 percent and the low score was at the 49th percentile. The median for this class was within the high 10 percent.

It can perhaps reasonably be said that the Emporia Scholarship Examination tended to be mostly factual in nature, whereas the *Brown-Woody Civics Test* tended to examine more for understanding of the vocabulary of civics, for recall of the facts of civics, and for application of principles to practical situations.

It is evident, therefore, that this reflectively taught class seemed not only to achieve many of the outcomes which the class was primarily designed to achieve (as shown by the informal measures reported) but also achieved much better than normal expectation in terms of their ability to recall items of factual information and in their retention of understandings. This is the outcome anticipated by those who have carefully studied the nature of reflective teaching, and it seems to have been clearly demonstrated by this experiment.

It may be well at this point to anticipate a criticism which is likely to be raised with reference to this and the following studies. It may be objected that no control groups were used which would furnish a basis for comparison and thereby for judging experimental results. It is our considered opinion that such a criticism is ill-founded and will not stand careful scrutiny. In fact, the employed plan was adopted because of recognized faults in what was conventional in educational experimentation before and during the early 1940's.

The major control in each of these investigations was the group which furnished the standardizing base for each of the tests used. If the standardizing base was reported as representative of the nation as a whole, it was assumed that normal expectation for a normal class conventionally taught would be the standard norm for the test; sometimes the median, and sometimes percentile ranks. Class-median scores on intelligence examinations were compared with national medians for the grade-levels in question, such as eleventh or twelfth, in order to reach a conclusion as to whether a given class was approximately above, equal to, or below the standard group. Thus, a group with IQ's approximately equal to those of the standardizing group would normally be expected to make scores approximately equal to standard on the achievement tests, and variations above or below would be interpreted accordingly.

This plan may not be as neat numerically as certain other plans in use around 1940, but it was thought to be more valid. If, for example, a given teacher teaches both experimental and control classes simultaneously, he or she is bound to be partial to one method or the other. And such partiality is extremely likely to influence classroom results in favor of the favored method, regardless of its effectiveness otherwise. If, on the other hand, different teachers taught the different classes, then the differences in teacher capacity would be likely to outweigh the differences due solely to method. Whatever may have been our progress in methodology up to now, it seems that we still must face the brute fact that a good teacher may outteach a poor one regardless of the particular "method" he may use. This, however, does not deny that a good teacher with a superior method is practically sure to outstrip a teacher with equally good natural endowments but who employs an inferior method.

It may be suggested that recent developments in the statistical treatment of data might have made possible a better plan than the one used by these investigators. This we neither deny nor admit, for to do either seems unnecessary. In the first place, they were not readily available at the time all but one of these investigations were conducted and, second, the obtained differences were sufficiently large to make minutely refined measures unnecessary. A butcher does not need an extremely accurate chemical balance to weigh a pound of beef steak.

THREE STUDIES IN AMERICAN HISTORY

During 1941 and 1942, three experiments in the reflective teaching of a first semester of American history were reported.[3,4,5] The three teachers were experienced, as with Mrs. Droll were perhaps in their thirties, and also as with her had taught conventionally prior to the experimental semester which they report. All were able teachers and likable persons. The Avery study was with a class in a small high school, whereas the Johnston and Sailer studies were conducted in somewhat larger, though still small-town, high schools.

Prior to these studies, Lawson M. Roberts[6] had formulated plans

[3] Torry C. Avery, "An Experiment with Teaching a Class in American History According to the Pragmatic Theory," unpublished Master's thesis, University of Kansas, 1941.

[4] Laura C. Johnston, "An Experiment with the Problem-Raising and Problem-Solving Method of Teaching American History," unpublished Master's thesis, University of Kansas, 1941.

[5] Roy L. Sailer, "A Third Experiment in Teaching a Semester of American History in Accordance with the Roberts Plan," unpublished Master's thesis, University of Kansas, 1942.

[6] Lawson M. Roberts, "Ten Units in American History Formulated in Accordance with the Pragmatic Theory of Teaching," unpublished Master's thesis, University of Kansas, 1941.

for ten units in American history extending from discovery and colonization through the Civil War. The unit titles were as follows:

I. Exploration and the discovery of America
II. Colonization of America
III. The American Revolution
IV. Establishing a national government
V. Winning respect at home and abroad
VI. The Jacksonian period
VII. The Westward Movement
VIII. American society at mid-century
IX. Slavery and sectionalism
X. War for southern independence

All three reports, especially the one by Miss Johnston, describe in considerable detail the way the units actually developed in class. They also included suggestions as to how the various units might be improved. To give even a sketch of those class discussions is out of the question here. We can only say that it was almost amazing to see how closely Mr. Roberts' plan actually worked in class, even though there was no attempt toward strict following of those plans. In reflective teaching, it is necessary to follow a thought-line as it actually develops in a given classroom. The *study itself* needs to determine the line of study, and circumstances alter cases. Nevertheless, imaginative planning ahead of time can be considered a necessity, in which the planner persistently tries to think as students would think under the anticipated circumstances; and Mr. Roberts' anticipations turned out to be highly accurate and usable. Students took hold from the very beginning and participated with interest, even enthusiasm.

The Avery and Johnston classes were small, 10 or 11 students each. The Sailer class had about 20 students.

Since each investigator reported findings in a way somewhat different from the others, it will be necessary to take the reports one at a time. All three, however, in making comparisons with their own previous experiences with classes similar but taught in a more or less conventional manner, noted distinctly heightened interest; greatly increased voluntary use of library facilities and other reference sources outside of the textbook; increased interest in current national affairs; increasing participation, especially by the more reticent students, in classroom discussions; increasing tendencies to question statements made by fellow students or teacher or authors;

and other characteristics which reflective study is thought likely to promote.

The Avery Study

There were ten members of the class taught by Mr. Avery. His measure of mental ability was the *Army Group Examination Alpha,* given at the beginning of the experimental semester. Intelligence Quotients ranged from 110 to 74, with a median of 92. Since a report of the U.S. Office of Education indicated a median intelligence quotient of high school juniors and seniors of 108,[7] it appears that this class was of considerably less than average capacity. Whether this measurement was accurate is a distinct question in the mind of the present writer, but it seems probable that the class was below average, though possibly not as much as a median IQ of 92 would indicate.

Two tests were employed to measure achievement. The *Kansas American History Test,* published in 1938 by the Bureau of Educational Measurements, Kansas State Teachers College, Emporia, covered the period of American history included in this study. Form A was given at the beginning and Form B at the close. The median class-score at the beginning was equal to the 5th percentile standard test-score. The median class-score at the close of the period of study was equal to standard percentile 62. Form A was given on September 4 and Form B on the following January 21. On January 24, the *Emporia Every-Pupil Scholarship Contest Examination* was taken and the median score of the class was equal to the standard 75th percentile. Since both of these examinations represented largely the recall of facts in American history from colonization to the close of the Civil War, the evidence from these measurements is that, in this regard, achievement of this class was markedly above what could reasonably be expected of it. And the class evidently made great advancement during the period of study.

The Johnston Study

Miss Johnston used more measures of the standardized type than did Mr. Avery. Three tests of mental ability were administered: Army Alpha, Henmon-Nelson, and Terman Group. Army Alpha, given at the beginning of the experiment and representing the entire class of 11 students, gave a median of 103 and a mean of 108.

[7] Kefauver, *op. cit.*

The other two intelligence examinations had been given earlier in connection with the regular all-school testing program and included records of only 8 of the 11 class members. Omitted were two who were above the median and one who was below. The averages of those two examinations (Henmon-Nelson and Terman) gave a median of 105 and a mean of 106. Therefore, it seems reasonable to conclude that, in comparison with national standards, the class was about average.

Miss Johnston took 25 weeks, 7 weeks more than one semester, to complete the ten units. She had one achievement test which covered the entire time and represented the material covered. This was the *Kansas American History Test* (see above) with Form A given on September 11 and Form B on the following March 4. The median score of the class at the close of the study was equal to standard percentile 50. In other words, on this examination, the class after instruction apparently remembered as many facts in American history as would ordinarily be expected of it.

The *Columbia Research Bureau American History Test,* published in 1926, was also administered at beginning and end of the experiment. This test, however, covered the period from colonization until 1926. Besides testing the facts of history, this test also seemed to require a considerable amount of reasoning ability and discriminating judgment. However, 50 percent of the questions related to post-Civil War, a period not covered in the experiment. The median of the class rose from a standard percentile rank of 12 at the beginning to a percentile rank of 37 at the close. When this test was ordered, Miss Johnston did not realize that 50 percent of it covered material subsequent to what was to be included in the course. But she administered it anyway, and it should be noted that the class gained 22 percentile-points during the study and ended only 11 percentile-points below the standard median, presumably based on study of the entire course.

The *Emporia Every-Pupil Scholarship Examination* was given on January 8, two months before the close of the study. On that examination, the median score of this class was equal to the 72nd percentile of the 176 medians (presumably class medians) reported for the examination. In other words, the January median for this class was equal to or higher than the medians of 72 percent of all classes reported. A total of 4754 scores was reported by the 176 schools used for determining standard test-scores.

On April 8, another such examination was given for which standardization included 4457 scores from 148 different classes. On this examination the median for this class was equal to the 75th percentile of all medians. Thus, at both times Miss Johnston's class, having average capacity, ranked well above average in performance on examinations requiring primarily recall of factual information.

However, during the year prior to this experiment, Miss Johnston taught an American history class of eight students having a median IQ approximately five points higher than the experimental class. On the January examination the previous-year class achieved a median equal to the 75th percentile of all medians. Of the preceding class Miss Johnston says, "The method of teaching last year was based principally on the Morrison plan which stressed facts and included some drill. There was no drill in the remembering of facts in this experiment." It is evident that Miss Johnston did well, regardless of what method she was attempting to use.

Moreover, during January the experimental group took an annual current-affairs test published by the Searight Publications Bureau of Lincoln, Nebraska. Only two members of the experimental class made scores lower than the score indicated by the publisher as the average to be expected of such students. As Miss Johnston says, "This showing seemed to indicate that our class, although of average capacity, is better informed than average on current affairs."

Among Miss Johnston's informal observations regarding her experience with this experimental class is the following:

The problem-solving method of teaching is no panacea; it is no cure-all for the ills of teaching. Members of our group were more willing to hypothesize and, by research, to test out hypotheses and follow through to a conclusion. There was a tendency to do the guessing and let it go at that. This might be expected, since the method was new to the writer and to the pupils. There seemed to be an adequate realization of the problems and perhaps that is all one could expect from beginners. Pupils felt free to express their opinions and to challenge those of others. Discussions were lively and interesting. As was pointed out . . . the pupils raised many questions. For example, "Why didn't we include Lower California in the Mexican Cession?" and "Why did Spain allow only native Spaniards who were Catholics to enter her colonies?"

Not all pupils worked up to their several abilities; there were some who gave little and seemingly gained little. However, perfect correlation between ability and achievement may be too much to expect of any method.[8]

---

[8] Johnston, *op. cit.*, pp. 113–114.

Miss Johnston summarized her feelings about reflective teaching as follows:

1. It stimulates wider reading. Pupils read to find the solution to a problem rather than to meet a required assignment.
2. It arouses interest to determine the "why" of things and ideas, and leads the pupils to substantiate their conclusions and opinions.
3. It promotes the recognition of problem situations.
4. It provides opportunity for wholesome "give and take" in the discussion of controversial issues.
5. It seems to result in greater retention of factual information, even without coaching for such retention, than is ordinarily achieved.[9]

The Sailer Study

In the Sailer study, two measuring devices were used in addition to those employed in the Droll, Avery, and Johnston studies: (1) a class group in a nearby community was obtained to serve as a control; (2) a published examination, which represented an attempt to measure reflective thinking and was to a degree standardized, was administered to both experimental and control groups.

As we have indicated in each case, the method used by the three preceding investigators to obtain a "control" to serve as a basis for comparison is, first, to find how the median IQ of the experimental class compares with the national median IQ for students in grades 11 and 12 combined. This, as noted, was recorded by the U.S. Office of Education as about 108. Second, the class-achievement medians are compared with nation-wide norms for the examinations by indicating what percentile ranks on the national norm the median score (50th percentile) of the experimental class equals. Thus, when a class of average IQ makes a median achievement-score equal to a national 70th percentile, it is taken to have achieved considerably more than normal expectation.

In addition to such comparisons, Mr. Sailer used a class from a nearby community with which he was familiar and with whose teacher he was acquainted. Of course, Mr. Sailer also reported his own personal impressions, as had the others, and found himself quite in agreement with their observations.

Measurement of intelligence was obtained by use of the *Schrammel-Brannen Revision of Army Alpha, Form A.* The medians of both control and experimental groups were the same, 112, four points higher than what was taken to be the national median for grades

9 *Ibid.*, p. 115.

11 and 12 combined. Moreover, the 75th percentiles were nearly the same (122 experimental, 119 control). However, there was considerable difference in the 25th percentiles to the disadvantage of the experimental group (89 experimental, 102 control), there were 9 more students in the control than in the experimental group (29 control, 20 experimental). Thus, the Sailer class was about the size of the Droll class and almost twice the size of the Avery and Johnston classes. Moreover, due to difference in policy between the two schools on the age required for entering first grade, students in the experimental group averaged six months younger chronologically than those in the control group. Thus, it seems that, except for the control being a somewhat larger group, the two groups were approximately equal in capacity.

To test for factual knowledge, the *Emporia Every-Pupil Scholarship Contest Examination* was again used, and on January 28 was given to both groups. The standard test-percentiles were determined on the basis of 3987 individual scores reported from 633 different schools in 29 different states. For the experimental class, the national percentile-ratings of the individual students ranged from 2 to 99 with a 25th percentile of 15, a median of 55, and a 75th percentile of 92. For the control class, individual student-scores ranged in national percentile ranks from 2 to 85 with a 25th percentile of 16, a median of 38, and a 75th percentile of 50. Thus, on fact recall the experimental-class 75th percentile was 7 national percentile-points higher than the top score of the control class, the experimental median was 5 percentile-points higher than the control 75th percentile, and the two 25th percentile scores were about the same, even though the 25th percentile IQ of the experimental group was 13 points lower than that of the control group.

Comparing, as did Miss Johnston, the experimental-class median score with the class-median scores for the 144 schools reporting, the experimental-class median reached the 67th percentile for all class medians. The median score for the control class was equal to the 30th percentile of all class medians.

These results indicate that, on fact recall, Sailer's and Johnston's results are approximately the same—distinctly better than normal expectation even though no attention had been paid in either class to whether facts were remembered or not. Facts were obtained because they were needed in problem-solving and were so used, but that was all. If Mr. Avery's class was as low in capacity as his obtained IQ's indicated, his class made a remarkable showing.

Mr. Sailer also gave the *Every-Pupil Scholarship Contest Examination* on April 8, some time after the close of the formal experiment. The result for his experimental class was the same as to median (55 in both cases) as the January 28 examination but with a somewhat lower 75th percentile and a somewhat higher 25th percentile. Mr. Sailer suggests the possibility that the drop in the 75th percentile might have been caused by numerous absences from his class by top-ranking students who were drilling for the contest in the work of other classes. His own class was not drilled for the contest.

In order to obtain a standardized measure of reflective ability, Sailer found one instrument which seemed to be at least partially satisfactory—the *Cooperative Test of Social-Studies Abilities,* Experimental Form 1936, by J. Wayne Wrightstone. The test was divided into four parts with available norms based on the scores of 1250 students. Part I dealt with obtaining facts, Part II with organizing facts, Part III with interpreting facts, and Part IV with applying facts. The total score was found by adding together the four part-scores. The same form of the test was given twice, once at the beginning of the school year when the experiment was started and once near the close of the school year, some time after the close of the experiment. It was given to both experimental and control groups at about the same time. It was expected that a different form would be given the second time, but, since no second form was available, the first had to be repeated. However, during the entire intervening period nothing whatsoever was said in either class about the test or that it would be given again, so that the practice effect in favor of the second would probably not have been very large, if any. We merely mention this test to show that an attempt at such type of measurement was made. The very make-up of the test was such as to be rather unsatisfactory both to the investigator himself and to his advisor, the present writer. Those four factors may indeed be aspects or elements of reflective thought, but it seems hardly sound psychologically to assume that a true measure of reflective ability can be obtained by a summation of scores which purported to measure those four factors in separation from one another.

For what they are worth, however, the results of this test are given. At the beginning of the year, for some reason, the control group scored considerably higher than the experimental: for the control group, the 75th percentile was 155, the median 115, and the 25th percentile 90. For the experimental group, the 75th percentile was 156, the median 89, and the 25th percentile 60. Near the close of the year, for the control group the 75th percentile was the same, 155, the median was 7 points higher, 122, and the 25th percentile was 4 points lower, 86. For the experimental group near the close of the year, the 75th percentile was 19 points higher, 175, the median was 52 points higher, 141, and the 25th percentile was 20 points higher, 80. Thus, according to this measuring instrument, during the year the control group made little progress in reflective capacity while the experimental group was improving considerably. The announced norms for the test, based on 1250 cases and for the *close of the senior year,* were 75th percentile 162, median 141, and 25th percentile 119. Since it is not known what type of students composed the 1250 to whom Dr. Wrightstone administered his examination for standardization, we have no way of knowing or of surmising why the results for both classes participating in the study were no higher comparatively than they were.

Two Studies in Upper Elementary Grades

The Trefz Study

The foregoing studies dealt with classes in senior high school. The two remaining deal with upper elementary, the Trefz Study[10] with Grade VI and the Reader Study[11] with Grade V. Moreover, because in these grades a single teacher was in full-time charge of each class, the experiments cover all of the subjects studied by these pupils, for almost an entire school year at a time. And, in addition, two successive years of work are included in each report which comprised the master's thesis. Furthermore, the Trefz study can here be extended for four additional years (six years in all) due to informal reports made to the present writer by Mrs. Trefz at the close of each year. Thus, evidence is given as to whether a teacher may profit by experience in reflective teaching and secure better results a sec-

[10] Ida R. Trefz, "An Experimental Study of Teaching a Sixth-Grade Class for Seven Months Employing a Pragmatic Program," unpublished Master's thesis, University of Kansas, 1941.

[11] Edna C. L. Reader, "An Experimental Study of Reflective Teaching in a Fifth-Grade Classroom for a Two-Year Period," unpublished Master's thesis, University of Kansas, 1953.

ond, third, fourth, fifth, or sixth year than were secured on a first attempt. Both teachers had not previously attempted reflective teaching as such, and have more than once indicated that they had been largely unaware of it, other perhaps than the ordinary conviction that we ought to do what we can in helping children learn how to think.

In order to give the reader an idea of what led to Mrs. Trefz' study, we shall let her tell it.

The method used by the writer in teaching previous to this experiment was confined more to factual learning, the textbook method being used. Questions were asked and answers were given, with little discussion. Reports were made by class members and accepted by the others without agreement or disagreement. Maps were used for memorizing locations, not as sources of information for continual reference in solving problems. Rules were memorized; not formulated or "arrived at" by the pupils themselves. Particularized learnings [were] the major objective; not development of an enhanced ability to learn for one's self. School and life were not as closely related as they might have been, even though field trips were taken and community projects talked about.

Then, during the summer of 1939, through the study of teaching procedures and through reading books by Dewey, Bode, Kilpatrick, Wheeler, and others, ideas and words such as democracy, discussion, agreement, harmonization, enhancement, relationships, problem-solving, and reflective thinking began to take on new and different meanings. In the fall of 1939 the pragmatic program became the basis for our teaching procedures.

I had this same group the year before (1938–39), having been promoted from the fifth to the sixth grade with them. Unconsciously, in September, 1939, my teaching was changed to fit a somewhat higher level of mental capacity, because I changed my objective to reflection-level thinking. Before, it had been recollection and recognition (understanding) levels.[12]

It might also be noted here that, after Mrs. Trefz had taught this class in fifth grade, it came with her to sixth grade somewhat below the achievement-norm for beginning sixth grade. As a result, however, of her teaching this same class during sixth grade but reflectively rather than conventionally, the class finished the year above normal in achievement. This is a rather significant comparison because *the only factor which differed materially was the method of teaching. Both years it was the same class and the same teacher.* Moreover, when the teacher taught conventionally, she was convinced that that was the way to teach and had been teaching that

---

[12] Trefz, *op. cit.*, pp. 3–5.

way for a number of years. The altered teaching method came *after altered convictions* regarding teaching. Hence was avoided the difficulty which arises, when a teacher is simultaneously handling two different classes in two different ways, of his conviction that one way is better than the other and of his consequently favoring the preferred method. It is for this very reason that the present writer has advised experimenting teachers not to use classes taught by themselves as control groups.

Mrs. Trefz tells as follows of her first experimental year.

Group intelligence and achievement tests were given. In the 1939–40 class of thirty-six sixth graders, the I.Q.'s ranged from 69 to 143. The median was 97. There were twelve pupils whose I.Q. fell in the normal range (90–110), eleven were above normal (111 up), and thirteen were below normal (up to 89).

Results on the achievement tests taken in October seemed to indicate that teaching was still pitched at too low a level to challenge the better students because the thirteen pupils ranking below normal in intelligence were achieving more in proportion to their ability than those with the higher I.Q.'s. This conclusion was reached after reading an article by Bayles.[13] He says, "We believe that the interests of a class as a whole are best served when teaching is pitched above the median of the class, say at the level of the second quartile, and made sufficiently flexible to challenge the best pupils. If the more competent members of a class, usually the most influential in determining the general class attitude, are convinced that a class is worth while, the remainder usually follow along and gain considerable benefit from the instruction, whether they comprehend all that goes on or not. The writer's general impression of teaching today is that it is focused upon too low a level to present a wholesome challenge to pupils."

Hereafter teaching was pitched on a higher level. Class work was made more challenging for the brighter pupils, yet interesting to the duller ones.

In the spring of 1940, Form B of the achievement test, of which Form A had been used in the fall, indicated that those whose I.Q.'s lay in the range of normalcy (90–110) for their grade made an average of nine months advancement in the five months between tests, those whose I.Q.'s lay in the above normal group (111 up) made an average of seven months and a half advancement in the five, and those in the below normal group (up to 89) made an average of ten months advancement in the five.

Should the teaching have been pitched at a still higher level, or was the test a satisfactory criterion for judging the advancement of the higher group? We were bothered by this question. The test covered practically the same ma-

[13] Ernest E. Bayles, "The Relativity Principle as Applied to Teaching," *University of Kansas Bulletin of Education*, Vol. 4 (February, 1940), p. 10.

terial as Form A on which these higher pupils had made good scores at the beginning of the study. In order to have secured a complete picture of the gain of all groups, we felt that another test should have been given the superior group to test the depth of their gain.

The children of this class (1939–40) did come to know democracy as more than a form of government. They enjoyed attacking problems, searching for data, discarding irrelevant material, and then accepting solutions that were most in keeping with available data. Sensing that a degree of success had come with this experiment, yet feeling it an unfinished task, we decided to continue using the pragmatic program into 1940–41, profiting from the experience gained in 1939–40.[14]

The present writer can well remember Mrs. Trefz' concern with the relatively poor showing of her upper-IQ group in terms of progress during the period between tests. To have the high-capacity group registering only seven and a half months improvement in five while the low-capacity group registered ten months improvement was to her a shock. For, if IQ means capacity for rate of growth, then with equal treatment or opportunity a high-capacity group will surely register more advancement than will one with low capacity. When the opposite occurs, something must be holding back the high-capacity group. Mrs. Trefz finally decided that *her teaching was still not pitched on a level high enough to give the upper two-thirds of the class the challenge it needed.* Hence, during the second year, she sought to have her class delve more deeply and study more difficult problems than they did the preceding year. Space cannot be taken here to give descriptions of the studies as they were pursued by Mrs. Trefz' class in the second year of her experiment. She gives such descriptions in her thesis.

In presenting the test results for the second year of Mrs. Trefz' experiment, though not quoting exactly we shall follow very closely her own report. During the first year, 1939–1940, Forms A and B of the *Metropolitan Achievement Tests, Intermediate Battery, Complete (Revised)*, were used: Form A in the fall and Form B in the spring. In the second year, 1940–1941, Forms C and D were used, Form C in October and Form D the following April. The tests were given approximately seven calendar months apart. Intelligence quotients for the class, taken from school records, showed a high of 127, a low of 63, and a median of 105. Thirty pupils composed the class. As shown by the October achievement test, the class was then at

[14] Trefz, *op. cit.*, pp. 5–8.

grade-level—six years and one month (6.1)—as shown by the calibration chart for the test.

In April, almost 7 months later, the class median was found to be 5 *months above* grade-level. Therefore, since advancement of the class was 5 months more than the 7 which was normal, it is evident that median class-achievement showed *12 months improvement in 7*.

The largest gain made by any class member during the 7-months period was 15 months and by the student having the highest IQ, 127. Gains of 14 months were made by 4, having IQ's of 121, 108, 87, and 64, respectively, the latter being a repeater in the grade. Gains of 13 months were made by 2, with IQ's of 105 and 110. Twelve-months gain each were made by 11 students with IQ's ranging from 121 down to 85. Those having IQ's from 111 up made a mean gain of 11.6 months during the 7, those with IQ's from 90 to 110 made a mean gain of 12 months, and those with an IQ of 89 and below a mean gain of 10.3 months in 7. The mean gain of the entire class taken together was 11.3 months during the 7 months between tests.

It would seem, therefore, that *pitching the level of difficulty higher the second year than the first did accomplish the anticipated result—* the middle group outgained the low group by almost 2 months, whereas the preceding year the low group had gained 10 months while the middle group was making a gain of 9. Moreover, the upper group this year outgained the low group, although by only 1.3 months on the average, whereas during the first year its gain was only 7 months while the middle group was gaining 9 and the low group 10. However, the showing by the upper group was still unsatisfactory since its mean gain during the 7-months period was .4 month less than that of the middle group although it should seemingly have been perhaps at least 2 months more than that of the middle group.

Nevertheless, the overall showing of the class was indeed remarkable. This was a widely used test, well standardized, and calibrated in terms of 10-month years. That is to say, the median showing of the class—12 months improvement in 7—means that the class on the average improved 1.2 years during .7 year. In other words, the median gain of the class was about 72 percent more than normal expectation. And it is very clear that *the overall gain of the class was not at the expense of the low-capacity members,* for their mean gain was 47 percent more than normal expectation for *average*-capacity pupils.

It would seem that this showing by low-capacity class members deserves emphasis, due to common conviction and indeed frequent claim that reflective teaching (or teaching so as to make pupils think) may be fine for the best students in a class but it will work a hardship on average and poor students. Mrs. Trefz' experiments for both years clearly showed almost the opposite, that *lower-capacity students were profiting from reflective teaching more than were higher-capacity students.*

Thus, at the close of two years' experience with reflective teaching, this teacher was still wrestling with the question, "What must I do to enable my best students to achieve as nearly up to their capacities as my poorer students do?" In studying this problem, Mrs. Trefz analyzed improvements made on the various parts of the test—that is, in the various subjects which were covered—and found that at the beginning of the year the 1940–1941 class was below grade in both arithmetic and spelling. Regarding this analysis she had the following to say:

Because of the very low median on the fall tests in arithmetic and spelling, special effort was made to help the children do reflective thinking in these subjects. Many questions were asked both by the teacher and by the pupils. Searching of data for the best answers kept the children interested, alert, and wanting to learn. Why they were missing problems, and not spelling words correctly, became individual problems. Each pupil was encouraged to find his trouble. Often the class helped him, and then, sometimes, the pupil had to have the teacher's help to straighten him out. This was often done in a supervised study period, the period being provided, not at fixed times, but when a "felt need" seemed to indicate it. The children enjoyed the supervised work period, and often asked questions on what had been bothering them. Many times during the class recitation periods the children recognized their need for more problems in the different fundamentals and asked for drill in these.

In spelling, visualizing the word, pronouncing it correctly, being aware of the syllables, noticing silent letters, and spelling orally, helped the children feel an answer to the question: "How does the word *have* to be spelled?" They enjoyed a baseball game of spelling very much, the game being played like regular baseball, using words for balls.

Indeed, it was gratifying to discover the results as indicated by the spring achievement test in these two subjects especially. The median for the class in average arithmetic went from seven months below grade to four months above grade, indicating, in all, eighteen months gain in seven months time—the seven months below grade, the seven months interim (between tests) and the four months above grade. In spelling there was a like result, from six months below grade to three months above grade, sixteen months gain in all.[15]

Mrs. Trefz' analysis led her also to make the following comments regarding the social-studies aspect of the year's showing.

In the sixth grade we have social studies instead of history and geography, and even though the class was most interesting, and social studies perhaps the best adapted of all the subjects for reflective thinking, the tests in geography and history did not cover social studies subject matter. Because of the nature of the tests, being of the multiple choice type of objective tests, they required mostly recognition-level thinking (understanding) and not reflection-level thinking. As a result, we believe that the outcomes of some of our very best work are not reflected in our test results at all. We believe that if our test battery had included one in the social studies proper, the class would have shown high level achievement in that test.

Throughout the year there have been unmistakable indications of an increased ability to think straight. The members of the class see their problems more quickly, and are better able to use the facts they possess in arriving at correct generalizations.[16]

Following are the conclusions of this experimenter at the close of two years' experience with reflective teaching.

We have conducted classes the last nine months, using to the best of our knowledge pragmatic teaching, which seeks to promote reflection-level studies of ideas in contrast or conflict, looking toward development of enhanced and more harmonious outlooks on life.

1. We found it to be very interesting both to pupils and teacher. The children enjoyed the privilege of discussion. The teacher needed to keep up with the affairs of the day, to be able to contribute her share in discussions.

2. We found changed attitudes. The class became more cooperative. The children were led into respecting the rights of others, not only in the room, but also on the playground and at home.

3. We found enhanced and more harmonious outlooks on life. The rendition of the play "I'm an American" revealed this enhanced outlook. Through the study of the European countries and contrasting them with America, the children realized what it meant to be an American. Because of this realization very little coaching was necessary in putting on this play successfully. The children's art project taught them that things are neither good nor bad in and of themselves, but in the relationships in which they are seen.

[15] *Ibid.*, pp. 61–62.
[16] *Ibid.*, pp. 62–63.

The study of budgeting both time and money was shown as carrying over into the home by reports of parents who remarked about instances of planning and budgeting at home.

4. We found improvement in self-reliant, reflective thinking. Radio news of the day were sometimes discarded as propaganda and reasons given why they were evaluating them as they listened, and the next day shared what they thought was worth while.

5. We found marked improvement in subject matter knowledge. In 7 months time the class made 18 months progress in arithmetic, 16 months progress in spelling and an average of 11.3 months progress in all subjects.

6. *We found that pitching teaching on an upper level of class ability increased the achievement of all groups; low as well as middle and high capacity.* In 7 months, the ten pupils with the highest I.Q.'s in the class (112–127) made an average of 11.6 months improvement, and the ten pupils with the lowest I.Q.'s (63–100) made an average of 10 months improvement. Moreover, the higher the level of ability aimed at in the teaching, the higher the correlation between ability and achievement on the part of all groups; high, middle, and low.[17]

Mrs. Trefz' formal report, which represented her master's thesis, was made in 1941 after two years of experience in reflective teaching. But her interest was aroused and she continued her measurement program for four more years, each year using one form of a test-battery in the fall and a different form in the spring, six or seven calendar months later. In some years the Stanford test was used and in others the Metropolitan. Each year she would send to the present writer an informal, though careful and accurate, report of her findings.

In her *third year,* 1941–1942, the tests were given in October and March, 6 months apart. The median grade-placement in October was 5.8, or the eighth month of the fifth grade, which was at that time 3 months below the grade-standard of 6.1. The results of the March test showed median grade-placement of 7.8, or 11 months above the standard grade-placement of 6.7. This year her class was made up of 25 pupils, and *its gain was more than 15 months in median grade-placement during a 6-month teaching period.*

Average (presumably mean) gains in grade-placement made by each IQ group for the six-months period between tests were as follows:

Above normal IQ (111 up)	17 months
Normal IQ (90–110)	18 months
Below normal IQ (up to 89)	9 months

[17] *Ibid.,* pp. 66–68. Italics added.

Thus we note that, in her third year of reflective teaching, this teacher—a mature and experienced teacher at the outset—made a large gain over her second year, an average gain of three times normal expectation or 18 months' improvement in 6. During this third year her below-normal group continued to do approximately as well as the first two years but her middle and upper groups did much better than before. Yet her top-capacity group still fell short of her middle-capacity group regarding gain during the period.

During the fourth and fifth years, results continued on this remarkably high level, even showing some gains. Mrs. Trefz' final report to the writer was for the year 1945–1946, her sixth year of reflective teaching. In this case the tests were given about 6 months apart and the gains were as follows:

Above normal IQ, average gain	21 months
Normal IQ (90–110), average gain	19 months
Below normal IQ, average gain	14 months

This was with a class of 25 pupils. The class started with a median of 2 months below standard grade-placement and ended with a median of 11 months above standard grade-placement. It is evident that this year the objective of getting students to achieve approximately in accordance with their several capacities was accomplished. The average of the top-capacity group was 2 months higher than that of the mid-capacity group and its average in turn was 5 months above that of the low-capacity group.

Thus, it is seen that a teacher, even though mature and experienced at the outset, can, by getting hold of a fruitful idea or plan, greatly improve the achievements of her pupils as measured by available standardized tests, and can continue steadily to improve those results over a period of at least six years. This is indeed a splendid record of achievement and it is evident that this teacher is deserving of highest commendation for her efforts. The question, of course, arises as to whether others could do the same. The findings of the Droll, Avery, Johnston, and Sailer experiments appear to give an affirmative answer, although for only one year.

The Reader Study

Miss Reader was a mature and personable young woman, younger than Mrs. Trefz, teaching fifth grade in a midwestern town in the 5000–15,000 population group. This was a two-year study, performed during 1951–1952 and 1952–1953.

As with Mrs. Trefz, *Miss Reader had to follow essentially the course of study required in her school system. Modifications could be effected only within that general framework.* As she says, "The units of reflective thinking have been worked out following the interests of the pupils, guided by the teacher so that required material in the course of study would be covered."[18] Later she enlarges,

The course of study follows fairly closely the basic textbooks which are provided for each child. There was a definite shortage of supplementary and reference material, but some was provided by the school during the year and the County Librarian was generous with library books, checking out twenty-five or thirty at a time for use over two-weeks periods or longer if needed.

The children were accustomed to the traditional type of teaching and had learned, as most children do, to take textbook and teacher's word as final. An effort was made to lead them into thinking their own way through the questions they normally raise, and to bring to light incompatibilities in their outlooks. It was rather hard to do this, for many children seldom expressed their own ideas in the classroom for fear of being laughed at or thought impertinent, or just from force of habit. But, after the teacher had said several times, I'm not sure, let's find out, they began to feel that perhaps after all their ideas were worth expressing.

The writer had, previous to this study, been using broad social units for two or more years so decided to continue this method, *adding to it reflective teaching.* At first the children did not notice much change and a casual observer who might have stepped into the classroom would not have been likely to notice much difference. The subject matter was related directly to everyday experiences outside of the classroom so that it would have meaning to the pupils. Then, as they followed the trend of thought from the familiar to the unfamiliar, questions were asked about things outside the realm of their knowledge, and incompatibilities in outlook were brought out. At first this only astonished the pupils for, when they could not find an immediate answer, they turned to the teacher and said, "What *is* the answer?" When they were not told but were challenged to find their own answers, their next question was, What shall we do now?

But they were instantly alert and eager to meet the situation. Even the slower pupils, who were accustomed to sitting quietly with their minds on something else until the correct answer was given by better students, looked up in surprise at this turn of events. If the challenge or conflict had been planned ahead of time by the teacher—and most of the first ones were—material was made available in the classroom so that each child could find information on the subject under discussion, at his own reading level.[19]

[18] Reader, *op. cit.,* p. 7.
[19] *Ibid.,* pp. 32–33.

Earlier Miss Reader says, "Of course, in most instances the teacher knows what the answer will be, since she has seen the data tested many times before. But the children should be permitted, within suitable or reasonable limits, to find the answers for themselves. Thus they will learn not to accept just any theory that is advanced, but will insist that it be tested. And they will gain a feeling of confidence in their ability to find answers for themselves."[20] Miss Reader has this further to say,

The incompatibilities in the pupils' outlooks which were brought out in the daily lessons led far from the textbooks, although such were still used for reference work. They were, in fact, the best reference materials available and it was easy for the teacher and pupils alike to slip back into the habit of accepting statements in these books as correct and final, without challenge. But, by constant questioning, the habit was formed of checking to see whether the children had beliefs or opinions differing from those stated in the text, then checking other material for additional data. The children also learned to form hypotheses or, as they said, to guess at the answer, then defend such hypotheses or guesses until proof was found that they were not tenable. Of course, at first the guesses were inaccurate and many times unreasonable. But, as the habit of testing these opinions grew, the youngsters found that, if in the first place they considered the problem from all the angles which they could see, their guesses were more nearly correct.

Reflective thinking *had* to be used when the data on hand were under consideration. Memory alone could not help a pupil decide which of the hypotheses he had formed was most in harmony with the data. Not only did the children face problems, they also gained insights into how to work out solutions for themselves.[21]

The 1951–1952 class had an enrollment of 34 pupils, an IQ range of from 75 to 131, and a median IQ of 102. The mean IQ was 98. The 1952–1953 class was composed of 34 pupils with an IQ range of from 81 to 141 and a median of 106. The mean also was 106. Both years the achievement test used was *Metropolitan Achievement Test, Intermediate Battery*, with Form S given in October each year and Form R given the following April. IQ's were taken from the permanent record cards of the students and were determined in the course of the regular testing program of the school.

For the first year of the experiment (1951–1952), the October

20 *Ibid.*, pp. 13–14.
21 *Ibid.*, pp. 35–36.

achievement test showed the class to be a little below standard grade-placement—4.8 instead of 5.1. Both the median and the mean for the class were 4.8.

When the second form of the test was given 7 months later, the mean grade-placement was 6.3 as compared with the standard at that time of 5.8, or 5 months above grade-standard. The median again corresponded to the mean. Thus, *in the 7-months period between tests, the pupils had gained 15 months in grade-placement as compared with standard expectation of 7 months*. Since, as explained before, grade-placement on this test is computed on the basis of a 10-month year, this gain is a bit more than *twice normal expectancy*.

During this year the high-capacity group (IQ's above 110) gained an average of 19 months during the 7 months between tests; the mid-capacity group (IQ's between 90 and 110) made an average improvement of 12 months in 7.

It is evident that, even *during her first year of reflective teaching, Miss Reader's class not only greatly exceeded normal expectation but also made gains which correlated highly with pupil capacities,* the high group averaging 4 months more than the middle, and the middle averaging 3 months more than the low. Miss Reader had read of Mrs. Trefz' experiences.

The 1952–1953 class was evidently an unusually capable one. In October when standard grade-placement was 5.1, this class made a mean grade-placement of 5.5 and a median of 5.8. The median grade-placement was 10 months, or one year, higher than the median grade-placement of the previous class. Only in arithmetic and spelling was this class below grade-placement during the second month of the experimental year.

When the second form of the test was given 7 months later, late in April, the class achieved a mean grade-placement of 7.6 and a median of 7.9. At that time standard grade-placement was, of course, 5.8. Thus, using either mean or median grade-placement in comparing October and April tests, this class made an *average gain of 21 months during the 7-month period between tests*. This is a gain of *three times normal expectancy*. In this case, the high-capacity group made an average gain of 23 months in 7, the mid-capacity group an average of 19 months in 7, and the low-capacity group an average of *17 months improvement in 7*.

Test results for achievement gains shown by pupils during the 7-month period for the two years of the Reader experiment are summarized as follows:

	In 1951–1952	In 1952–1953
Mean class gain	15 months	21 months
Median class gain	15 months	21 months
High-capacity group mean gain	19 months	23 months
Middle-capacity group mean gain	15 months	19 months
Low-capacity group mean gain	12 months	17 months

The *Metropolitan Achievement Test, Intermediate Battery,* was used both years. Form S was given early in October and Form R late the following April.

I cannot refrain from speaking further of what this second class did. In the first place, it *might* be thought that a class which started above grade-expectation would hardly be expected to make as much improvement with altered teaching as one which started below grade-expectation. This is a feeling rather commonly held even though careful thought shows it to be theoretically fallacious; with equal treatment a faster group should progressively widen a gap between it and a slower group. This class, although beginning the experimental year a full year in advance of the first class, outstripped the average gains of the first-year class by six months. Looking at it another way, *the class, although starting approximately a half-year above grade-placement, made a gain during the seven months between tests of 300 percent normal expectancy.*

It should also be noted, and emphasized, that *the mean grade-placement of 7.6 for this class in April was a very conservative rating* since many of the individual grade-placements had to be below the scores actually made by the pupils. The reason for this is that the highest grade-placement given on the conversion scale for the test was 9.0, whereas test scores could be and were made which were higher than a grade-placement of 9.0. Of the 34 test scores made on the science part of the test, 17 could not be charted at their actual value because they had a grade-placement higher than 9.0. In addition, there were 16 scores in geography, 13 in history, 10 in literature, 8 in English, 2 in arithmetic-problems, 5 in vocabulary, and 10 in reading which ran off the top of the chart and had to be computed as only 9.0 when they actually were higher—81 in all. How much higher than 7.6 the class mean would have been if the grade-placement chart had been calibrated above 9.0 is a matter for conjecture.

However, it should be noted that the final median of 7.9 was doubtless closer to the true central tendency of the class than was the mean of 7.6 because, as statisticians understand, of the tendency of atypical scores at the extremes of the range to influence a median much less than they do a mean.

Miss Reader terminates her report of test results with the following interesting item:

> The children in the class the first year of the experiment, 1951–1952, were given an achievement test at the beginning of the next school year, 1952–1953, when they were in the sixth grade with a different teacher. The Stanford Achievement Test, Intermediate Battery—Complete, Form G, was both given and checked by the elementary supervisor. The subject-matter fields of this test were similar to those of the Metropolitan Achievement Tests which had been used for fifth-grade testing. However, both the tests and the conditions for the test were different from those of the previous year.
>
> The results of the Stanford Achievement Test showed that the median grade-placement for the class was 6.1. Since the class median grade-placement of the Metropolitan Achievement Test given the preceding April was 6.3, this was a difference of two months on different kinds of tests, one given before and one after the summer vacation. Compared with the median grade-placement at the beginning of the fifth-grade year, the children still had a median gain of thirteen months. And, compared to the average grade-placement of all the schools in the city, they were five months above the system average.
>
> This appears to indicate that *knowledge gained by reflective teaching is not easily forgotten and is applicable to different kinds of tests.*[22]

It would indeed be interesting, and profitable as well, to know what happens to youngsters after an experience of this kind when they return again to conventional teaching. Regarding this question we have no data, although Mrs. Trefz once reported to the writer that a teacher who had her pupils in a following grade spoke to her of the rather unusual interest and capacities of the pupils. Moreover, during the summer session of 1959, a fellow teacher of Mrs. Trefz volunteered to the present writer the comment that she had noticed unusual interest and capacity on the part of pupils who had previously been taught by Mrs. Trefz. The real question is, of course, not what youngsters would do when returning to conventional teaching, but what might reasonably be expected from pupils who had had teaching of this kind during their entire public school and even college experience.

[22] *Ibid.,* pp. 99–101. Italics added.

In completing our report on Miss Reader's experiment, I should let her speak for herself. Following is her entire chapter entitled, Summary and Conclusions.

There are two steps in reflective teaching, problem-raising and problem-solving. The important object of the whole program is to challenge the children with an I-don't-know situation so they want to find the answer, then help them realize that they must consider all relevant data they can find before they decide which answer is correct. The children are led to question and compare, instead of just memorize facts which the teacher or the textbook presents to them.

It is not an easy way to teach as far as the expenditure of energy is concerned. It is far less work to make page-by-page assignments for the children to read and to accept without question. But the results of teaching reflectively are so much more satisfying that, because of this satisfaction, it might in the end be considered the easier method. To see children develop the ability to think through a problem, to see their interest and determination and their looks of satisfaction when they have met the challenge, is worth more to a teacher than the extra effort put forth in making and carrying out plans to give them the challenge.

During the two years of this experiment, in a fifth-grade classroom, the results have been most satisfying. In the first place, during a seven-months period between tests, the median gain in achievement—fifteen months the first year, or two times normal expectancy—would be enough to merit continuation of this type of teaching. But even more important is the all-round development of the children. No grade cards are given in this school system, but parent-teacher conferences are held. Many parents voiced the opinion, I don't know just what you are doing, but my child really likes school this year. And he seems to be learning, doesn't he? Usually this question was asked because there is still a tendency on the part of the public to doubt whether children can learn quite as much when other than traditional methods of teaching are used. When given a brief explanation of teaching methods in use and of consideration given to development of the whole child, then given actual proof of the gains their children were making, the parents were more than satisfied.

As far as the children themselves were concerned, they improved in their ability to think clearly, and enjoyed the work. School no longer seemed to be an isolated portion of a day, for home experiences were used at school and school experiences were used at home. The children had come to realize that everyone has a right to his own opinions; that no answer should be scoffed at for it might prove, when tested, to be the correct one. They learned that there is a reason for doing most things as we do them, and that those reasons can be found if we shall but search for them. Some pupils accepted the challenge of reflective teaching better than others, but even those who did not always respond gained in many ways.

The question might be asked, Was drill or practice ever necessary on fundamental combinations in arithmetic? Only after the pupils realized the need for practice was it introduced. They were never given drill just to learn a certain combination or process. But this type of teaching helped a child to realize his weakness. One child aptly remarked, I knew how to work that problem the same as the others did, but I just missed my multiplication. Boy, I'm sure going to learn that tonight. There was no need for the teacher to require drill.

The role of the teacher as a guide was a pleasant one. Sometimes the problem became so large that the children became discouraged rather than challenged. It was then that the teacher needed to help make the problem more simple by advancing theories which would lead toward solution and start the children thinking along profitable lines. She worked only as a group leader, so was never afraid of losing the respect of the children by admitting that she did not know. She was just another person and had a right to make a mistake once in a while.

There were very few disciplinary problems in the room either year, and certainly *no* serious problems. Of course, the children were normally cooperative and, had traditional methods been used, there would probably not have been many problems. However, in several cases it is quite certain that the challenges given the pupils changed their attitudes toward school and perhaps also effected better adjustment in their social life in school.

The interest, sparkle, and enthusiasm which could be seen on the faces of the children as they started each school day and attacked new problems; the acceptance of each child as an important member of the group; the growing confidence in ability to meet new situations successfully both in school and out of school; the improved ability to make right guesses after considering a problem; and the actual gain in achievement in subject-matter fields; all combine to provide evidence that the reflective method of teaching is far superior to traditional methods. Moreover, it would seem to be the way to achieve democracy in the school room.[23]

GENERAL COMMENT

In this survey six experiments in reflective teaching are reported. All of the experiments were conducted in connection with master's theses at the University of Kansas under the advisorship of the present writer. The first four dealt with social-studies classes in high school, grades 11 and 12, the fifth with sixth-grade classes, and the sixth with classes in fifth grade.

[23] *Ibid.*, pp. 102–105.

The major question raised in each case was how well pupils do in school work when taught reflectively as compared with achievement in classes taught conventionally. Reflective teaching is described and illustrated as that which starts with a problem—an "I-don't-know" situation or one in which the class members are faced with a question which they cannot answer, yet would like to answer. Hence, *problem-raising* is the first step.

Problem-solving then involves, first, formulation of possible solutions by the students; second, logical deductions as to what practical consequences the various proposed solutions imply; and third, testing the various proposals by determining which, if any, is successful in deducing correctly (1) data which already are known and (2) data which are not already known but have to be discovered by search, or produced by experimentation. Thus, reflective study begins with a question and, after study, ends with an answer to the question. Facts are gathered in profusion but not for the purpose of memorization and later recall; they are to be used only in solving problems. Whether they are remembered is a matter of no immediate concern for a teacher whose major concern is promoting reflective ability. *In none of the foregoing experiments did the teacher concern himself or the class with the recall of factual information.* Few, if any, fact-recall examinations were given during the experimental teaching.

An experimental question of each and all investigators was, however, "How well do the members of classes taught in this manner compare with those taught conventionally with regard to what is covered in conventional, standardized examinations?" Analysis of such examinations shows that they test predominantly for fact recall, together with some testing for understanding of principles. The results of the formal tests reported in this chapter answer, for the most, these questions only. In other words, they tell whether the members of classes taught reflectively recall facts and retain the ability to use ideas or principles as well as, better than, or not as well as members of classes taught conventionally.

As far as these six experimental studies supply an answer to this question, the answer is unqualifiedly that *students taught reflectively do better—a great deal better—than students who are taught conventionally,* even when, as is doubtless shown in all cases wherein the Emporia Scholarship Examinations were used, conventionally taught students are given considerable coaching directly focused upon the examinations.

Statistical devices to show the significances of obtained differences have been quite unnecessary in these reports because the sizes of the differences have been so large as to make their significance obvious.

A second point, evidenced mostly by informal yet careful observations, was that objectives particularly sought in reflective teaching gave reasonably dependable evidence that considerable progress had been made; that students actually made distinct and more than normal progress in achieving the kind of self-reliance in the face of difficulties which reflective teaching would be expected to engender. If it is suggested that these measures were "purely subjective," we would ask a reader to examine the basis for each such conclusion, noting the actual observations that were made and the care which the observer used in stating what conclusions he reached in light of the observations which he made.

A third major point to be noted is the one, indicated by the Trefz and Reader studies (particularly the Trefz study), that *even an experienced teacher does not do as well during the first year of reflective teaching as, with reasonable effort, she or he can expect to do in subsequent years.* Mrs. Trefz' classes showed *steady achievement-gain over a period of six years* and Miss Reader's second class made considerably more gain during the experimental period than the first one, even though the second class came to her one full year in grade-placement higher than the first class. It is reasonable, therefore, to expect that the first four teachers reported herein would also have been able to show greater gains by their classes after they had been teaching reflectively for two or three years.

A fourth point to be noted, although not emphasized previously in this chapter or the reports on which it is based, is that *many benefits of reflective teaching may be achieved within the framework of courses and of school organization already in existence.* No individual teacher has to upset a given school or its curriculum in any way, yet he can greatly improve his own teaching. Doubtless it would help to have other teachers doing the same because of the enhanced effectiveness of coöperative endeavor. But it should be remembered that in each of the foregoing investigations a single teacher was working within the conventional framework of subject-matter and school organization and was working by himself. This fact might be remembered when one reads of the results obtained through many of the curricular innovations which have of late become popular in certain quarters and have been widely heralded as modernization of the curriculum.

Finally, as to whether a teacher can stay in a community after conducting classes in such way as to promote reflective thinking on problems which are challenging to their class members—problems which frequently represent matters distinctly controversial in the community—the answer with reference to Mrs. Trefz and Miss Reader is that one is still teaching (as this is written) where she was during the years reported herein and the other has long since moved voluntarily to a much better position, where she has been considered an outstanding teacher from the very beginning. As to the other four, the writer knows of all four. During the experimental year they experienced no difficulty in the communities where they taught, and later moved by their own choice to better positions. And it is to be expected that *genuinely reflective, democratic teaching tends not to stir up a community even though controversial matters are considered* because all conclusions and convictions reached by class members are those which the studies indicate are necessary; not those which a teacher brings to a class and proceeds to indoctrinate, whether in light of evidence which is favorable or unfavorable. I once had one of my students—a social-studies teacher, also superintendent, in a very small town in rural western Kansas—say to me, "Teaching reflectively, I don't need to have the slightest hesitation in having students out here study anything that they ought to study; even labor unions." The point is that, in this nation, teachers who understand how to teach democratically and do so in a competent way are likely to have *less* trouble with a community than other teachers and will probably be able to stay in their jobs as long as they wish to do so.

This is not to say, however, that reflective teaching—or any other kind, for that matter—will of itself be guarantee for holding a job. Ill-considered and thoughtless actions, exaggerated claims or much discussion of what one is doing or attempting to do, exhibitionism or rambunctiousness, unnecessary interference with the rest of the school, failure to maintain "discipline," going out of one's way to be argumentative, boasting about better than ordinary results, and other breaches of what is ordinarily thought of as good taste may well promote situations which quickly become intolerable. But to go one's way, quietly and ably and in keeping with democratic procedure, will go far toward enabling one to choose for himself whether and when he will go to another position.

CHAPTER 2

How We Behave

SINCE educational theory should seemingly focus upon the processes of teaching and of learning, and since learning is an aspect of behavior in general, it would seem advisable to proceed at once to the question of how we behave. Human behavior is, of course, one of those matters which we all know about, yet what is supposedly known by everyone very frequently has a way of being not very well known by anyone. It may well be that this is true of human behavior; true enough, at least, that we may be justified in making explicit what we think we know about it. After dealing with behavior as a whole, we can then turn to the question of learning.

What assumptions ought to be made about human behavior? In other words, what interpretation should be adopted? This depends, of course, on what we are wanting help in doing—and that is to get people educated. We want to handle learning situations in ways which will render them highly fruitful, and to do this requires knowledge of the probable outcomes of adopted procedures. This means having a pretty good idea ahead of time of "what will happen if . . ."; in other words, *anticipatory accuracy,* the test to be applied to any directive if we wish to determine whether it be a true one.

How must we view or interpret human behavior if we are to be as accurate as possible, at a given time and place, in predicting what course it will follow? You will note that we do not ask for absolute accuracy; we do not consider that possible, either now or in the foreseeable future. We ask only for a principle which will enable us to win most frequently or consistently when placing bets against those who base their predictions on other, alternative principles.

In order to derive such a principle, we should perhaps first consider what factors it would require us to take into account. When this question is raised in class, I ordinarily try to bring it thoroughly down to earth by singling out a class member toward the front of the room—someone, of course, who can "take it"—and supposing that we are laying a bet as to what he will do at the time which normally marks the close of the period. The question is not what the prediction actually will be, but what factors must be taken into account in reaching the prediction. This makes it kind of a game and promotes enthusiastic participation by most of those present, but it also has a quality of immediacy which promotes active and aggressive thought.

At first, only stilted "pedagoguese" results; for instance, that we must know his "normal personality." This is counteracted by stipulating the use of words having no more than four syllables, preferably not more than three. A variety of proposals is forthcoming, among the first being *what he wants to do.* This is so obvious that it is never questioned, except for qualification of the word "wants," to divest it of mere whimsicality or passing fancy. Usually, the expression, "what he wants or intends to do," is satisfactory.

"His environment" is a second proposal which comes early, but the word has four syllables and is so diffuse and almost limitless in scope that it is changed to "what does or will confront him" or "what he will run into." Discussion quickly brings out the point that many factors which are "inside of one's skin" are really part of what confronts one, such as a broken leg when stairs must be negotiated, a heart which has to be humored, or a splitting headache when a heavy date is impending. This tends to raise the question of what is *self* and what is *nonself* but, unless there is ample time for side issues, that has to be pushed aside.

This, after screening out duplications and nonessentials, tends for the moment to leave us with two factors: (1) what one wants or intends to do, and (2) what one will run into. By this time, if not before, a third factor will enter the discussion: what our class member is *in the habit* of doing. Ordinarily, I let this proposal stand for the time being, hoping for an additional proposal which sometimes comes but more often (without some previous tip-off) does not. This proposal is, how he *sees* what does or will confront him.

Somehow, until after we think it over, we are not usually impressed with the significance of this factor in determining how we behave. After looking at it a bit, however, we can hardly fail to become convinced that it is highly important. Newly arrived in a strange hotel and taken to my room by elevator, I may wish right away to meet a friend who I know has a room on the floor below. The elevator is some distance away and it is quite busy at the moment, and just around a nearby corner but unbeknown to me is a stairway down. Will I take elevator or stairway? Under the circumstances, I am practically sure to take the elevator, whereas, if I knew about the stairway, I would be just about as sure to take it. Not only must a possibility exist; it must also be *seen or sensed as* a possibility, before we take advantage of it. How can we possibly take advantage of a short cut if we do not know of its existence? Of course, by chance we might blunder or fall into it, but usually such chances are very small and our present context has to do with designed or intentional behavior, anyway; not with blind or stumbling chance.

Thus, a third factor forces itself into our deliberations. If we are to predict behavior successfully, we must take into account not only what a person wants or intends to do and what he will run into, but also *how he will sense or see* the confronting situation in terms of what he is wanting or intending. These three factors seem to be necessary. Are there any others?

We now come to the effect or significance of what one is *in the habit* of doing. This is a matter considerably more complex or involved than the foregoing ones; at least, not so immediately obvious. It may even imply a commitment as to why we do what we do. It may mean that we tend to do later what we have done before, for the reason that each time we perform an act we wear deeper the neural path which controls the act and so make it more likely to occur again. Thus, we act in a given way later—on habit level—*because* we have acted that way before. A path has been worn—a path of lowered synaptic resistance—through the nervous system, and we "follow the path of least resistance."

It should be noted that this is the conventional or traditional view regarding the kind of human behavior which is spoken of as *habit*. It deals with the actions we take when we really are not paying attention to what we are doing; when we are not "thinking." It is a view which, whether under the aegis of idealism or realism, has prevailed for thousands of years and, for many of us, is so completely taken for granted that it is not even thought of as a theory. Most textbooks in psychology and physiology even today ostensibly take it for granted, not even suggesting that there might be another way of looking at the matter. Our language usage itself implies the view,

The American College Dictionary (the first one I happened to pick up) having, "1. a disposition or tendency, constantly shown, to act in a certain way. 2. such a disposition acquired by frequent repetition of an act." Thus, *repetition* is given causal status as well as being used descriptively.

Twentieth century connectionism and behaviorism both enthrone the repetitional theory of habit-level behavior and furnish a fully worked out mechanism—the S-R bond or reflex-arc theory—to account for it. "We learn to do by doing," an expression wrongfully imputed to John Dewey, might well have been the theme song had we had radio and television in 1900. Even William James accepted the theory without question.[1]

But let us give habit-level behavior a really close look. Have you ever in your whole life seen anyone perform a given line of action exactly the same way twice? Or do you have any knowledge of anyone who has? You had better be very careful of your answer, for much hangs upon it. "Life is forever new" and "You never step in the same river twice" are expressions of the ages, representing explicit denial of the very heartbeat of the repetitional theory of habit. From time immemorial mankind, including professional psychologists, has both averred and denied this theory—averred it as theory yet denied it in basic fact—without clear realization of so doing.

Take as simple an action as tossing up a coin or other small object and catching it as it falls. Is the sequence of acts ever twice the same? If you have to be convinced, take a movie of the action in slow motion, several catches one after another. Actually, if arm and hand should follow every time an exactly set path without deviation, the object probably never would be caught (unless an expansive catching device were employed), due to variations in the flight of the object after leaving the hand. Keen, open eyes must follow the flight, relaying information as to its progress, so that fine and precise adjustments of position and motion of hand may continue until even after the catch is made. Note how different will be your actions if eyes are closed as the toss is made and kept shut until after the attempted catch. Moreover, think how the whole body enters into the act—eyes, head, neck, both arms, torso, and certainly legs and feet.

To believe that the essence of habit-level performance is repetition

[1] William James, *Talks to Teachers and Students,* New York: Henry Holt and Company, 1900, chaps. 6, 8, 9.

would seem to be about as absurd as one can imagine. To repeat is what we should avoid doing, if it were even possible. For, in learning as in performing, wrong acts must be eliminated and right ones adopted; hence keen sensitivities and split-second adjustments must be continuously and coöperatively at work.

How then did we ever get the idea that repetition both characterizes *and* causes habit? Probably because we never stopped to think that a later performance could be much like an earlier one, not *because* of the earlier one but *for the same reason that* the earlier one was as it was. This is not hairsplitting—a distinction without a difference. This is a distinction which makes "a whale of a difference." Let us examine it closely.

Suppose we return to the three factors previously accepted, albeit tentatively, as necessary to accurate prediction of behavior. The first, what one intends or wants to do, may be spoken of as *goal* or *purpose,* and it must be recognized as patterned or configurational. The second factor, what one will run into, may be spoken of as the *confronting situation,* and it too must be recognized as patterned or configurational. The third factor, how one senses or sees the confronting situation in terms of purpose or goal, may be spoken of as *insight,* and it also must be recognized as patterned or configurational.

Is this all we need? Not at all; we have also to know how these factors are to be related one to another. We need a predictive principle. Given a certain pattern of goal, situation, and insight, how will a person act? We can hypothesize that *he will act in such a way as to achieve what he is after* (*goal*) *in the quickest and easiest way that he senses or comprehends* (*insight*) *under the circumstances* (*confronting situation*). This we may speak of as the *principle of least action,* following the lead of Raymond Holder Wheeler who called it the *Law* of Least Action.[2] You will note that we present this as a hypothesis; that is our reason for calling it a principle instead of a law. We do not take it in any sense as a final pronouncement. We only propose it as an instrument which may be found highly useful in the perennial pursuit of outguessing other people and possibly outguessing life itself. In fact, we are not going to occupy the reader's time, or space in this book, with a recital of evidence already gathered which we feel gives the hypothesis sufficient support to merit high confidence in its use. What supportive evidence we cite will be

[2] Raymond Holder Wheeler, *The Science of Psychology* (2nd ed.), New York: Thomas Y. Crowell Company, 1940, pp. 38–40, *passim.*

only for the purpose of clarification; of helping a reader to develop a working idea of what the whole proposal means.

Our hypothesis, then, is that, in order to predict or anticipate behavior with accuracy, we need to bring to bear an adequate fund of pertinent knowledge regarding the three factors—goal, confronting situation, and insight—and then apply the principle of least action. This means that later behavior will be like earlier only if and when, and in the degree to which, the three influencing factors are the same. This makes clear how one can perform on habit level, yet do something never done before, and indicates what Wheeler meant when he said that any purported explanation of human behavior which fails to account fully for correct and effectual action the first time is no explanation at all. We indeed have good reason for wanting to know how a person is "in the habit" of acting; how he has acted before. But the function of such knowledge is to give information or cues as to one or more of the three factors, particularly perhaps as to his goals or his insights; not to indicate what the prediction should be. Attention needs to be focused on getting a present job done; not on how past ones have been done. Altered goal means altered action, as does altered situation or altered insight; else, a job does not get done. If later behavior is much like earlier, it is *for the same reason that* the earlier was as it was; not *because* of the earlier behavior.

Many terms now crowd in, demanding discussion. Perhaps most demanding are *least action* and *insight*. Let us take least action first. To choose a satisfactory name for this principle is not easy. Wheeler uses least *action;* another writer uses least *effort*. Neither may be entirely satisfactory. Wheeler states the law as follows: "When action is defined as units of energy multiplied by units of time, movement occurs from one position to the other, over the shortest possible path."[3] The other writer also chooses that which is "least possible," making it least possible *effort,* which is perhaps essentially the same as Wheeler's "units of energy multiplied by units of time." To both of these we have applied the corrective of what is "sensed or seen as" possible. For no one will design behavior on the basis of anything of which he is not aware. This would seem obvious, is amply supported by experience and experiment, and should be specifically written into the theory. Our expression, "the quickest and easiest way," is adopted because we feel it to be more easily and more widely understandable

[3] *Ibid.,* p. 40.

and usable than other expressions. It can be rendered mathematical if necessary, but most users seem to prefer a nonmathematical form.

But what about this "least" business? Are we really, you may ask, as lazy as this? However, do we have to call it lazy? Might it not be just good sense, or discernment? If you or I take what we afterwards realize is a long way round to get something done, are we not ordinarily a bit embarrassed, if not chagrined, about it? And why did we take the long way, if we did not at the time fail to realize that there was a shorter one? Of course, we are not unmindful of the saying, "The longest way round is the sweetest way home." But this is something else entirely; our goal is not to get home. Is not the saying perhaps a recognition of the principle of least action, rather than a denial? Customarily, if you or I see a person taking a long way or a hard way to get something done, do we not suspect either his motives or his judgment? Motives represent goal; judgment represents insight.

And what of insight? This should be a highly serviceable term, yet by many psychologists it is meticulously avoided for the expressed reason that it means so many different things. The writer is aware of this difficulty, but believes it to be not insurmountable. Moreover, the word enjoys common usage, much of it essentially along the precise line which fits our purposes. Let us give it a precise meaning and then use it that way and that only.

Insight is here defined as *a sense of, or feeling for, pattern*. It is not what impinges upon our sense organs—light rays, sound waves, tactile imprintings, etc.—but *what we make* of them; not what they are, but what we take them to be. We get the "feel" of the way our automobile is running; we "catch the point" of a joke (if we do); we "get the sense" of an explanation; we first want to "get the heft" of a heavy-looking object which is to be carried; we "see" how a principle applies to a given case; we "catch on"; we "get the meaning" of a word; we comprehend or understand a proposition; we "get the run" of a matter; we "get the idea"; and so it goes. We have a great variety of ways to express the conviction, "I have an insight."

It should at once be noted that an insight may be false or it may be true; it may be shallow, superficial, trivial, or it may be deep, penetrating, significant; it may be vague or it may be sharp; it may be particularized or it may be generalized; it may be good or it may be bad; it may refer to an intellectualized principle or it may be something largely motor or muscular; it may be expressed in words or it may not. Whatever form an insight takes, it is what we make of what comes to us, and it is on this that we design whatever behavior pertains thereto.

As the term is employed here, insight is never to be equated with any verbal expression which may be used in an attempt at communication. It is that which words are marshaled and used to express, but which cannot be transferred from one person to another in any way analogous to transfer of a baseball from pitcher to catcher. The only way to convey an insight is to handle or deal with a person in such way as to get him to formulate or work out a sense of, or feeling for, the pattern which we ourselves have in mind. Each person has to create his own insights; no one else can do it for him. And mere capacity to repeat the right words is no guarantee whatever, in and of itself, of possession of an insight. This is something which the makers and users of classroom tests or examinations should certainly appreciate more thoroughly than they seemingly have done or now do (see Chapter 14).

In using the expression, "a feeling for pattern," the writer is not using the word "feeling" as we do when we speak of a feeling of satisfaction or of dissatisfaction with something. The latter is emotional, and seemingly a dependable accompaniment of every evaluative insight. This matter will be discussed rather carefully in Chapter 8, so it will not be dwelt upon here. In order to differentiate, we may call the latter—an emotional response—a *feeling tone*. Thus, we may say without ambiguity that a sense of, or feeling for, pattern—an insight—which is at all evaluational is bound to be accompanied by a feeling tone of satisfaction or dissatisfaction, approval or disapproval, respect or disrespect, like or dislike, or of neutrality; depending on whether what is under consideration appears to be favorable, unfavorable, or neutral to whatever aspect of our value-system is under scrutiny.

Insights have to do with what psychologists call the *cognitive;* that which is intellectual or mental. Feeling tones or emotional responses are designated by them as the *affective;* they are what is often called "visceral," what seems to be mainly under glandular and autonomic control. Speaking colloquially but perhaps quite understandably, it may be said that insights, or the cognitive, have to do with our heads, and feeling tones, or the affective, with our hearts. We shall return to this matter after we have dealt with learning. In Chapter 8 it is pointed out that the way to a man's heart is not through his stomach, but through his head.

A page or so back, it was noted that an insight may be an intellectualized principle or it may be something largely motor or muscular. For the latter, the term *kinesthetic insight* has occasionally been used. However, following my mentor, the astute philosopher and psychologist, the late Dr. Boyd H. Bode, I am not satisfied with making such a distinction. For it tends to cause us to "give our heads a rest" when we are dealing with what used to be called matters "neuromuscular" as contrasted with matters "ideational." And I have found that, in the interests of high-quality achievement, it is just as disastrous to "leave our heads at home" when trap-shooting or playing billiards as when dealing with matters akin to the theory of special relativity. In any case, one needs to "get the run of the thing," and that calls for keen and attentive wits. Abstracting some particular aspect of a total situation or configuration and dealing with it in abstracted form is always an insightful process, whether mental or manual; as important for basketball as for biology.

To "get the feel" of how a baseball must leave the hand in order to throw a curve requires the same approach as to get the feel of where a prospective Pluto must be in order to account for an "improper" deviation in the observed path of Uranus. The details of the two are greatly different as well perhaps as their relative difficulties, but to treat one as nonintellectual and the other as intellectual is probably highly unwise. At any rate, the meaning of the present proposal or theory seems logically to imply a similarity between the two, and demonstration of the wisdom or unwisdom of its employment may well constitute a significant facet of the evidence to support acceptance or rejection of this proposal in its entirety.

In the foregoing pages, it has been repeatedly noted that insight is what we make of what comes to us, not what it "really is." This point also will be further developed in later chapters (Chapters 4, 5, 6). It also raises the question of Dewey's principle of *interaction* or *transaction* (use whichever one you wish) which will repeatedly appear as we proceed. If we are to avoid philosophical solipsism as well as to possess insights which are truthful in the sense of being accurately predictive, our insights have to represent "working agreements" between ourselves and the situations which confront us, or our environment. We have to deal with a world as it is, whether we like it that way or not; to deal successfully with that world we have to keep asking, "Are my insights satisfactory to you?"

But the world itself does not seem to be entirely adamant on this score. It also seems disposed to coöperate if we ourselves shall do so.

There are hosts of confronting situations which are highly flexible in terms of what (insights) may be made of them. For example, a rabbit or quail may be in full view of a hunter yet, as long as it remains motionless, not be seen by him at all. Of course, the hunter may not consider this coöperation but evidently the hunted does. Or, a drawing of a landscape may be artfully contrived so that, as one looks at it, previously unseen faces successively "jump out" at one and, whereas at first none was evident, afterwards one can hardly see the landscape because of the faces. As you well know, "motion pictures" are not in motion at all; but they certainly look that way and, in this case, the viewee is pretty uncoöperative at letting the viewer see it as a series of stills. Kelley's *Education for What Is Real* has been a popular source of information on experiments which demonstrate this interactive quality of human vision.

The point of all this is that, if we are to predict behavior accurately, we have to recognize insights as the outcome of an interactive or transactive process, but have also to recognize that a person will *design* his behavior on what he *takes* the confronting situation to be. If we then can accurately anticipate whether and when a developing situation will require a change in the "take" (the insight), the accuracy of our prediction will be heightened. So the answer to the original and central question of this chapter is that we seemingly must interpret human nature as purposive or goal-seeking, as insight-directed, but as taking place in an environment which may or may not be circumvented but which, in any case, has to be dealt with on pretty much its own terms (see Chapter 6). And, to repeat the principle, it is assumed that a human individual will always design his behavior so as to achieve what he is after (or satisfy his wants) in the quickest and easiest way that he senses or sees as possible under the circumstances. Because goal and insight play so important a part in this theory as well as significantly distinguish it from its most active competitor, the bond or reflex-arc theory, the writer feels justified in giving it the name *goal-insight theory*.

SELECTED REFERENCES

Adrian, E. D., *The Physical Background of Perception*, Oxford: The Clarendon Press, 1947.

Bayles, Ernest E., *The Theory and Practice of Teaching*, New York: Harper & Brothers, 1950, chap. 4.

Bode, Boyd H., *Conflicting Psychologies of Learning*, Boston: D. C. Heath & Company, 1929, chaps. 11, 12, 13, 14, 15.

Bode, Boyd H., *Modern Educational Theories,* New York: The Macmillan Company, 1927, chap. 9.

Bruce, William, *Principles of Democratic Education,* New York: Prentice-Hall, Inc., 1939, chaps. 5, 8, 9.

Coghill, G. E., *Anatomy and the Problem of Behavior,* New York: The Macmillan Company, 1929.

Dewey, John, *Human Nature and Conduct,* New York: The Modern Library, 1930.

Dewey, John, *Logic, The Theory of Inquiry,* New York: Henry Holt and Company, 1938, chap. 2.

Dewey, John, *The Reflex Arc Concept in Psychology,* in Dennis, Wayne, *Readings in the History of Psychology,* New York: Appleton-Century-Crofts, Inc., 1948, no. 41, pp. 355–365.

Hartmann, G. W., *Educational Psychology,* New York: American Book Company, 1941.

Hartmann, G. W., *The Field Theory of Learning and Its Educational Consequences,* in National Society for the Study of Education, Forty-First Yearbook, Part II; *The Psychology of Learning,* Bloomington, Illinois: Public School Publishing Company, 1942, chap. 5.

James, William, *Psychology,* Cleveland and New York: The World Publishing Company, 1948, chap. 10.

James, William, *Talks to Teachers and Students,* New York: Henry Holt and Company, 1900, chaps. 6, 8, 9.

Kelley, Earl C., *Education for What Is Real,* New York: Harper & Brothers, 1947, chaps. 3, 4.

Koehler, W., *The Mentality of Apes* (trans. E. Winter), New York: Harcourt, Brace and Company, 1925.

Lashley, K. S., *Brain Mechanisms and Intelligence,* Chicago: The University of Chicago Press, 1929.

Snygg, Donald, and Combs, Arthur W., *Individual Behavior,* New York: Harper & Brothers, Part I.

Wheeler, Raymond H., *The Science of Psychology* (2nd ed.), New York: Thomas Y. Crowell Company, 1940, chaps. 1, 7, 10, 11, 14.

Wheeler, R. H., and Perkins, F. T., *Principles of Mental Development,* New York: Thomas Y. Crowell Company, 1932, chaps. 2, 4, 5, 6.

Wiener, Norbert, *Cybernetics,* New York: John Wiley & Sons, Inc., 1948, chaps. 4, 5, 6.

CHAPTER 3

Learning and Transfer

LEARNING

IF we assume the goal-insight theory of behavior as it has been developed in the preceding chapter, what view should we then adopt as to the nature of learning? To define learning as a change in behavior (as is frequently done) would seem to be about like saying that Shakespeare and Hamlet are the same thing. A change in behavior may indeed come after something has been learned, but the behavior change is the *result;* it is not the learning itself.

If, as we have concluded, behavior is dependent upon three different factors, then a change in any one of the three will bring about a change in behavior. And is this not obviously the case? My ordinary time for getting out of bed may be 7:00 A.M. There comes a morning, however, when I want to be in the blind, ready to hunt ducks, at opening time of one half hour before sunrise. My altered getting-up time has not come from anything learned; this morning I simply have a different goal. My change of goal may, of course, have come from learning that ducks are flying or that classes have been canceled for the day. But, regardless of the reason for the change in goal, it is the change in goal which is immediately responsible for my change in behavior.

Again, my customary way of driving to work is up Fourteenth Street, which is a steep grade. On a morning after a heavy snow, I take a different route: a change in behavior. True, I have to know that the street is too slippery to negotiate. But the immediate cause of my change in behavior is the change in the confronting situation— the altered street surface. And by no stretch of imagination or logic is one likely to say that learning is to be thought of or defined as a change in confronting situation.

Hence, by the method of indirect proof, we reach the proposition that, if learning is influential in changing behavior at all (and it surely is admissible that it is), it is so by way of a change in insight. And this seems tantamount to saying that learning is to be defined as *a change in insight;* a process of developing insight; building new insights or modifying old ones.

. Although we speak above of "proof," it does not seem necessary to claim the foregoing as constituting grounds sufficient for adoption of the insight definition of learning. It may be well, however, to recognize that adoption of the goal-insight theory of behavior does carry with it the logical consequence of commitment to the definition of learning as development of insight. For, if behavior is affected by three and only three factors, of which one is insight, and if behavior changes induced by changes in the other two factors are not recognized as the result of learning, then it follows that learning has to be taken as a change in the third factor—insight.

Since it is generally recognized that experimental or experiential justification is the real "court of last resort" on whatever matters can possibly be referred to it, we should doubtless use it if possible in seeking justification for our definition. The question then becomes whether the insight definition will lead to better prediction and consequent control of learning situations than will competing definitions. When we come, however, to a canvass of the experimental and experiential evidence available, we find it so voluminous that comprehensive summarization is out of the question. An entire volume could be devoted to that matter alone. Our purpose in this book can reasonably be served by calling to mind a few typical and significant studies.

The pioneering study by Max Wertheimer, father of German Gestalt theory, of the two alternating light flashes seems to be as good a starting point as any. When the alternations were slow, they were "seen" as such; first one, then the other. But with gradual increase in the alternation rate, a frequency was reached above which the flashes could no longer be seen as separate and distinct from one another, but only as a single light moving rapidly back and forth between the two locations. This principle, of course, has for decades been utilized to produce motion pictures; a series of similar but slightly different stills thrown upon a screen in a succession so rapid that the human eye can only see them as connected, flowing movement. If the speed of projection is retarded sufficiently, the succession of disconnected stills becomes evident.

What this coterie of experiments and experiences seems to show is mainly the unitariness of insight. It is essentially an all-or-none matter; you either have it, or you don't. This is why the expression, "flash of insight," seems so descriptive. James spoke of "flyings and perchings"—one perches on one insight, then suddenly flies to the next. As early as 1897, Stratton reported experimenting with the wearing of spectacles equipped with combination lenses which first caused objects to appear upside down. After two or three days there were occasional periods during which things turned right side up, but with reversals frequent and easily produced. By the eighth day, however, stability had been achieved and the world dependably "looked" as it ought to look—right side up.

When I was a youngster, there was for a while a vogue of drawings which depicted hidden faces. A roadside, or some other scene, would be portrayed with trees, bushes, clouds, dust swirls, etc.; a placid, unthreatening, pictorial pastorale. Then, of a sudden, out of a bush would appear a face, then one in a cloud, then several out of the foliage of trees, and so it would go. Afterwards, one could hardly see the landscape because of the plethora of faces. Finally, Earl Kelley tumbled to all of this after spending ten weeks with the Ames demonstrations at the Hanover Eye Institute and reported it in his little book, *Education for What Is Real,* which became popular overnight.

These experiments all bear out Dewey's fundamental principle of perceptual *interaction* (or transaction)—as I find it, the one basic theoretical innovation of Dewey for philosophy as well as psychology —that it is *what I take* the world to be that serves as the foundation upon which I fashion my *design* for living. I may be pushed and pulled about by forces many of which I am unaware—my "world of effect." But always certain of the building materials which I use for formulating plans or designs are what I take the world to be— my "world of insight." This is a long cry from solipsism; it is *not at all* a case of asserting or assuming that the world is made by my thought processes. But my thought processes are taken to be exactly that; and it certainly does not take a sage to comprehend that I could not possibly (except by remote chance) base any plan or design of my own on something of which I was not cognizant.

If, therefore, learning can truthfully be construed as a process of developing insight, we must, for one thing, expect to find it exhibiting this above-noted all-or-none quality; this "flash" characteristic. Deductively, we are led to expect that one can long be mulling over a mystifying matter, seemingly getting nowhere. Each lead we get runs afoul of data already possessed or newly disclosed. Things just are not "adding up." Then suddenly the key factor emerges, the whole "picture" undergoes reorganization, and the matter "jells." This is all very mysterious, of course. What happens inside of our nervous systems to effect such a miracle is largely beyond the scope of human knowledge. We do not assume it to be a part of that supposedly far-off realm of the finitely unknowable. We are optimistic; we feel that we are making progress and shall continue to do so; we even have a notion that some day we shall achieve a major breakthrough. But this is only one of the myriad mysteries of life; birth, death, conception, chemical change, energy transformation, inertia, electromagnetic induction, atomic fission, hereditary stability, racial evolution, why "my heart leaps up when I behold a rainbow in the sky."

What is important for educational theory is not acquaintance with the whole physical-chemical-physiological *structure* which accounts for an act of intellectual creation. A seventh-grade teacher probably would not be helped much if he knew all about it; little more perhaps than if he knew exactly the parts of the body which are affected by the workings of the fifth cranial nerve. What *is* important is how to work with Mary in order to get her to see how to locate a decimal point accurately at the culmination of an arithmetical maneuver. *We need to know what we can possibly do to help a new insight form, as well as what to do afterwards to test its validity.*

Is there evidence that sudden "jelling" is a rather vital characteristic of learning processes and should therefore be looked for and encouraged? There is really so much that we might better turn the question around and ask whether it ever occurs any other way. Koffka's *The Growth of the Mind* and Koehler's *Gestalt Psychology* and *The Mentality of Apes* are replete with examples. Read the account of Sultan when it dawned upon him that he could telescope one stick a bit into the open end of another and make of them a single stick long enough to reach the desired banana.

Even Thorndike's cat in the puzzle box probably did not act as Thorndike indicated. Seemingly, Thorndike's eyes were on his stop watch rather than on the cat. Adams' later report on a similar experiment, wherein the investigator actually did watch the cat, pretty well substantiated the rather astounding observation that indeed the cat did act very much like a cat; certainly not like the disorganized, random scatterbrain which Thorndike reported. And motion pictures of cats undergoing learning situations which are adapted to their levels of potential insight certainly show them to be amazingly humanlike in what appears to be the sudden jelling of an insight and the fluent, competent, and effectual behavior which ensues; behavior on the habit level.

Thus, we see that habit-level behavior is not at all the routine, repetitional, humdrum process which has for millennia been imputed to it. It is indeed a highly creative process. The only difference between habit-level behavior and that which we call reflective is that in the former the insights arise immediately, along with the situations to which they are referent, whereas in the latter the insights are not immediately forthcoming but require a period of time in which to form. As H. Gordon Hullfish was wont to observe more than a quarter-century ago, "When a situation and its meaning occur simultaneously in experience, we behave competently and on habit level." It is this interpretational pattern which Bode called the "flexible-habit theory," as contrasted with the "fixed-habit theory" of psychological conditioning.

Does learning ever occur in a way which would cause one to think of it as a gradual process rather than a sudden one? Yes, it does. In the first place, one may have to throw a dart at a target a good many times before getting the "feel" which is requisite to accuracy in making hits. But this is not the gradualistic, path-wearing process which is necessary to substantiate the theory of *conditioning*. The writer has, rather late in life, taken up trap-shooting as a recreational outlet, though, it must be admitted, in rather desultory fashion. At first I read some good explanations of the theory of hitting the birds (the clay pigeons), particularly the factors necessary in determining the amount of "lead" (how far to aim in front of the flying target). Then I practiced; I'm still doing that.

After the study of theory, the percentage of hits took a big jump over what it was before. But there are many factors, all of which must be correctly executed if a hit is to be made; correct lead, which varies for each bird; keeping both eyes open instead of only one; correct placement of stock against cheek so that the gun barrel is not canted to right or to left; correct vertical alignment of gun barrel with target (how high or low to shoot); correct timing of the shot (neither too quick nor too slow)—all of these in their infinite variety and others as well.

When all of these factors require thought each time, when one must keep telling one's self *in words* what to do, then factors are missed. And improper execution of any one will be responsible for failure to hit the target. Use of some device which would each time supply the reason for the miss—whether the shot charge went above or below, before or behind—would greatly speed improvement. When no such information is readily obtainable and one has to surmise each time just what he did wrong and try to correct it next time, he is working much in the dark and progress is slow. A capable, experienced shooter who is able each time to tell the novice what he did wrong should help considerably, although emotional strain can easily arise from such procedure and make things worse rather than better.

After a more or less extended period of practice, however, one begins to get the "feel" of the whole process—often called the "feel of the gun"—and then not only do scores take a spurt upward but confidence rises, one relaxes, and scores creep up further. Moreover, judgment of what one did right or wrong each time also mounts, and this helps.

In reviewing the foregoing, it should be noted that, though scores are undergoing an overall *gradual* improvement, the gradualness is not of the kind which a path-wearing interpretation would require. It is more of a case of "going steady by jerks," a common Midwestern expression. The skill or ability in question is complicated; influenced by several factors. All must finally be fused into an integrated, coördinated whole, but not all of them jell at one time. This means that development of even a highly muscular skill is basically a cognitive process; an insightful one. One is working gradually toward an overall "sense of pattern," but it is often via one insight at a time. There are, of course, those naturally favored individuals who seemingly grasp the whole thing at once; many are the top-quality athletes who are, or could be, equally proficient in a variety of sports. With these, gradualism is far from evident. But we less favored ones should not fall into the path-wearing (conditioning) pattern of "sheer repetition," for that will assuredly slow us still further and may even stop us completely.

A study was once made with rats learning a rather complicated maze. Of course, improvement was gradual. But the experiment was planned so as to make the learning of any given crucial turn identifiable, together with its effect on total time. Under these circumstances it became clear that the gradualness was indeed a case of "going steady by jerks." Total time did take a small but perceptible drop with the learning of each crucial turn, with plateaus between.

To continue citation of data here seems unnecessary. (Philosophers aren't supposed to use data anyway, are they?) Obviously, practice is needed; but not repetition. Each succeeding trial is indeed a "trial." Something is tried. A pattern is "caught," tried, and accepted or rejected. If found acceptable, the job is done; if not, something else is tried. Whenever it is sensed that a given trial was in some way defective, the next trial is based on another pattern and the whole line of action is different from before. Repetition is what is *avoided*. Hence, "drill" in the time-honored sense is not to be tolerated.

When an insight to be gained is a very simple one, with few if any complications, one successful trial is all that is needed. Not even one is necessary if the correctness or efficacy of the insight is obvious to the learner without trial. For example, how many of us are entirely satisfied as to what would come if we should jump off the top of a 12-story building? Yet how many of us learned that by doing? The *doing* of a simple act in the learning of it is likely to be little more than performance of what is necessary to assure us that our anticipation of outcomes is accurate. We are seeking truth—anticipatory accuracy.

When, on the other hand, an insight to be gained is somewhat, or highly, complex, then we are far from likely to achieve a correct combination the first time. Hence, repeated trials are necessary in order, first, to find a fairly workable combination. This, of course, represents practice. But once such a combination is achieved there is still much to do. One then seeks to polish it up, looking for unneeded elements which may be eliminated, for modifications which may be more suitable, for a "feel" for the entire act as a whole. This represents more practice. But all such practice is a far cry from repetitious drill. It is far from routine. It is indeed to a degree creative. One's head is continually at work, cybernetic "feedback" is functioning, all one's sensitivities are keyed to reporting back the efficacies of experimental acts, new and better ways are continually being sought.

When classrooms become places in which development of new or improved insights is paramount, many present practices will no longer prevail: repetitious memorizing of word combinations, whether they be rules of grammar, foreign-language vocabularies, letter sequences of words to be spelled, multiplication or other mathematical tables, set statements of scientific principles such as Boyle's Law, geographical names and places, or historical names, dates, and events; science laboratories in which cookbooklike recipes are slavishly followed from a manual or reports are prepared which represent only drawings or word descriptions of laboratory specimens; visual-education materials viewed merely because they are at hand and a schedule calls for their showing; notebooks prepared merely because a workbook calls for them; 15 mathematical "problems" to be handed in by youngsters who caught the point with the first few; "projects" carried out because we must "learn to do by doing" when in so many cases few insights are gained during the last two-thirds of the time spent; and so, *ad nauseam*. The point is merely that there should be no more "doing" than is necessary to establish the insight or insights in question. Informational details are not to be hoarded for their own sakes. "Love 'em and leave 'em." They'll be around when they're needed again. If not, reflective teaching will have developed in pupils enough of an insight into how to obtain such items when needed that they will be quickly available. And why should an able teacher not supply a lot of such details anyway? After all, young people stand in need today of so much in the form of widely transferable or useful generalization or principle that we can ill afford to waste a moment on the acquisition of untransferable or unusable item-details.

A few pages back we were speaking of the "jelling" of an idea; the getting of an insight. This is really a matter of considerable importance for teachers who would conduct classes insightfully, and especially for those who would teach reflectively. For what good is it to be able to *test* insights if we do not know how to *get* insights in the first place? Perhaps the two examples most likely to come to mind are of Archimedes' formulation of the principle of flotation and Newton's formulation of the principle of universal gravitation. Whether either of these stories is a really true one in terms of details of involvement by the stipulated parties is a question which need not concern us here. What is important is that the related incidents are true to life in general.

In both cases, the individual had a problem on his mind. And what is a problem? An ongoing action-line or thought-line has been, at least temporarily, arrested and its continuation is desired. Progress has stalled because an obstacle has arisen. Metaphorically, we are faced with a forked-road or no-road situation. Archimedes had to inform the king whether the gold in his crown was pure or adulterated, yet the crown was to be in no way injured, damaged, or altered. Newton was at work on a perplexing principle which would accurately deduce the orbits of planets and satellites. A third example, less known but just as informative, was Kekule and the benzene ring—a problem in organic chemistry.

In all three cases the individual had been at work upon his problem for some time and was absorbed with it, carrying it with him at work or away from work. But in each of these cases the idea formed during a period of relative relaxation. Archimedes in his bath, Newton under an apple tree in his garden, and Kekule drowsing before a dancing fire after a good meal and a stein of beer. Obviously, neither the bath, the apple, nor the beer did the trick. A fertile mind, absorbedly at work, did that. But the lesson may well be not to push too hard. Relaxed tension together with high sensitization to the problem area seem highly important.

Also, we have just mentioned a fertile mind. This would mean one possessed of a large fund of ideas which have been useful in other areas, some closely related but others only remotely so; a mind appreciative also of the efficacy of widely generalizable ideas and looking for one of that kind. This is perhaps a more reasonable, down-to-earth, true-to-life interpretation of the *intuitive* than is the idealistic one of revelation from on high. But it certainly is recognition of the intuitive, albeit in modernized form. Some call it a vivid and fertile imagination, even a poetic one. And is it not high time that we give able scientists some credit for being poetically imaginative, and cease making them forever logical, mathematical, and practical? What was the biological genius of Pasteur if not an aggressive, leaping imagination? He certainly did not know a great deal of biology, nor was he overly meticulous in controlled experimentation. And what else can be the import of Einstein's principle of "free invention" (see pages 84 and 88)? A fertile, imaginative mind, preferably already in possession of a large fund of widely generalizable, tested insights, seems highly important.

It would also seem that at this point a comprehensive and penetrating knowledge of history is important; of history concerned primarily with the fortunes or fates of ideas, not with mere chronicling of names, dates, places, and events. If an investigator is uninformed regarding the history of his investigation, he stands in high likelihood of merely repeating the errors of his predecessors. Knowing what has been tried before and the fate of those trials, he knows, first, what not to try again, but second, he possesses a reserve fund upon which he can draw for counters which may be scattered about so that possible new combinations may "jump out" at him. Having this in mind, the writer gets rather impatient with those who take Dewey to task for not giving a true place to history in his philosophy or in school curricula. His feeling is that Dewey has made a far more significant place for history than have most of those who berate him.

As for teachers in schools who would ask for suggestions on what they should do to heighten student capacities for creativity, one might say this: (1) Always practice reflective teaching; teaching which begins with a problem and progressively builds up to culminate in an answer. (2) Keep clearly in mind that a problem represents a mental perplexity—things just don't "add up"—and that prospective problem-solvers will not be in a position to make much headway toward solution until they get a pretty genuine appreciation of just what their problem is, just what is causing the difficulty. (3) See in the first place that the students do already know a few things, that is, have a fund of ideas relevant to the general area of subject matter under consideration; and that they then realize the possibility of drawing upon such funds for old ideas which may possibly be used intact or for old ones which may serve to suggest new combinations or completely new ideas. Here is where history is needed. (4) Be relaxed; do not push too hard for immediate closure. (5) Do some card-stacking. Adroitly throw various possibilities into the ring, those which you are confident will bear fruit once they have a chance to dawn on someone. (6) Be slow to frown upon wrong answers. Let the study determine. Remember that if you give a calf enough rope he will sooner or later hang himself. (7) Always keep the field open for surprises to yourself. Remember that a teacher who has ceased to learn is not likely to be greatly promotive of learning in others; and that the hit-and-miss process of "brain-storming" has possibilities of turning up excellent ideas from the most unexpected and unlikely sources. Even the "dumb ones" may come up with astoundingly fruitful creations if only given a chance. Remem-

ber that Edison was discouraged from continuing school, and why.
(8) Finally, if and when certain ideas needing consideration—
whether likely ones or not—are not forthcoming, you had better
suggest them yourself. It is not where ideas come from that counts;
it is where they lead. All ideas, regardless of source, are to be subjected to the tests of problem-solving, and it is always well, as
quickly and effectually as possible, to separate each idea from the
person who proposed it. In this way personal involvement is mini-
mized and class members learn disinterested objectivity. Toward
this end also, a teacher needs to make sure that many of his own proposals are among the rejects, so as to remove status-value from his
own proposals.

There is one further matter to note regarding teaching which
is designed to promote development of insight. Although insight
learning works so beautifully into the pattern of reflective teaching,
it should be noted that teaching can be insightful and not be reflective at all. It is of great importance that this point be emphasized;
the writer knows from experience that many students, graduate as
well as undergraduate, get the idea that any teaching which is insightful is also reflective. Therefore, he would like to do some table-
pounding when he says that *teaching for development of insight
can be either reflective or nonreflective.*

A very promising methodological proposal of the mid-twenties
was of the nonreflective kind, yet one which, if really followed,
would be genuinely insightful. This was the unit method of Henry
Clinton Morrison, presented in his book, *The Practice of Teaching
in the Secondary School,* and for many years practiced in the University of Chicago middle school. Briefly, high school courses were to
be reorganized into "units," each one (for "science-type" at least)
to represent an area of subject matter the study of which would even-
tuate in a given *understanding.* Hence, this was a long step beyond
memory-level teaching, and the whole plan and program, if strictly
followed, would virtually guarantee what we have seen appropriate
to call *understanding-level* teaching, as well as insightful learning.
The insights sought were of a broadly generalizable kind, with wide
possibilities for transfer to life outside of school, thereby taking classroom learnings off the shelf and out of the ivory tower.

But the teaching program was a far cry from being reflective. The
five-step plan for "science-type units"—exploration, presentation, assimilation, organization, and recitation—was one of presenting the

question and the answer at the same time (the second period, presentation) then handling students on an individualized basis by means of worksheets in such a way as to get the answer really established in each student's thinking (assimilation). No alternative answers were ever systematically brought into consideration; only the one presented in the "overview" or "preview" was studied. The "mastery test," marking the close of the assimilation period, was genuinely one of *using,* rather than repeating, what one knew. Not only was problem-solving—in the sense of fairly considering a variety of alternatives and finally reaching whatever one or ones the study might justify—*not* written into the plan and program; Morrison was explicit and emphatic in its denial.[1]

In a context somewhat different from the present one, Morrison's plan would deserve extended study. We refer to it now only to emphasize the point that teaching can be insightful without being reflective. Teachers of science and mathematics, to name only two fields, can easily fail to appreciate this point. For, in those fields, authorities can reach such high agreement on fundamental principles that it is forgotten that alternatives ever did, or possibly ever could, exist. This situation led Dewey once to remark, "We have become so enamored with the spoils of our science that we have quite forgotten the method." When a science teacher's attention is concentrated exclusively on clarifying a given scientific principle, he may establish the matter very clearly in the minds of his students, yet fail completely to give them any feeling whatever for the very quality which makes science scientific—scientific *method.* Failing this, students may have merely substituted one idol for another and, instead of bowing in deep obeisance whenever hearing the expression, "the Bible says," they come to do the same at the invocation, "science says." And, among others, advertisement writers in the popular magazines for many years took full advantage of this unquestioning acceptance as a sales device.

The Transfer of Training

Finally, we close this chapter with a brief consideration of the almost forgotten problem of transfer of training, or the *use* and *employment* of learnings. In a textbook by the writer, published in

[1] Henry Clinton Morrison, *The Practice of Teaching in the Secondary School* (rev. ed.), Chicago: The University of Chicago Press, 1931, pp. 247–248, 250.

1950,[2] the sixth chapter deals with the topic, The Transfer of Training. In that chapter was presented a hypothesis which was a step in advance of the one presented by the writer in 1936,[3] one which received some recognition on the part of educational psychologists. As discussed in both these publications, theories prior to 1936 were based on one factor only: an opportunity for transfer must be presented by the environment and, if it were, transfer would occur. It had been recognized, of course, that the principle was not 100 percent dependable. Hence, customarily appended to its employment was the qualification, "other things being equal." But what the other things were was never indicated; not, at least, in an overtly systematic way.

In the writer's article of 1936, he proposed a second factor: that to a trained person not only must an opportunity be presented; it must also be *seen or sensed as* an opportunity. So obvious is this second requirement that, once it is called to attention, little question arises and those who are theoretically inclined are likely to incorporate it quickly. It is one of those matters which are so familiar that, although we continually take note of them and gauge actions accordingly, we are not focally aware of so doing. In common parlance, we just don't really see them. Hence, they somheow get left out of consciously formulated theory. As frequently happens when we are asked orally to spell a familiar word, we suddenly realize that we must first write it down and look at it. Why? Simply because what is familiar is the configurational word-picture; we have not acutely recognized the various letters.

It was not until three or four (or maybe more) years after the 1936 article that the writer realized the necessity for taking account of still another factor, a third one. This again, like the second, is so obvious as to elude focal attention. It is the factor of *purpose* or *goal*. Not only must the opportunity for transfer exist and be recognized as existing; there must also be a *disposition to take advantage of* the opportunity. What is the circumstance of a lie-telling episode if not of having an opportunity to tell the truth, seeing it as such, yet being disposed not to tell it? Most experienced teachers can recall cases wherein pupils have known the correct answers to questions yet, be-

[2] Ernest E. Bayles, *The Theory and Practice of Teaching,* New York: Harper & Brothers, 1950, pp. 85–98.

[3] Ernest E. Bayles, "A Factor Unemphasized in Current Theories Regarding the Transfer of Training," *Journal of Educational Psychology,* September, 1936, pp. 425–430.

cause of disgruntlement or some other reason, have refused to give them or even to admit knowing them. Are further examples needed?

It is not surprising that the identical-elements theory of the connectionists should have omitted goal from the reckoning, for refusal to recognize purpose at all was a cornerstone of connectionist theory in general. But, after realizing his omission, the writer was a bit chagrined because he had for a decade incorporated goal as an essential part of his own theory of behavior in general. If three factors are necessary to a generalized theory of behavior, they should also be necessary to a particular application of that theory.

For a number of years subsequent to realization of this omission, the writer kept a weather eye out for publications calling attention to it. But none appeared. Finally in 1950, as previously noted, his own emendation was made public. But, by that time, transfer theory had seemingly been permitted by educational psychologists to fall into the limbo of forgotten things. The desire to be experimental rather than "philosophical" may account for this circumstance. Yet, since life is forever new, it is perhaps never a specific item of training—in its own specific form—which gives it educational value. Its value indeed lies in its transferability, whether it be to new situations much like the original or to those which differ greatly therefrom. Newton, for example, made a tremendous jump when he transferred the concept of falling bodies from apples to planets, but it was transfer nonetheless. What fundamentally is application of any generalization to a particular case but a matter of transfer of training?

Thus, the theory or hypothesis proposed here can be stated as follows: *Any given item of training will transfer if and when—and only if and when—(1) opportunity offers, (2) a trained individual sees or senses it as an opportunity, and (3) he is disposed to take advantage of the opportunity.* This, of course, is a theory of designed or intelligent behavior, wherein a person's mind is at work even though he may not be acutely conscious of each and every move he makes or why he makes it. It is not meant to apply to cases of inanimate push and pull, wherein like a clod or stone one falls victim to circumstances unforeseen or unintended.

In this theory, factor (1) refers obviously to an individual's surroundings or environment; to what confronts him. Hence, we may call it the *confronting situation.* We prefer the latter term to the more generalized ones because it tends to direct attention to pertinent matters. It may indeed be claimed that one never acts or behaves except as influenced in greater or lesser degrees by the entire universe, past and present. But most of such influence is, for a given occasion, negligible, and it is to focalize on pertinent matters that the term confronting situation is preferred.

However, it should be noted that "what is underneath one's own skin" may also be part of a confronting situation. A broken leg or left-handedness may be a potent factor in the design of a given action, just as much as a series of stairs to be negotiated or script to be written from left to right, slanted toward the right, and in general "naturally" fitted to right-handed persons. A whole theory of the self is herein involved, one in which "the self" is taken as essentially referring to factors (2) and (3) but essentially excluding factor (1).

Factor (2) refers to what we wish to call insight. We hope that by now we have made clear our use of the term. To recapitulate, we do not imply deep and penetrating discernment; nor is truthfulness even implied. What we mean is *a sense of, or feeling for, pattern;* getting the "heft" of a thing. It is "intuitive" in a way, if we employ this term in a nonabsolutistic manner.

Factor (3) refers to purpose, end, or goal; to what we are after. As with the other two factors, the patterned or configurational character should always be held in mind. Practically never will a purpose or goal be functioning singly and alone. Many may, for a given occasion, be negligible, but the pertinent ones are usually several. Moreover, for any given occasion, the several will be hierarchical; they will be held in an order of precedence or importance. Furthermore, they will be fluid, not static; the hierarchical order may change, new ones may be added, and old ones may drop out, all in the process of moving from earlier to later stages of accomplishment.

Hence, our transfer principle may be restated, though less smoothly or precisely, to say that we transfer training when (1) the confronting situation offers an opportunity, (2) a trained individual's insight is to that effect, and (3) his pattern of goals is such as will lead him to take advantage of the opportunity.

We present this restatement for the purpose of making clear the logical kinship between our theory of transfer and our theory of behavior in general. The latter we choose to call the *Principle of Least Action,* and can state as follows: We assume that we act in such a way as to achieve what we are after (our goal pattern) in the quickest and easiest way that we sense or comprehend (insight) under the circumstances (confronting situation). Thus, the three factors—goal, insight, and confronting situation—are present and functioning in our theories both of transfer and of behavior in general.

It may be asked why one concerned primarily with educational philosophy should be dabbling in psychology (and it may be that "dabbling" is a fitting term). The reason is that we approach educational philosophy from the angle of teaching theory, and for teaching theory a functional psychology—particularly of learning and of transfer—is essential. Furthermore, since such is our concern, it may be appropriate to close this chapter with a few observations on what this transfer theory means for teaching.

Obviously, this theory of transfer is essentially a matter of employment of insight. We use a learned insight if and when opportunity offers, we note the opportunity, and we wish to take advantage of it. If and when these three factors occur simultaneously on a given occasion, we proceed on *habit level* and continue in such manner as long as the unfolding occasion maintains such simultaneity. Thus, action is always suited to confronting situation and purpose, even though the series of acts or, better, the behavior-pattern has never before been performed.

It follows, therefore, that if we would teach for transfer we have to teach for insights which are widely applicable or generalizable. We must concentrate attention on broad generalizations or principles, rather than on a plethora of mutually isolated informational items with no attempt at considering how they are, or may be, related one to another. In other words, we must teach for understanding rather than for memory. In fact, if transfer-capacity be our aim, we shall probably be wise to terminate the practice of giving memory-level examinations at all, thereby leaving a clear field for the pursuit of understanding. Thus, classroom instruction would concentrate upon the *use* of knowledge, rather than on its retention.

But teaching for transfer means more than this. It means that learners must be sensitized to transfer as a possibility, must learn how to take advantage of opportunities as they arise as well as how even to make them arise, and must develop the dispositions necessary to promote taking advantage of opportunities and capacities. Without the latter, opportunities even though recognized will go for naught. Educational objectives such as this are achievable only over a considerable period of time. They represent ends to be sought at all educational levels—kindergarten through graduate school. Their manner of pursuit must be adapted to maturational development at each stage, but the pursuit should be persistent, nonrelenting.

Finally, since the question of transfer involves what one does with what is learned, it would seem reasonable to assume that the way in which a given matter is learned would considerably influence its transferability. Therefore, the whole question of learning theory should go hand in hand with that of transfer theory. The transfer theory presented here would seem to be logically compatible with the theory of learning as development of insight; not with conditioning.

Thus, a configurational or field theory of behavior in general which recognizes the significance of goal and insight as factors and least action as the principle of prediction, a theory which takes learning to be a process of developing insight, and a transfer theory which takes into account three factors—confronting situation, insight, and goal—are all presented in this and the preceding chapter as integral parts of a psychological outlook which gives promise of soon becoming, if not already so, a leading candidate for acceptance as a dependable interpretation of how human beings behave.

SELECTED REFERENCES

ON LEARNING

Bayles, Ernest E., *The Theory and Practice of Teaching,* New York: Harper & Brothers, 1950, chap. 5.
Bode, Boyd H., *How We Learn,* Boston: D. C. Heath & Company, 1940, chaps. 13, 14.
Cole, L. E., and Bruce, W. F., *Educational Psychology,* New York: World Book Company, 1950, chaps. 13, 14.
Dewey, John, *Logic, the Theory of Inquiry,* New York: Henry Holt and Company, 1938.
      Chapter 2 contains much on interaction.
Brownell, W. A., and Moser, Harold E., *Meaningful vs. Mechanical Learning: A Study in Grade III Subtraction,* Durham, N.C.: Duke University Press, 1949, Duke University Research Studies in Education, No. 8.
Fullagar, W. A., Lewis, Hal G., and Cumbee, C. F., *Readings for Educational Psychology,* New York: Thomas Y. Crowell Co., 1956, readings 4, 5, 9, 10, 11.
Hartmann, G. W., *Educational Psychology,* New York: American Book Company, 1941.

Hilgard, Ernest R., *Theories of Learning.* New York: Appleton-Century-Crofts, Inc., 1948, Chaps. 1, 7, 8, 9, 12.

Judd, Charles H., *Education as Cultivation of the Higher Mental Processes.* New York: The Macmillan Company, 1936, chap. 8.

Katona, George, *Organizing and Memorizing,* New York: Columbia University Press, 1940, pp. 137–260.

Koehler, W., *The Mentality of Apes* (trans. E. Winter), New York: Harcourt, Brace and Company, 1925.

Koffka, Kurt, *Principles of Gestalt Psychology,* New York: Harcourt, Brace and Company, 1935.

Morrison, H. C., *The Practice of Teaching in the Secondary School* (rev. ed.), Chicago: The University of Chicago Press, 1931, chaps. 2, 6, 11, 14, 15, 16.

National Society for the Study of Education, Forty-first Yearbook, Part II, *The Psychology of Learning,* Bloomington, Illinois: Public School Publishing Company, 1942, chaps. 5, 6, 7, 12.

Swenson, E. J., Anderson, G. L., and Chalmers, L. S., *Learning Theory in School Situations,* Minneapolis: The University of Minnesota Press, 1949, University of Minnesota Studies in Education, College of Education, No. 2.

Wheeler, R. H., and Perkins, F. T., *Principles of Mental Development,* New York: Thomas Y. Crowell Co., 1932, chaps. 13–20.

ON TRANSFER

Bayles, Ernest E., *The Theory and Practice of Teaching,* New York: Harper & Brothers, 1950, chap. 6, also references therein cited.

Bode, Boyd H. *Fundamentals of Education,* New York: The Macmillan Company, 1921, chap. 8.

CHAPTER 4

Idealism, Realism, and Pragmatism

WHEN one who is inclined to be thorough-going in his thinking begins to delve into the question of desirable educational procedures, he is likely to run soon into the realization that he must decide what he expects to accomplish. There seems to be little question among educators nowadays that educational objectives are a matter of high importance to all serious workers in the field.

Moreover, meticulous thinking about educational objectives will quickly divulge the necessity for becoming acquainted with the aims and aspirations of those who constitute the jurisdictional group wherein the procedures are to take place. It is hard to imagine a situation in which an educational worker is entirely free to pursue whatever ends he may personally desire.

Together with ends one realizes also the necessity for consideration of means. If certain ends are unachievable with the means at hand, such ends will probably have to be abandoned or postponed. Or, if certain ends require means which for some reason appear undesirable or unsatisfactory, such ends should doubtless undergo reconsideration and possible modification. Ends and means should seemingly be compatible with each other; else, matters will go awry. Moreover, ends and means in one field of endeavor should seemingly be compatible with those in other fields; else the totality of one's work may be vitiated because one's various endeavors will tend to oppose, obstruct, or nullify one another.

If we should define *philosophy* as a program for living and *educational philosophy* as the educational aspects of such a program, matters to which we have just referred would appear to be an essential, if not a major, part of educational philosophy. For what is a program if not a plan for action? And what plan of action can give promise of success if not formulated in light of desired ends and suitable means? So viewed, educational philosophy obviously should be given serious study by any and all who enter the educational profession, be they teachers, administrators, or specialists of any kind. For who can do well his part if he fails to envision it as participating in the total enterprise?

Some consider philosophy as contemplation of the unknown, others as search for ultimate reality. I consider the former—contemplation of the unknown—more the domain of science than of philosophy. The quest for knowledge is essentially a scientific one, and it would seem that contemplation of the unknown is a phase of such. This does not mean that philosophy is not concerned with knowledge; only that that is not its major concern.

On the other hand, to consider philosophy as a search for ultimate reality is to stack the cards at the very beginning. It simply means that any view which denies the validity of the assumption of ultimate reality has no philosophic standing; no part in philosophy. If such be the case, then what I have to say is not philosophical, and I shall have to let you place it in whatever category you will. Search for final, ultimate, absolute reality has been pursued with futility for at least 2500 years, and gives promise of being as futile in the years to come. For, if you should get it, how would you know you had it? Practical reality is subject to practical, tangible tests, but not ultimate reality. Many are those who have been convinced that they had found the latter, but have been unable so to convince the world at large.

And there is the further malconsequence of the assumption of ultimate and final reality—its very ultimacy and finality. Should it be known, there would be nothing more to seek. Historically, every person or group of persons which has become convinced of having somehow gotten hold of ultimate reality has from that time forth become a proponent of the status quo, a foe of progress; progress, at least, within the realm of that conviction.

Define philosophy as a process of formulating a program for living—of working out the purposes, plans, and specifications for conducting the day to day, month to month, and year to year affairs of life; then science will represent the knowledge which becomes useful in formulating this program, and art can refer to the process of carrying it out. Such a definition of philosophy seems to express the common usage of the term and does not stack the cards against any particular formulation.

Historically, there are three major philosophical points of view—idealism, realism, and pragmatism. Of course, if we give attention to all of the shades or nuances of difference, we find hundreds of published philosophies. But all appear to be variations of one or another of these three. Let us begin by considering a few points of pragmatic doctrine.

Just at what point we start is perhaps of importance only as it serves the occasion. For the present it seems most convenient to say that pragmatism holds to the basic principle of configurational psychology, that nothing is either perceivable or conceivable as a thing-in-itself, but only as it is related to other things—as a figure against a background and from a given angle or direction of envisionment. The relationships of an object, both to its background and to the viewer, are as essential as the object itself. Is iron heavy? It is, if compared with aluminum. It is not, if compared with platinum. Is this room well or poorly lighted? The answer depends to a great degree on what the terms are taken to mean. It seems wholly justifiable to say that pragmatism is relativity taken seriously; an attempt to be consistently relative in one's thinking. In other words, pragmatism is relational, configurational, or contextual; it is a foe of absolutism in all its forms.

To repeat an example which has been widely used to explain the principle of relativity as it applies in the realm of physics, let us imagine a ball dropped by a person standing in the aisle of a passenger coach of a train which is moving north. Does the ball fall in a straight line? To a person sitting in a nearby seat the ball will certainly appear to fall in a straight line, and from that vantage point will fulfill all of the conditions necessary to justify such an interpretation. To a person standing along the right of way beside the tracks and presumably possessed of X-ray vision, the ball would appear not to fall in a straight line but in a parabola. To a person returning from Mars, far enough from the earth not to be carried along by the atmosphere, the ball would appear to follow a different path, one with an eastward component. The illustration could be further complicated but that is unnecessary. We might add that, to a very tiny spider resting on its surface, the ball would appear not to be moving at all. Just which of the observations is the really, truly, ultimately correct one? It is evident that none is. Yet each interpretation is correct, and is the only correct one, from a given vantage point.

In this sense, therefore, we adopt the both-and, rather than the either-or, outlook. A statement may be both true and untrue at the same time, depending upon what it is presumed to take into account or what it is presumed to mean. A statement never can be adopted as finally and forever true or untrue, under all circumstances and conditions. The Newtonian conception is just as true now as it ever was. It is thoroughly and dependably true for building bridges, railway locomotives, and automobiles. It becomes untrue only when one is dealing either with the realm of the microcosm or with that of the macrocosm.

Since Lobatshevski's work of 1830, geometricians have no longer been inclined to speak of the axioms of Euclid as self-evident truths, requiring no proof. Those axioms are now considered merely as assumptions or postulates on which one system of geometrical thought is based. If other assumptions are made, other systems are the result, which are just as true in terms of logicality or internal consistency as the Euclidian system. And some, incidentally, are more true if agreement with nature is taken as the criterion. Riemannian geometry, not Euclidian, was the one used by Einstein.

If relativity is to be taken seriously, we cannot limit it to psychology, physics, and mathematics. Many absolutists are quite willing to grant relativism title to the domains of physics and mathematics, and even other fields including psychology. But when it comes to morality, they usually draw the line. Moral principles are not to be tampered with. It is not right, so they say, to tell lies or to kill human beings; it never was and never will be, regardless of circumstances. To persons born and raised in a moral climate such as Americans have been, such an assertion may at first appear to have merit. We are so thoroughly opposed to homicide that we hardly dare, even in our own private thoughts, to think of the taking of human life as ever justifiable.

Yet the cry against capital punishment for certain major crimes is by no means universal, slaying which is proven to be in self-defense is not illegal, many of even the most moral among us are inclined privately to condone certain mercy slayings, and it seems that a majority of the American public is apt to classify as "crackpot" that small number of persons known as conscientious objectors who hold that war is no excuse for the taking of human lives. I cannot bring myself to respond to the Mosaic Law, "Thou shalt not kill," other than by saying that circumstances alter cases. I find no reason, philosophical or otherwise, for considering this Commandment an "eternal verity."

Nor can I bring myself to believe that a lie is never justifiable; that falsification is always bad. In fact, I am quite delighted that American womanhood is widely given to the art of falsification in the matter of facial appearance. I presume that the Ninth Commandment, "Thou shalt not bear false witness against thy neighbor," could hardly be taken as failing to condemn the bearing of false witness in favor of one's self. Yet I have never heard it used as an argument against women wearing rouge.

You may be inclined to ask how we can bring up children if we adopt the attitude that telling lies is not always wrong. I am willing to admit that to adopt an absolutistic attitude with them on all moral questions, including lying, is the easy way. But, like many apparently easy ways, it is a very short-sighted one. It is certainly true that I cannot explain the principle of relativity to a 4-year-old. But it is also true that I do not need to take seriously his innumerable petty falsifications. To him there is no moral issue involved, and he probably simply will not understand me when I tell him that he must always tell the truth. Later on, when he does understand, he will find so many highly respected adults, possibly including myself, stating more or less serious falsehoods from time to time that he will be bound to wonder why he should not do likewise. He will probably also begin to wonder about me; whether I am being genuinely honest with him, or whether I simply am not wise to the ways of the world. In either case, his respect for me tends to deteriorate, and I may make more of a liar out of him than he otherwise would become.

I might convince him that God considers lying a sin, that God will know whenever he lies and will keep a record of it, and that sins must be answered for on the Day of Judgment. This might be effectual in keeping certain children from telling lies, but I doubt that I know of a more vicious method of bringing up youngsters. If and when practiced, it may sooner or later result in some form or forms of mental illness, many of them decidedly serious.

My method of dealing with a child on the matter of lying will be and has been tied up as part and parcel of my dealings with him on all other matters. It will be on the basis of democratic fairness—what goes for him goes for me, and vice versa. Much (though not all—that is another matter) of what I expect of him he should expect also of me. Often I have to tell him wherein he is wrong, and on the level of his insight I should tell him why. But I should also put the obligation upon him to do the same with me. Whenever I accuse or scold him unjustly, he should tell me so and why. Thus, we have to talk the point out.

If he lies to me on matters which make a difference to me, he must also expect that I shall do the same with him—that if I promise him a nickel for doing an errand I am obligated to live up to my promise only as long as he lives up to his. My own sons, I believe, have never gotten the impression from me that they should not tell falsehoods because "it is wrong to tell lies." I have simply refused to be seriously moralistic about it, and have frequently in a rather joking way simply said that if you are going to tell a lie tell a good one. Don't be a sap about it.

I have even helped them fix up a story that they might tell to casual questioners about some matter which may have been embarrassing and regarding which the questioner perhaps had no real business asking. Many are the rough spots in my own experience which would have been smoothed if someone whose judgment I respected had given me help of that kind. If I tell a whopper to someone who knows what I am doing and knows that I know that he knows, I am harming neither him nor myself. In fact, it could even be a means of cementing friendship if I used that method of answering a question which he had no business to ask, rather than if I told him bluntly that it was none of his business.

Thus, it would appear just as reasonable to deal with moral principles on a thoroughly relativistic basis as to deal in that way with scientific or other principles. I insist upon my right, as long as I stay within the spirit of the law, to determine my own moral code and to accept or reject Biblical or other moral doctrine as I see fit. I believe children should learn the value of doing right as they see it to be right and because they see it so, not because they need to please or to placate God or because the Bible says so.

Discussion along this line we might prolong indefinitely. But let us study a few contrasts in order to bring into sharper focus the differences between pragmatic and absolutistic theory. If we propose to deal with all things relativistically, what of truth itself? Truth may be taken as a proposition or an insight—call it whatever you will—which somehow gets itself woven into the warp and woof of our living. It changes our feelings or attitudes, and it modifies the way we do things.

Assumptions as to the nature of these propositions or insights—the nature of truth—and as to the method of their attainment differ with differing philosophies. It may be assumed that truth is something which has an essentially objective existence of its own, separate and distinct from any particular embodiment in which we may find it. The term *idea* is conventionally used to designate such a matter.

Circularity is taken to be one such proposition or idea definable as a line which passes through all points in a plane equidistant from a given point. Such a matter seems to have a peculiar set of properties, quite unlike those of any material thing. Since a line is taken to be unidimensional, having length only, a circle which has breadth or thickness cannot be a true or perfect circle. In fact, it cannot be a circle at all. It can only be an imperfect representation or an approximation of a circle. Since any and every material circle which ever has appeared or is likely to appear has both breadth and thickness, we can never hope by searching among material things to find a true circle. Therefore, we must go elsewhere, to the realm of the immaterial . . . nonphysical . . . (metaphysical?). Apparently, a perfect circle can exist only in imagination, in the mind. Moreover, any kind of stuff with which we could even hope to get a true picture of the metaphysical must itself, seemingly, be metaphysical. Hence, mind must also be immaterial or metaphysical.

Furthermore, although all material circles differ from all other material circles and, through undergoing change, differ from themselves from one time to another, it is only in the realm of idea that we can find perfection, that is, the things which by being perfect and complete do not undergo change and therefore represent Ultimate Reality. They are absolute—final and utterly unchanging. Therefore, ideas and ideas alone represent Ultimate Reality; the Absolute. This is the philosophy of *idea-ism,* with an "l" inserted making it *idealism.* We should note this particular derivation of the name, and that it does not signify that idealists alone have ideals or that this philosophy alone has a place for ideals. I have seen and heard it argued that pragmatic philosophy has no place for ideals for if it had it would be idealism; a thorough misconception both of idealism and of pragmatism.

With ideas conceived as metaphysical stuff—disembodied, having an existence independent of any finite mind—yet somehow necessarily connected with some mind, it would seem that these ultimate, original ideas must reside in an Infinite Mind which would be the source of all ideas, at least of all true ones. Moreover, since ideas are taken to be immaterial or nonphysical, no material or physical test may justifiably be applied to determine their truth or falsity. It would be bland presumption, if not worse, to test immaterial things on material bases. How, therefore, shall we obtain truth?

There is only one conceivable way to get truth in the original, or at first-hand, and that is for a finite mind to receive an impression from the Infinite. And the most widely used term for designating this process is *revelation*. Philosophy also makes wide use of the term *intuition*. For the present reader, I believe it unnecessary to enumerate the various forms which revelation or intuition has been assumed to take during the past two and one-half millennia. The major and, I believe, undeniable point is that this view has caused men to close their eyes and their other physical senses, so as to shut out the material world about them, and seek truth through "sheer contemplation."

I have been speaking solely of presumably original truth. Once such is obtained, then other truths may be derived by the process of deduction, or deductive reasoning. If such-and-such be true, then such-and-such follows. But, although ideas derived from other ideas by the process of reasoning may be thought of as relatively true, nevertheless they are basically absolutistic because they are derived from absolutes.

Let us now look at truth in a somewhat different way. A proposition or conception may be considered as inextricably welded to material things rather than as having no conceivable or possible connection with them, or at least as being independent of them. It may be thought of as one of the laws of the universe, with atoms and molecules so completely and indissolubly bound by it that they can do naught but follow. Such laws then may be thought to represent the intelligence of the universe—the order thereof—and the function of human minds in search of intelligence (or truth) is to become aware of these laws. The term now most used to designate this view is *realism*, possibly from medieval Latin *realis,* meaning *thing*.

Since truth is presumed to reside in things, it is to things that we must go in order to find it. Hence, the search for truth becomes a matter of opening our eyes, together with all of our other physical senses, and seeing (using the term loosely) all that we can possibly see. Not only do we use our unaided natural senses, but we also use whatever devices we can invent to improve those senses and make them more discerning. Therefore, the method of obtaining truth is *observation.*

By one observation, of course, we cannot hope to get final and ultimate laws or truths. We have to make thousands upon thousands of observations, or perhaps, as when taking a picture in very poor light, we must make exposures for relatively long periods of time. In either case, truth is achieved in the process of obtaining a summation of impressions of some presumed original. And since the original is assumed to be the immutable Laws of the Universe, the logic of the conception is that the outcome of the search, once you have been finally and ultimately successful, is a conception which is final, ultimate, utterly unchanging, absolute.

Although Galileo, Newton, and others spoke from time to time of hypotheses, the view and process which I have just indicated is essentially that of science from the sixteenth through the nineteenth centuries. It represents what is widely called the Newtonian Conception. Scientists who thought in those terms were indeed inclined to recognize that theories, ideas, or hypotheses seemingly had to be used in scientific investigations, but always such recognition was decidedly deprecatory. Theories were only for those who could not be sure. After you were sure you called them laws, even though perhaps few realistic scientists, at least in later times, were willing to deny that even laws might not sometime have to be changed. But the change would be made because someone had made a mistake, calling something a law when in fact it was not. Was it not Laplace who bemoaned his fate at coming after the great Newton who had left nothing further to be discovered in the realm of physics? I find the following statement in boldface type in a twentieth-century textbook for college students: "A fact is the direct result of observation unmodified by any act of reason. Facts are eternally true. Theories come and go."[1]

I believe that Newton never did really make an unequivocal statement about the place of theories or hypotheses, but I believe it is fair to say that his basic method was to "gather the facts and let the facts

[1] Cady, H. P., *General Chemistry,* New York: McGraw-Hill Book Co., Inc., 2nd ed., 1926, p. 77.

speak for themselves." He always seemed rather ill at ease when he thought he was indulging in theorizing. The following is from a paragraph near the end of the third book of *Principia Mathematica,* in which he is speaking of the cause of universal gravitation: "But hitherto I have not been able to discover the cause of these properties of gravity from phenomena, and *I frame no hypotheses;* for whatever is not deduced from the phenomena is to be called an hypothesis; and hypotheses . . . have no place in experimental philosophy. In this philosophy particular propositions are inferred from the phenomena, and afterwards rendered general by induction."[2]

Just what can be the burden of the intent when one says, "I frame no hypotheses," "hypotheses have no place in experimental philosophy," and "particular propositions are inferred from the phenomena"? Study of the total passage from which the above is taken does show that in this connection Newton did not necessarily mean that he never made hypotheses. He was simply refusing here to enter into controversy about the cause of gravity; he wanted to hold the discussion to the fact of the mere existence of gravity. But there is unquestionable generalization in the above passage, and it was characteristic of Newton that he would first gather all of the facts he could in a given realm, then mull them over and over, trying to read nothing into them, but letting the law finally reveal itself after persistent and prolonged study.

John Locke, contemporary of Newton, presents this view in his *tabula rasa* theory of mind. After first developing the conception of no innate ideas, making the mind at birth a thorough blank, he assumes its passivity by thinking of it as a tablet upon which impressions descend from the outside by way of the physical senses. As these impressions come, they tend to fall into patterns, just as ripples are left on a sandy beach after the tide goes out. Those patterns represent primary ideas. This is the process of *induction,* expressed about as clearly as it can be.

Looking at idealism and realism together, although they seem at first to be diametrically opposed to each other, we find points of fundamental similarity. We have already noted the absolutistic nature of both conceptions. Truth is something which is taken to be ultimate and final—quite unaffected by the process of human minds becoming aware of it. After you once get it, provided you

[2] Italics added.

really get it, there is nothing more to do. The final stage, perfection, is a static one.

Again, the method of obtaining truth, although representing large practical differences in the history of human thought, discovery, and invention, is the same in both cases in the sense of being a discovery. In one case the discovery, regarded as intuitive, is by means of the "inner eye"—the mind's eye—and in the other by the outer or bodily eye. But it is quite reasonable to speak of either one as a revelation of truth. We said above that Newton sought to have natural laws "revealed" to him through extensive and critical study of the observed facts. And certainly we are told that Moses *listened* to the voice of the Lord from the burning bush and *observed* the Ten Commandments by reading them from the two stone tablets received by him atop Mount Sinai.

This similarity is attested by Thomas Paine. In his book, *The Age of Reason,* in which after first rather devastatingly disproving the Bible as being a true revelation of the word of God on the basis of its own inconsistencies, he goes on to say that he is in no wise opposed to the principle of learning God's will by the process of revelation. He wishes only revelation which gives evidence of its divine source by not contradicting itself. This, he says, can alone be found by studying the Laws of God as revealed in nature. This is the Deism of Paine, Hobbes, Franklin, and others. I wonder why the churchmen of the time were so upset by Tom Paine. Moreover, much of the teaching of science in the nineteenth century was predicated upon the belief that it was basically religious, by virtue of its revelation of the laws of God through the study of nature.

As a bit of practical advice, we might suggest that one will be wise always to be very circumspect in passing judgment of his own as to whether a given philosophical writer is realist or idealist. Name him either one or the other, one can be almost sure sooner or later to run into impressive authority to the contrary. Plato, for example, is ordinarily classed as idealist and in our account of idealism we gave pretty largely the Platonic version. Yet many are those who consider him a realist, presenting the case that, since his disembodied ideas are the only ultimate reals and since they also are existents independent of any finite being, Plato's basic doctrine is that of "independent reals," so he is obviously a realist, even a neorealist.

We spoke above of the Deism of Paine. About the same could be said of the philosophy of Thomas Aquinas for, although he has the universe as completely and utterly a creation of the thoughts of God —supposedly the position of objective idealism—Thomists are agreed that Aquinas' doctrine (Thomism) represents philosophic realism and Aquinas himself derives much of his doctrine from Aristotle, the realistic deviant from Plato. Furthermore, John Locke with seeming ease arrives at "spirits" and God even though he abjures the possibility of having any ideas except those which secure original entry into the mind by way of bodily sensations.

Rather than argue such matters—which I refuse to do either here or elsewhere—it would seem the part of wisdom simply to be highly agreeable on the matter of who is realist and who idealist. Take the person's own word for it, or the word of whomsoever wishes to pose as authority, and proceed to the matter at hand.

Philosophical enterprise might be materially advanced by employment of the two categories of *absolutism* on the one hand and *relativism* on the other. This would be analogous to psychology's adoption of *connectionism* and *field theory*. I recognize the unlikelihood that this will soon be done by professional philosophers, for large vested interests are at stake. But it is suggested as a way to keep one's own thinking straight or clear. One can then use whatever names given situations require and at the same time keep one's own bearings.

As to the names suggested—absolutism and relativism—there are disadvantages to both. On the one hand, I certainly get the feeling that realists and idealists do not generally like to be called absolutists. Not long ago a Thomist friend gently chided me, "Remember that absolutism is a smear term." On the other hand, relativism is a term which for some means solipsism—the doctrine that whatever *I myself* think a thing is, that it really is. Not uncommon is the remark, usually off-hand, "Let's be relative; anything goes."

Yet, try as I may, I have not been able to arrive at better ones. As long as we wish to communicate with people we have to use terms with which they are at least somewhat familiar or on which they can get help from Webster. To concoct and employ new ones is to sever contact. With both these terms, recourse to Webster Unabridged or to a college dictionary furnishes the definitions which I wish to employ.

As to the term "relativism," or "relativity," it is in wide use scientifically to designate essentially the scientific outlook which corresponds to the one we are employing in philosophy. Relationalism or contextualism or configurationism might be used, the latter revealing the essentially corresponding outlook in psychology. But, since none of the latter three terms has anywhere near the commonness of usage of relativism and relativity, it seems reasonable that they occupy second, third, and fourth places.

"Pragmatism," "experimentalism," and "instrumentalism" are the three terms generally used by Dewey. The original one, pragmatism, was first employed by Charles Sanders Peirce, first of the Peirce-James-Dewey line of modern pragmatists. It is the term ordinarily employed when the idealism-realism-pragmatism triad is under discussion, as incorporated in our chapter title. Over the past half-century, however, this term has been subjected to such widespread misuse—usage which designates an outlook completely different from that of Peirce, James, and especially Dewey—that it has really become almost a smear term and has tended to fall into disuse. When the public as well as even a large percentage of professional philosophers introduces some comment with the expression, "Now, let's be pragmatic," it comes close to a sure bet that the meaning will be to think only of narrow, short-term, strictly monetary, or otherwise nonidealized ends, any and all of which are thoroughly at odds with Peirce-Dewey thought, though James did indeed use the expression, "the cash value of an idea." "Anything is O.K. if it works" is an attitude which we later take pains to show is not that of philosophical pragmatism. All of this has tended to cause genuinely pragmatic philosophers to look for another name.

"Experimentalism" and "instrumentalism" have both received considerable usage, with preference perhaps to the former. Instrumentalism tends to be unsatisfactory because it gives undue emphasis to the very point which in the preceding paragraph we indicate is objectionable. It tends to support a truncated value-theory, one which recognizes only what things are good *for* and fails to recognize that many of the goods of life (indeed, maybe all of them) also embody the value aspect of just being a *good*—something enjoyed on its own, not because of what else one can get with it. This matter is treated in Chapter 7.

Experimentalism tends to give accurate connotation in the sense that pragmatic epistemology—theory of knowing—is basically supportive of commitment to the experimental (broadly conceived) as the only way of knowing. That is to say, experimental justification alone is taken as the basis for support when one says, "I know," and the claim is never taken as exceeding the degree justified by experimental demonstration. *Belief* may go further, but pragmatists take great care to distinguish between the expressions, "I believe" and "I know." On the latter, they will never go "the whole way."

But the term experimentalism is somewhat unsatisfactory because it is not sufficiently inclusive. It tends to make of pragmatism a truth-theory only, and to minimize or deny its coverage of *ontology* (existence or being) and *axiology* (value) (see Chapters 6 and 7). Experimentalism should give way, therefore, to a name which has the more inclusive connotation, and that is why we have come to employment of *relativism*. From the professional, historical-minded few who are bothered by the earlier, subjectivist employment of the name, we ask generosity in recognizing that our employment is not a subjective, solipsistic one. For their benefit we might add the adjective, objective —*objective relativism*.

Returning now to the idealist-realist orientation, we cannot quite see how absolutism can be taken as a smear term. It seems to focus exactly on the point at issue. The philosophically precise meaning of the term "absolute" is that a given matter—be it object, event, or idea—is taken as a thing-in-itself, independent of all else; absolute, *ab soli*, by and of itself alone; *absolvere*, to set free, to be independent. Derived meanings which are legitimate as well as common are: utterly unchanging; final; perfect. A philosophical absolute is something taken to be of such kind—truth, beauty, morality, justice, or whatever is considered to be *not* subject to alteration by man or by any other finite agency.

That there are many who claim to be idealists or realists who, at the same time, have misgivings, and wish to, and do, introduce exceptions to the absolutist position, we freely recognize. To these we can only say, "If you don't like the position, then why assume it? If in some areas you like it and in others you don't, simply say so and let it go at that. We shall all be helped by keeping our categories as clear as is humanly possible." This, of course, does not settle the matter, but we feel that it does make for clarity. Perhaps we may be permitted to say—even though we know that many will not believe us—that this book is not written for the purpose of making converts. It is written for the purpose of adding a bit, if possible, to clarification of a point of view regarding American educational theory.

There is a point which needs attention because it is often one of confusion. It is not infrequently argued, and by some who it seems should know better, that pragmatism does have and has to have its absolutes. That some so-called pragmatists tend to luxuriate in a few absolutes I do not deny. But that such is necessary, I believe is deniable. The issue seems to be a case of mistaken identity.

In order to view anything relationally (in fact, to size it up at all), it is necessary to establish a point or frame of reference. By taking a foot-candle as a point of relative fixity, we can pinpoint the illumination of a room to a degree of fineness determined by measuring instrument and observer. And, unless some point of fixity is assumed, no fixed statement regarding the illumination of that room is possible. Hence, some argue, an absolute is necessary. But it should be noted that a point of fixity, such as the foot-candle in measuring illumination, is not a *philosophic* absolute. It is indeed a point of fixity, but only for a given purpose and at a given time; it is *relatively* fixed. It may indeed be called relatively absolute, merely meaning relatively fixed. But it can hardly be called absolutely absolute, which is the philosophical meaning.

Some try to bridge the gap by use of the term, "relative absolute," using the word "absolute" as a noun. Such a term would seem to contradict itself. In the philosophical sense, an absolute is something which is taken as unequivocal, unaltered by space, time, or circumstance. But to call something relatively absolute is to change the word absolute from a noun to an adjective and to employ it in the sense of unchanging. To say that a foot-candle is relatively unchanging (hence relatively absolute) as a measure of illumination makes perfectly good sense and appears to be accurate. But to call it an absolute, or even a relative absolute, seems to be neither sensible nor accurate.

To say, for example, as certain educationists have done, that democracy is "one of" the absolutes of pragmatism seems to be a misinterpretation which might even be termed flagrant. Democracy need not be taken, and usually is not, as a frame of reference which is inexorable. Pragmatic educationists are usually careful to specify that they are thinking in terms of education in a democratic society, implying by such specification that other assumptions are possible and, if assumed, would probably make a difference. That democracy is held to, rather firmly, is merely recognition of a presumably observable situation, that the United States of America seem to be committed to the democratic principle and, until they change, educational thinking should be fitted into such a frame of reference. If it should ever come that we the people change our minds, then indeed the frame of reference for educational thinking will have to be altered. To consider that, as long as democracy is taken to be the national commitment, educational policy should be so oriented has all of the characteristics of relational thinking. There is nothing absolutistic about it.

What of pragmatism on the nature of truth or of its attainment? Again we look at a proposition or insight, but this time we assume it to be the product of human minds. At once we are looked at askance. How can a mere human being be so presumptuous! But let us see. I, a mortal being, approach the world and find what I may conveniently characterize as objects, events, and ideas. The world has in a way an *existence* of its own. Each object, event, or idea has a knack of getting along, to quite a degree, without my help. I as a person do not deny that objects and ideas have an existence and events do happen, often quite without reference to, or being influenced by, me.

But suppose that I wish to know about them and approach them with that purpose in mind. I am on a quest for *truth*. There is a difference between existing and knowing, and now I am wanting to know. What do I do? Somehow or other, I am able to size up the world as I find it, often very poorly but sometimes more successfully, in such a way as to make things fall into a pattern, the parts of which appear to me to be related one to another—as parts of an integrated whole. (I doubt that William James was correct in saying that the world to a baby is a "booming, buzzing confusion." A baby simply does not catch the confusion.) I can only view things relationally. Often I do not see very much at a time, not even all of what is directly before my eyes (as my wife will bear enthusiastic witness). But what I do see is relational or *configurational; insightful.*

By *insight* I mean a sense of relationship or a feeling for pattern. I may later attempt to describe or explain this pattern by means of words, but the *sense of pattern* (or insight) is prior to and different from the words which may later be used to express it. I start to say something to a friend but stop because I cannot find a particular word. My sense of pattern—my insight—is there, but for the moment the word is not. Once I hear or think of the word, I immediately recognize it as what I want, and proceed. Words may be means of expressing insights; they are not the insights themselves.

I approach this world that confronts me, seeking truth. Let us say that on a beautiful day in early fall I approach my favorite lake seeking to catch members of the finny tribe. Where are fish to be caught? Ordinarily I think of the fish as feeding along certain spots close to the shoreline. I therefore try these spots, one after another, but today with little success. This must be a bad day for fishing, I decide. Perhaps I had better give it up. But, no, the day seems ideal, the water just right. Possibly I need different bait.

I change from minnows to grasshoppers, from grasshoppers to worms, from worms to plugs, from plugs to flies. No success. I look over the situation. Cooler weather is here. It may be that the top water has become sufficiently cooled to start settling and the summer stagnancy of deep water due to stratification has given way to the fall turnover. Maybe the fish are feeding in deeper water, toward the middle of the lake. I return to minnows for bait, put more weight on my line, start trolling back and forth straight across the lake, trying one depth after another. Soon I begin to catch fish but in a most unusual place, the middle of the lake.

I then envision the underwater situation—oxygenated water clear to the bottom of the lake at all depths, and a lush growth of algae which has not previously been available because of stagnancy. If true, fishing should be good at certain places. I try those places and catch fish. Was my envisionment, or insight, *really* true? I know no more than I have indicated, but I catch fish. And just how much more can we ever know, or do we need to know? We may make guesses or have beliefs that go further—that is our right—but we should distinguish between knowledge and conjecture.

What has all this to do with pragmatism? Possibly it means, as certain philosophers are inclined to believe, that pragmatism may be fine when it comes to catching fish, but it is not a philosophy. This may possibly be true; it is almost bound to be so if we consider philosophy only as a search for Ultimate Reality. I was not searching for Ultimate Reality, I was after fish. And in the process I had to do some searching for truth. Ideas popped into my mind from time to time. Where did they come from? I did not know nor did that question cause me particular concern. My concern was with what the ideas would do for me rather than with where they came from.

Each idea represented a *possible* truth. But whether indeed it was truth was taken by me to be ascertainable only on the basis of try-ing out the logical consequences of the idea and seeing whether those logical consequences, or implications, turned out after experi-ment to be the observed ones. The test of truthfulness of any of those ideas was taken to be the success with which it served as a guide to the kind of action which enabled me to obtain what I sought. If my conception of what those fish were doing led me to methods and places for catching them, the conception was to that degree truthful. Insofar as a conception fails to achieve what I intend that it should, it is untruthful. Truth, therefore, viewed pragmatically, is *that qual-ity of an insight which enables its possessor to design behavior which is successful in that it achieves what it is designed to achieve. Accuracy* in the *anticipation* of future events is the pragmatic test for truth.

The process of attaining truth is that of reflective-scientific thought. Faced with a problem, a forked-road or no-road situation, we look about for possible solutions which we treat tentatively, as ideas or hypotheses. We already have considerable data, else there would be no problem. We gather more data, arranging them and rearranging them in the light of our various hypotheses, asking which hypothesis causes them to fall together into the most har-monious pattern. Finding one which *appears* best, we do some rea-soning. If that be true, what follows? In other words we predict new data and the circumstances under which we should find them. Read the exploits at crime detection of Sherlock Holmes, Ellery Queen, or whomsoever is your favorite.

On the basis of the prediction we set up the necessary conditions and start things going. In other words, we perform an experiment. This is the crucial test. If the hypothesis which we employ causes us accurately to anticipate the experimental results, we say that *so far forth* our hypothesis has proven true. And this is our conclusion. This is the method of science, as scientific investigations are con-ducted today.

No longer do scientists wait until all of the data are in before attempting to tease out conclusions. Scientific investigators are con-tinually playing hunches, anticipating what they might find and then going out to see whether they find it; looking in certain spots for certain things, not simply sweeping the world with a dragnet and taking what they happen to catch.

No longer do scientists claim to approach the world without preconceived notions and without bias. They overtly assume that probably no human being is without bias, especially those who claim to have none, and if they would be genuinely successful in their investigations they must recognize and define clearly what biases they have and try to correct for them, possibly even by leaning a bit backwards against them. They are concerned with finding genuine truth, not mere justification for their own preconceived notions.

Thus, the pragmatic way of attaining truth is to make use, perhaps, of idealistic intuition, although it is simply called imagination. Thereby hypotheses are obtained. Claud Bernard, renowned French physiologist of the mid-nineteenth century, spoke somewhat as follows: "When you are outside of the laboratory, let your imagination wrap you round like a cloak. But when you enter the laboratory, lay your imagination aside as you would a cloak, less it interfere with your observations."

Then it is deductive reasoning, also employed in idealism, which is used to work out the implications of the various hypotheses. But the function of hypotheses and of deductions therefrom is not to settle truth; it is merely to obtain possibilities which shall be put to the test of experience and experiment.

The observations of realism play a real part in scientific investigation. All of the facts that possibly can be gathered are gathered, and they are certainly encouraged to do as much speaking as they will. But in a very real sense they are *made* by a scientific investigator to speak, when in less capable hands they would remain silent. Herein scientists often become poetically intuitive.

And one new step has been added, going theoretically beyond idealism and realism. That step is *experimentation*. Through the course of philosophic history, idealists and realists have both done much experimenting. But they have not admitted it in their theories.

SELECTED REFERENCES

Breed, Frederick S., *Education and the New Realism,* New York: The Macmillan Company, 1939. A fairly good presentation of realism, but a very faulty one of Dewey.

Broudy, Harry A., *Building a Philosophy of Education,* New York: Prentice-Hall, Inc., 1954, chap. 5.

Burtt, Edwin A. (ed.), *The English Philosophers from Bacon to Mill,* New York: The Modern Library, 1939.

Butler, J. Donald, *Four Philosophies* (rev. ed.), New York: Harper & Brothers, 1957.

Childs, John L., *American Pragmatism and Education,* New York: Henry Holt and Company, 1956.

Dewey, John, *Democracy and Education,* New York: The Macmillan Company, 1916.

Dewey, John, *Reconstruction in Philosophy* (enlarged ed.), Boston: The Beacon Press, 1948.

Durant, Will, *The Story of Philosophy,* Garden City, N.Y.: Garden City Publishing Company, Inc., 1926.

Edman, Irwin (ed.), *The Works of Plato,* New York: The Modern Library, 1928.

Fast, Howard, *The Selected Works of Tom Paine,* New York: The Modern Library, 1946, p. 329.

Gallie, W. B., *Pierce and Pragmatism,* Harmondsworth, Middlesex: Penguin Books, 1952.

McKeon, Richard (ed.), *Introduction to Aristotle,* New York: The Modern Library, 1947.

Mayer, Frederick, *Philosophy of Education for Our Time,* New York: The Odyssey Press, Inc., 1958.

National Society for the Study of Education, Forty-first Yearbook, Part I, *Philosophies of Education,* Bloomington, Ill.: Public School Publishing Company, 1942.

National Society for the Study of Education, Fifty-fourth Yearbook, Part I, *Modern Philosophies and Education,* Chicago: The University of Chicago Press, 1955.

Paine, Thomas, *Age of Reason,* New York: Freethought Press Association, Part 1.

Park, Joe, *Selected Readings in the Philosophy of Education,* New York: The Macmillan Company, 1958.

Wiener, Philip P. (ed.), *Selected Writings of Charles S. Pierce: Values in a Universe of Chance,* Garden City, N.Y.: Doubleday & Company, Inc., 1958, chap. 6.

CHAPTER 5

Is Modern Science Inductive?

IN a late-1950 issue of *The Science Teacher* an article appeared, written by a person who was characterized as "one of the 'deans' of science education in America," in which the case was pleaded for inductive teaching. Following are excerpts from the article:

In their required courses in psychology prospective teachers of science are taught the nature and importance of both the inductive and the deductive methods of instruction. Yet, later, when these young teachers begin their careers, they follow the practices of an overwhelming majority of high school teachers . . . in practically, if not completely omitting the inductive method.

In inductive teaching the pupil starts with some problem, the answer to which he does not already know. He then assembles, by observation or experiment, or both, evidence from which he can arrive at a tentative answer to the problem.

Then follows a quotation from the Forty-sixth Yearbook of the N.S.S.E.:

By inductive teaching is meant progressing from the particular to the general, or more specifically, from facts to concepts and principles.

The article then proceeds:

The inductive method is the one by which scientific knowledge has grown from its earliest beginnings; where the inductive method has inherited its logical place, as it has in a small but increasing number of high schools, these (deductive) procedures are reversed. The laboratory work comes first and the study assignments follow it.

This is not an isolated case. In fact, it is quite common. We find

eminent writers or speakers on American educational theory frequently referring to or thinking of the method of modern scientific
investigation as that of induction. In another 1950 publication, a
book on educational philosophy by a well-known author, the following expressions are typical—"experimental induction," "we study
inductively," "scientific (in the modern sense) and inductive," "an
inductive study."

Again, at a nation-wide educational meeting, a professor of physics and of the philosophy of science from a leading university, after
first commenting that science teaching at the general college level
should be deductive, characterized scientific procedure as inductively
arriving at principles and then deductively putting them to work.

In sharp contrast, Albert Einstein wrote as follows: "There is no
inductive method which could lead to the fundamental concepts of
physics. Failure to understand this fact constituted the basic philosophical error of so many investigators of the nineteenth century.
. . . Physics constitutes a logical system of thought which is in a
state of evolution, and whose basis cannot be obtained through
distillation by any inductive method from the experiences lived
through, but which can only be attained by free invention."[1]

The foregoing quotations are presented for the purpose of emphasizing a point in teaching theory which is at present the subject
of widespread confusion. The authorities first quoted are not alone
in their contentions. It may have been thought, at least hoped, that
the assertions in methods books of a half-century ago, on inductive
and deductive teaching, would by now have been corrected. But
such seems not to be the case.

In those earlier methods books, usually in a chapter of its own,
supposedly deductive teaching was described and assigned a place.
Another chapter would then deal with inductive teaching, with instructions as to when it, in turn, should be used. The thought was
that prescientific thinking was deductive and that it should be used
only for those aspects of a course in which a truth has presumably
been already established. The teaching procedure then would be to
start with the presumed truth (a general idea) and proceed by logical deduction to unravel its meanings for particular or concrete cases.

On the other hand, an inductive lesson would be one in which
observations of concrete cases would first be made, after which by

[1] Albert Einstein, *Out of My Later Years,* New York: Philosophical Library, 1950,
pp. 78, 96.

induction a generalization would be reached. This inductive method, as the two first-quoted authors indicate, was taken to be the scientific way to obtain truth and the major way in which science classes should be taught. It was a case of "gather the facts and let the facts speak for themselves."

That Einstein has spoken so emphatically against induction as the method of modern scientific investigation will come perhaps as a distinct shock to many. What can he possibly have meant? The meaning will be clear to those who have carefully considered implications of "the complete act of thought" as described and explained in 1910 by John Dewey and as supported and elaborated by certain of Dewey's later writings and by writers such as P. W. Bridgeman and Boyd H. Bode.

According to Webster-Merriam Unabridged Dictionary, induction is an "Act or process of reasoning from a part to a whole, from particulars to generals, or from the individual to the universal." And, according to Runes' *Dictionary of Philosophy,* " 'Perfect' induction is assertion concerning all the entities of a collection on the basis of examination of each and every one of them. The conclusion sums up but does not go beyond the facts observed." In the preceding chapter we have already noted the position taken by Newton.

Induction is, thus, considered in strict theory to be a process of gathering the facts and letting the facts speak. Be "thoroughly objective"; approach the facts with an "open mind"; read nothing of personal opinion or bias into them. This, in strictly theoretical expression, represents the Newtonian "method of science"—philosophic realism—and is what Einstein had in mind when he made the previously quoted statements in denial of the efficacy of induction. Eby and Arrowood, in describing the inductive method (or "New Organon") of Francis Bacon, point out that "Experimentation, as a process, is not different from observation, but involves merely the expert control of conditions, so as to facilitate or simplify observation."[2] We add this point in order to make clear that, although experiments were performed by those who considered the scientific method as strictly inductive, their interpretation of the nature of experimentation was quite different from the interpretation placed upon it by theorists such as Einstein and Dewey.

[2] Frederick Eby and C. F. Arrowood, *Development of Modern Education,* New York: Prentice-Hall, Inc., 1934, p. 239.

In contrast, the scientific-reflective process as envisioned as well as practiced today may be described as follows. First, a problem appears. Available facts or data, some of which perhaps are only newly discovered, appear not to be interpretable on the basis of previous theory. For example, during several years prior to the "discovery" of Pluto, the observed orbit of Uranus appeared to be slightly divergent from what it should have been if only the then-recognized planets existed. Fact and theory were a bit at odds with one another, and astronomers wondered why.

Second, hypotheses are formulated. In order to account for the evident discrepancies in the orbit of Uranus, the existence of an additional planet was assumed or posited. To this point, the process appears to be distinctly inductive. But the conclusion (a generalization) is still a considerable way off.

Third, implications (or logical consequences) of the new hypothesis are deduced. In our example, those of the old had long since been thoroughly worked out and found to be out of keeping with current observations, thereby creating the problem. Assuming a then-unknown planet, by logical deduction—in this case mathematical—determination was made of its size, location, orbit, and velocity. At this point the "deduction" was distinctly inductive in direction; it proceeded toward precise formulation of the generalization—the nature of the assumed planet.

However, it now took a deductive turn; but in two directions. The first was mere reversal of the just-noted *inductive* deduction. On the basis of precise assumptions regarding the new planet, could the facts already known be precisely deduced? To this point, there was little of what might have been termed experimentation.

Then deductions were turned toward the future; toward predictions of possible facts which were at that time unknown. Where, when, and under what conditions might the possible new planet be seen? Training the telescope upon the right places, at the right times, fulfilling other requisite conditions, and making the proper observations—these were all characteristics of modern scientific experimentation. It was not a mere case of gathering what could be gathered in the manner of a dragnet. The "blinker" technique, for example, was a manufactured one, designed to produce a set of facts highly peculiar to this particular investigation and unobtainable except by way of carefully executed design.

The fourth and final step in the scientific-reflective process is arrival at a conclusion. In light of the information which has been gathered, what interpretation or generalization is indicated?

There are many who fail to realize that scientists hold themselves accountable for living up to a certain set of rules or criteria in arriving at a conclusion. Scientists do not think of only one *right* conclusion as possible and of arrival at any other as a result either of gross incompetence or of vicious intent. Specifically, scientists insist that all obtainable facts be gathered and that, in reaching a conclusion, all such facts be taken into account. This we may call the principle of *adequacy*. Furthermore, the *interpretation* of the facts which is taken to be satisfactory and thus to conclude the study— hence the *conclusion*—is the one which causes all of the collected facts to fall together in a harmonious pattern, one in which the logic is clear so as to make deductions readily possible. This can be called the principle of *harmony*. Thus, the rule or criterion which scientists employ when they sit in judgment on hypotheses is that of *adequacy and harmony of conclusion in light of available or obtainable data.*

That this criterion does not represent what all persons take to be a universal good will be evident to anyone who will take a moment to consider how human minds work. Are there not those among us who insist that we *must* believe in God, even though they themselves admit that there is no scientific evidence to support such belief? Whether we should entertain such a belief, or should not, is not the question here. The point is that the scientific rules or criteria for determining what conclusions are good and what are not good do not represent rules or criteria which enjoy universal acceptance. In this sense they cannot be taken as representing a Universal Good, and it would perhaps be quite unwise or unjust to dub a person either incompetent or vicious who does not take them to be so. All we should say, seemingly, is that there are myriads of occasions upon which human minds arrive at conclusions on bases other than scientific. Whether they should do so is quite another matter.

To summarize the steps of the scientific-reflective method as we have described it: (1) a problem arises because available data seem to be out of harmony with one another in light of current interpretations or generalizations; (2) alternative interpretations are sought, new ones are invented if necessary, and all are taken into consideration (typically called hypotheses); (3) on the basis of each hypothesis, which serves as a generalization, concrete facts are deduced, some of which may already be known whereas others require experimental origination because they are not already known or may not previously have existed; (4) if one of the hypotheses is found to harmonize all known facts and to predict with accuracy unknown facts —the criteria of *adequacy* and *harmony* in the interpretation of available or obtainable data—the conclusion is that it has been found to be an acceptable hypothesis. On the other hand, with reference to step (4), if no considered hypothesis is found to satisfy the criterion, the conclusion is that the problem is not yet solved. This, it seems reasonable to say, is the method of modern scientific investigation.

The story of Einstein's arrival at his interpretation of the way the world runs is well told by Max Wertheimer in the seventh chapter of his posthumously published book, *Productive Thinking.* That account illustrates the process as above described. And it shows why Einstein could say, as noted earlier, that "physics constitutes a logical system of thought . . . whose basis . . . can only be attained by free invention." Hypotheses do indeed represent "free inventions," and it was for this reason that Newton declared, "I make no hypotheses."

The fact that science-education theorists have long been satisfied to characterize the scientific method as an inductive process, not a deductive one, is responsible for much of the puttering, time-consuming, uneducative busy work carried on in secondary school and college or university science laboratories. James Bryant Conant remarks that "the amassing of data does not constitute advance in science."[3] This remark we would commend for careful consideration by all teachers, as well as Conant's entire Chapter Four, in which it appears. Teachers would also do well to consider with care the following statement, made in a book review by J. L. Walsh, Perkins Professor of Mathematics in Harvard University: "The investigator should not fear the charge of 'arguing by analogy.' Perhaps the truest of the world's wisdom is embodied in parables—indeed, perhaps all wisdom consists in parables, including analogies and abstractions."[4]

To expect that high school and college students will be greatly educated by much of what they are required to do in their regular laboratory work seems unrealistic, to say the least. What, in terms of genuine scientific investigation, can be really achieved even in

---

[3] James Bryant Conant, *On Understanding Science,* New Haven, Conn.: Yale University Press, 1947, p. 103.
[4] *Scientific American* (August, 1949), p. 56.

college classroom-laboratories is not a great deal. If we, who are or have been science teachers, would take seriously a certain widespread attitude on the part of students, some rather fundamental changes in the conduct of classroom-laboratory work might soon be in the making. That attitude is that the educational value which students are expected to extract from laboratory work is a bit hard to divine; that the instructors themselves are far from clear on what it should be; and that the work, therefore, is to be done and the reports written with the least possible expenditure of effort and time.

If this attitude were entertained only by less capable students, those who generally are unappreciative of the value of intellectual effort, it might be brushed aside as unworthy of professorial consideration. But, although most science instructors may be able to adduce notable exceptions, it is an attitude held by hosts of highly capable and excellent students as well as by others.

A direct result of such an attitude is the widespread, long-standing practice, of employing, whenever students can possibly do so, extralaboratory sources for obtaining the information necessary to write reports—textbooks, other students' reports, etc. Much of the time, science teachers choose to ignore this situation. And much of the time when the situation is recognized as a problem, it is a presumed deterioration of the moral fiber of present-day students which is deplored. It is the sense of this discussion that *science teachers would do well to reconsider their basic conceptions of classroom science-laboratory work and see whether some fault might also reside there.*

Has it indeed come to pass that students are in large part viciously lazy? Are they fundamentally opposed to expenditure of intellectual effort? Or might it be that students are more critical than "in the old days" and, when they find certain supposedly educational requirements to be essentially noneducative, they circumvent them if possible?

Observation of natural facts and events is indeed an aspect, and an essential one, of modern scientific-reflective investigation. But it is far from all. Yet, to consider scientific investigation as essentially inductive—a case of gathering the facts so that the facts may speak—is to make observation of natural facts and events essentially *the* method of scientific investigation. In such a case, following instructions in laboratory manuals so that the particular facts envisioned by the author may be observed by the students is, logically, *the* method of science instruction. Generalizations will then follow as a matter of course.

But when a genuine problem—one which for students is a really I-don't-know situation—is a prerequisite, when *invention* of hypotheses and pursuance of thought for what can be logically deduced from these hypotheses are recognized as essential precursors to experimentation, then scientific investigation is much more than simple induction or the gathering of facts by observational methods. Classroom-laboratory work, when conceived in this manner, will be taken as an integral part of the entirety of classroom study regarding a given problem. And, when an experiment necessary to shed light on the overall study is impossible to perform in a classroom, it will be thoroughly justifiable to think of laboratory procedure as requiring careful study of a *report* of such an experiment, one performed by those who are competent and have the needed facilities.

For example, traditional and complicated nutritional experiments on growing plants and animals are practically out of the question for most high school and even college laboratories. Only the simplest, or incomplete, parts of such experiments can be performed during the time and with the facilities available. What should be done? Perhaps, in the context of a larger question under study, it would be well to perform such experiments, or such parts of them as can be performed, and then to read about how the whole experiment was done under ideal conditions. The actual performance of what can be done in a school laboratory, if in the context of a larger problem, will give students a certain first-hand experience which will help them achieve the insights necessary to read, with intelligence and wisdom, the reports of what others have done. Under such circumstances, it will be quite unnecessary to apologize to anyone insistent on scientific procedure for substituting such readings for mere time spent in laboratory puttering. In terms of improved student attitudes, the results may perhaps be astounding.

In this connection we would recommend perusal of Conant's proposals, in the previously cited book, of an overall study plan. Our only significant point of disagreement is his remark that the plan is suitable only for general education, presumably on the junior college level. The plan would seem to be highly advisable for advanced classes as well.

Closely allied to the concept of science as an inductive process is the tendency to hold hypotheses in low esteem. We have noted previously Newton's comment that "hypotheses . . . have no place in experimental philosophy." In an article from an issue of *Science Education* appearing in late 1950, we find the statement that "proper science instruction will help individuals to understand that natural laws, principles, and fundamental scientific theories have rather high worth, while hypotheses, superstitions, hunches, guesses, and deliberate lies are inferior ideas."

It is not often that a responsible writer publishes a statement which places hypotheses in the same category as superstitions and deliberate lies. But to publish statements which *imply* inferior status of hypotheses—inferior to established principles or laws—is not uncommon. Such statements imply that guesses or hypotheses are what one indulges in before achieving "real" knowledge, but are to be discarded as soon as a "law" is discovered. This attitude is a logical consequence of the belief that science is a strictly inductive process. When the present writer studied chemistry in college, there was considerable controversy as to whether it should be called Avogadro's *Law* or Avogadro's *Hypothesis*. The "status" of the principle would presumably have been greatly enhanced if it could without question have been called a law.

As a result of the Einstein revolution in physics, however, scientists who understand its implications no longer look down their noses at hypotheses. On the contrary, they recognize scientific generalizations of any kind as never getting beyond the realm of the hypothetical. They say, in effect, that the claim is not that atoms and molecules "really are" the way they are now envisioned. The claim is merely that they "act as if they were" that way. And they do not entertain any particular hope that it ever will be otherwise. That is the meaning of the Walsh statement, quoted earlier, regarding analogies and parables.

Relativistically speaking, the world's wisdom is taken to be couched in the form of hypotheses, free inventions of human minds; hypotheses in which greater or lesser degrees of assurance can be placed, dependent upon their degree of verification by human experience particularly in the form of scientific experimentation. Therefore, rather than placing hypotheses in the category of "inferior ideas," the attitude of competent men of science today is that hypotheses should be accorded all of the respect due to scientific generalizations of any and all kinds, because scientific generalizations never divest themselves of hypothetical status.

To view scientific procedure as strictly inductive is to fail to portray with accuracy the process of scientific investigation as it is carried on today. Such failure causes the teaching of science to fall far short of achieving the educational values which might otherwise be attained. If we wish to continue using the words "induction" and "deduction," we should recognize clearly the inductive-deductive nature of scientific method, what of it is inductive and what is deductive, and strive to achieve due recognition of the proper place and function of each.

SELECTED REFERENCES

Braithwaite, R. B., *Scientific Explanation,* Cambridge, England: Cambridge University Press, 1955.

Bruner, J. S., Goodnow, J. J., and Austin, G. A., *A Study of Thinking,* New York: John Wiley and Sons, Inc., 1956.

Conant, James B., *On Understanding Science,* New Haven, Conn.: Yale University Press, 1947.

Dewey, John, *How We Think,* Boston: D. C. Heath & Company, 1910.

Dewey, John, *Logic, The Theory of Inquiry,* New York: Henry Holt and Company, 1938.

Dewey, John, *Reconstruction in Philosophy,* Boston: The Beacon Press, 1948, chap. 6.

Einstein, Albert, *Out of My Later Years,* New York: Philosophical Library, 1950.

Frank, Philipp, *Philosophy of Science,* Englewood Cliffs, N.J.: Prentice-Hall, Inc., 1957.

Frank, Philipp, *Relativity, A Richer Truth,* Boston: The Beacon Press, 1950.

International Encyclopedia of Unified Science, Vol. I, Parts 1 and 2, No. 7, pp. 423–504.

Jeans, Sir James, *The New Background of Science,* New York: The Macmillan Company, 1933.

Oppenheimer, J. Robert, *Science and the Common Understanding,* New York: Simon and Schuster, 1953, 1954.

Reichenbach, Hans, *From Copernicus to Einstein,* New York: Philosophical Library, 1942.

Wertheimer, Max, *Productive Thinking,* New York: Harper & Brothers, 1945.

CHAPTER 6

Existence, Causation, and Intelligence

THE question of existence and causation is a persistent one in philosophy. What an object or an event *appears* to be is easily told. But what it "really is" is a question with which mankind has persistently struggled but for which no satisfactory answer has so far evolved. Yet the question is considered philosophically important; so important, in fact, that philosophy is often defined as a search for "Ultimate Reality." And, since pragmatic or instrumentalist philosophy is so frequently accused of begging this question and, in consequence, of not being a philosophy at all, it would seem not amiss to write down a few thoughts which involve a distinctly pragmatic or relativistic outlook. The question is one of *ontology*—the nature of existence or being.

Idealism carries the assumption that ultimate reality is of the nature of mind or idea. Thinking an object, whether by God or by man, is what brings it into existence or causes it to be. Hence, "mind is the explainer." The thought or idea of an object or event is reality; its tangible, sensible, or material form is merely a finite expression of that which is taken as fundamental (or infinite)—the idea or the thought.

Realism carries the assumption that ultimate reality is of the nature of essence or law. One can think of the universe as composed of some fundamental essence or essences—electrons, protons, and neutrons were so considered only a short time ago—and that these essences, behaving in accordance with fundamental or universal law or laws, cause objects and events to come into existence. Thus, the *laws of nature* cause electrons, protons, and neutrons to undergo certain combinations and thereby form atoms, atoms to form molecules,

molecules to form substances, substances to form objects, and objects by their action or activities to form events.

Therefore, it is evident that both idealism and realism posit a fundamental (or natural?) "order," which is the ultimate ontological existent and whose nature it behooves man to divine. This natural or fundamental order is not subject to time, place, or circumstance but, instead, accounts for them. Hence, such order is absolute— *ab soli;* dependent upon itself alone. Within the two foregoing philosophies, only a thorough-going solipsism avoids the assumption of a fundamental, objective order which exists prior to and independent of any finite knower, potential or actual.

The major purpose of this chapter is to consider the position of relativism—objective relativism, at any rate—on the matter of independent order or existence. What is it that exists or has being? And what "causes" it to exist?

When a potential knower, such as a normal human being, views an event and the objects which have participated in it, he receives a vivid impression that such objects and event are distinctly real. They do not appear ephemeral. They seem to be really there and to have really happened. Take, for example, an automobile accident. Even though the persons involved may not have intended it, they seem genuinely affected by it. They are bruised and hurt, a repair bill impends, and spectators shudder to think how they themselves might have been affected. All have been, or might have been, pushed or pulled about whether they wanted it or not. The phenomenon makes a real difference both to participants and to spectators. It seems to be real.

Reality, therefore, seems to be definable as something which might, should, or does make a difference to someone or something. The difference may be anticipated or known, or it may not. Thus, *knowing* and *being* are distinctly different from one another, and one who views reality in this manner cannot reasonably be dubbed a solipsist. Moreover, such a definition of reality implies that an idea or a thought may be as real as a stone wall. Thoughts or ideas make tremendous differences to most of us whether they are our thoughts or the thoughts of others; it may well be that they make more difference to human beings than does anything else.

But, as to being or existence, what is its ultimate nature? And what is the ultimate "cause" of all things? In other words, what constitutes Ultimate Reality? It is when the question of *Ultimate*

Reality arises that pragmatists or objective relativists in effect walk out on the discussion; and they do so because to them such discussions appear utterly futile.

It seems that this perhaps is the crucial point at which logical positivism balks at being thoroughly relativistic. In a recent symposium on operationism, Dr. Bergmann has the following to say:

All this [the procedure of operational measurement of a ledge taken to be three feet long] is completely noncontroversial. Equally non-controversial is, to my mind, the proper answer to an objector who voices, as it were, certain apprehensions of common-sense realism. "What you say," so the objection goes, "sounds suspiciously as if you thought you were somehow making the ledge's length when you measured it. Yet, the ledge has a length that is there and, in particular, the length of three feet whether or not you or anybody else measures it." Here is what I would answer. "The query for what there is, the so-called ontological question, belongs to first philosophy. It cannot even be discussed intelligently in this narrow context, and the logic of scientific concept formation, with or without the operationist footnote, has no bearing on it whatsoever. If it will help to convince you that this is so, I am prepared, as long as we talk in this very general fashion, to put the conditional in the subjunctive, 'if one *were* to do this and this, then one *would* observe that and that.' On the other hand, if you want to *know* how long the ledge is and have no means of inferring it from something else that you already know, then you will indeed have to measure it. This is perfectly commonsensical. So you need not fear that by admitting it you have fallen into a philosophic trap."[1]

Dr. Bergmann immediately dismisses operationism by adding, "Fundamentally, this is all that needs to be said about operationism as such." It would appear that, when he says "if you want to *know* how long the ledge is . . . you will indeed have to measure it," he is simply saying that, if you want *really* to know something, you must indeed *observe* it rather than *operate* upon it. In other words, you must disclose ultimate reality.

When an object or an event presents a convincing appearance of being real, an objective relativist for the moment at least takes it to be real and deals with it as such. It is so taken because it actually does, or can conceivably, make a difference to one. It has to be taken into account in whatever plans one might evolve relevant thereto. It cannot be disregarded without likelihood of one's plans going awry.

But whether it represents ultimate reality is a matter on which one

[1] Gustave Bergmann, "Sense and Nonsense in Operationism," *The Scientific Monthly*, Vol. 79, No. 4 (October, 1954), p. 211.

can make no plans at all. It might possibly be advantageous to know. But how can we know? Moreover, how can we know whether a given conception of what ultimate reality might be is even in the right direction? The idea that piecemeal discovery will assuredly at last disclose what has been at least vaguely indicated all along the way is one which is thoroughly at odds with human experience. Take, for example, the typewriter key "l." Is it to be taken as the letter or as the numeral? How can we know unless we know a larger configuration in which it is to appear? Moreover, how can we know beforehand whether a handwritten vertical line is numeral one, the nose of a face, or the left-hand side of a rectangular figure?

It can perhaps be considered common knowledge today that, for a potential knower, perception of a given object or event is as much dependent upon the configuration in which it is to be observed as on its own qualities. And a million observations of its qualities in a given configuration will be of little, if any, help in predicting what qualities it will evince in a new configuration. To try to predict with accuracy what we would know if we knew what we do not know now—before the overall configuration is known— would be futile. A relativist feels that he has far too much on his hands with the continuing task of doing his part in ordering the affairs of mankind to expend time and energy chasing the pot of gold at the end of the rainbow. And who can know but that the gold is really there?

Returning to the question of whether there is a cause-and-effect "order" in the universe independent of human intervention, a relativist readily and frankly admits that he does not know and that he sees no way ever of knowing. But, and this is a point seldom made explicit, *he assumes that there is*. The very fact that a thoughtful man, whether he be philosopher or scientist, attempts to *read order into* the affairs of the world is, in itself, evidence that he is assuming the universe to be independently orderly. Else, he would be embarked on an almost hopeless quest.

For example, a relativist—be he philosopher or scientist—assumes a gravitational order of greater or lesser universality and designs the affairs of his life in accordance therewith. But the strictly relativistic position is always, without exception, that any order *which he takes to act upon* is an order *which he reads into* the universe; not one that is "really there." *He neither asserts nor denies that it is really there*. He assumes that it is, but this assumption is based on his experiences and will be changed as soon as, but not until, his experiences warrant. It has none whatsoever of the characteristics of a philosophic absolute. For him it has reality. He orders the affairs of his life by it. To him it makes a real difference. But for him it is not ultimate reality. It has all the ephemerality of his own brain processes, which produced it.

The Baconian-Newtonian science of the several centuries prior to the twentieth has been insistent on assignment of natural cause-and-effect relationships to processes and events. A "natural law" was presumed to be an ontological existent; a given cause directly and dependably responsible for a given effect. The epistemological function of science was, in consequence, that of discovering such independently existing, cause-and-effect relationships. Logically, therefore, nature is determinate. If one had complete knowledge of all natural laws, one could predict with certainty the course of a given line of events and, by logical projection, could plot the complete course of universal history. Thus, natural law is *the* fundamental, ontological existent; it causes electrons, protons, and neutrons to cause, in turn, atoms, molecules, substances, objects, and events. Natural law represents, in consequence, ultimate reality. This is philosophical and scientific realism. Nature is determinate, and natural law or order is the ultimate determinant.

The relativistic upheaval of the twentieth century, both in science and in philosophy, raised again the possibility of indeterminacy. Seemingly, one cannot have both complete clearness and complete coverage at one and the same time. The point is well illustrated by one's experience with a compound microscope; the more clearly one is able to focus upon a given stratum of an object under magnification, the more thoroughly the rest is out of focus. On the other hand, when one is able (perhaps with naked eyes) to see an object as a whole, one is by that very circumstance unable to see the minutiae which a powerful microscope can reveal. In other words, one cannot have everything at once.

The relativistic assumption that the "order" which a given individual reads into the universe is his own concoction avoids the dilemma of determinism. Whether nature is ultimately determinate or indeterminate is no longer a problem. It may be either way. In any case, however, as far as man's designs or plans are concerned, it is *man's interpretation of* what is "out there" which counts, and these interpretations are in no sense absolutely deterministic. They serve man's purposes of prediction, and via them he orders his life. He assumes his "laws" to be accurate until experience demonstrates them otherwise. They are what he has to work with, and all he has. But are these "laws" ultimately true? There is no assumption that they are. On the basis of man-made laws, man determines his plans for action. Subsequently, such laws and plans are subject to review and revision if and whenever experience so indicates.

Briefly then, the relativistic position is that a natural, ontological "order," independent of human influence except as human beings function as part of it, is neither asserted nor denied. But, as a working principle, it is assumed. The solipsistic position is consciously rejected. Moreover, it is not covertly though implicitly functioning. Both objects and events are taken as existing, and being caused by influences, independent of human thinking except as human thinking is a direct participant. In a loose sense, it may be justifiable to say that people "discover" natural order, but, when speaking with care and precision, a relativist will use the word *invention* rather than discovery. Whether Cosmic Mind, or God, is responsible for ontological order, either by thinking it or by creating it in some other way, is a matter on which relativists are convinced that no finite mind does or can have knowledge and is one on which no commitment, either for or against, is required by the logic of the position which we see fit to call objective relativism.

It should be noted, however, that this ontological "order" or orderliness is not assumed to be necessarily a single one. It might be, but on the basis of present knowledge it hardly seems to be. For example, for an individual the size of a man, the large aggregation of molecules known as a billiard ball appears to behave in very orderly and predictable fashion. Yet there are ways, as far as physicists have yet been able to discern, in which the individual molecules of such a ball appear not to do so. Moreover, to an individual approximately half the size of one of those molecules, the orderliness with which he would have to deal would likely be far different from that of an individual who is man-size.

Again, to argue with a jeweler that, because the carbon atoms in a diamond are the same as those in a chunk of coal, he should sell you a diamond for the going price of coal would hardly be convincing. And, although human beings are assumed to be composed of chemical elements, it does not follow that the behaviors of human beings can be accurately predicted by the "laws" which appear to hold for chemical action. There is, of course, a sense in which the general formula of Einstein—$E = mc^2$—is taken to be a universal, but as such the formula is not of much use to a cultural anthropologist or to one who wishes to know what certain New York Stock Exchange prices will be six months from now.

Therefore, although in a given context or configuration we seem to be justified in assuming an ontological orderliness to which we *hope* our epistemological (man-made) "laws" closely correspond, nevertheless we hardly seem justified as yet in assuming any such orderliness to be a single universal, or an absolute.

Seemingly, the difference between the realistic and the relativistic position is not on the *assumption* of ontological, natural order, but is basically on the criterion for determining truth-quality and perhaps the nature of truth itself—therefore on epistemology. When one takes truth to be a "quality of a report on reality"—the quality of correspondence to reality—one makes truth-getting a process of discovery, of trying to find what is really, ultimately there. Thus, the truth-test becomes one of correspondence to something which, by definition, can never be known short of infinity—too late for mortal man. In consequence, realism commits man to a quest which he always has to admit, when pressed, is a hopeless one.

Contrary to recurrent claims, relativist ontology is not one of creation by a potential or actual knower. An object or event is neither true nor false; nor, inherently, either good or bad. It simply *is*. Epistemology is one thing, axiology another, and ontology still something else. It is quite reasonable, however, to speak of ontological existents in contrast with existents which are epistemological or axiological. A truth can exist, as can also a value or a norm. And herein comes to light an interesting difference. For, although objects and events are taken as not humanly contrived (with the exception previously noted), the relativistic position is that both epistemological and axiological existents are human contrivances. Here is where human creativity enters. Man makes his own truths and his own values. A relativist assumes that the "laws" of the world—both epistemological and axiological—are man-made.

Considering reality as that which makes a difference to one—as that which may not be pushed nor pulled about willy-nilly, which has resistivity of its own and which on occasions will itself do some pushing and pulling—it follows that reality can be either ontological, epistemological, or axiological. For items in all three categories do make a difference to human strivings. But, as far as intelligent or humanly designed action is concerned, the reality which is crucial is of the man-made varieties—epistemological and axiological, insights and values.

When a person designs a given behavior-pattern preparatory to execution, he does so in light of his goal or goals and of the situation which confronts him. Goals, of course, are axiological; what one wants or considers worth seeking; hence, self-made. On the other hand, the confronting situation wherein goals are to be achieved is not self-made; it appears to be an ontological existent, to be dealt with on its own terms regardless of the wishes of the person. However, the behavioral design which a person formulates or invents is *not* on the basis of the confronting situation *as it is*. It is, rather, on the basis of the confronting situation *as he sees it to be*. Experiment, as well as experience, have by now certainly demonstrated this point beyond reasonable doubt. If you or I see a door as locked, our next steps with reference to that door will be as if it were locked regardless of whether it actually is locked or not, and will so continue until experience convinces us to the contrary. Hence the "reality" which serves as basis for behavioral *design* is axiological (goal) and epistemological (insight); both self-made, both creations of the designer.

An objector immediately exclaims, "Ah, yes, just what I have been insisting. Solipsism!" But I reply that this is not solipsism at all, because a relativist who remains true to his premises never takes an insight to be final or absolute. All are tentative or hypothetical, subject to change the moment the resistivity of ontological reality registers its mark upon his insights or sensitivities. This is Dewey's principle of perceptual "interaction," perhaps the one crucial point at which Dewey's philosophy differs from those which preceded it. I take the ontologically existing world for what it *appears* to be, and *on that appearance* design my behavior. I *hope* that my insights are accurate, that such appearances "correspond" to ontological reality. But this is only a hope.

The *test of accuracy* of my insights, however, is not one of correspondence. The test is that of *anticipatory accuracy;* does the behavior-pattern which my insights lead me to design actually turn out, upon trial, as anticipated? To say that an insight is true *if it works* is not a sufficiently precise rendition of the relativistic-scientific test of truth. It includes too much and makes valid the rejoinder that a lie will then be a truth, if it works. There is only one way in which an insight has to "work" to imbue it with truth-quality; it must work to achieve anticipatory accuracy. In the degree to which an insight accomplishes this end, it is truthful.

And now we are ready to attempt a definition of the term intelligence, and to do so in light of a seemingly necessary contrast with the term "wisdom," or discernment. For I have found that much of the confusion which intelligence-test makers have long sought unsuccessfully to avoid is clarified if this contrast is made clear.

We would define intelligence as *the capacity to form insights,* and wisdom or discernment as possession of, and ability to use, *tested* or *dependable* insights. Considering insight as a sense of pattern or design—whether clear or vague, true or false, comprehensive or limited—we can easily conceive of achieving an insight without going to the further trouble of testing or proving it and thereby determining its dependability. In so doing we are exercising intelligence, but hardly gaining wisdom. I have found that much of educational literature would be greatly clarified if we would cease calling behavior intelligent when indeed we mean that it is wise or discerning. Taken in the sense here proposed, to say that behavior is intelligent is merely to say that it is designed; that it is planned or envisioned to achieve a given end, whether the plan is good or not. And the further-flung and more harmonious the plan, in terms of time as well as space and of past as well as future, the more intelligent it is. And intelligence tests should be designed to evince this capacity.

SELECTED REFERENCES

Broudy, Harry A., *Building a Philosophy of Education,* New York: Prentice-Hall, Inc., 1954, chap. 5.

Butler, J. Donald, *Four Philosophies* (rev. ed.), New York: Harper & Brothers, 1957, chaps. 8, 13, particularly the sections on metaphysics.

Dewey, John, *Logic, The Theory of Inquiry,* New York: Henry Holt and Company, 1938, pp. 520–526.

Dewey, John, *The Quest for Certainty,* New York: Minton, Balch & Company, 1929, chaps. 5–9.

Dewey, John, *Reconstruction in Philosophy,* Boston: The Beacon Press, 1948, chap. 5.

Fullagar, W. A., Lewis, H. G., and Cumbee, C. F., *Readings for Educational Psychology,* New York: Thomas Y. Crowell Co., 1956, No. 4.

Kelley, Earl C., *Education for What Is Real*, New York: Harper & Brothers, 1947, chaps. 3, 4.

National Society for the Study of Education, The Forty-first Yearbook, Part I, *Philosophies of Education*, Bloomington, Ill.: Public School Publishing Co., 1942.

National Society for the Study of Education, The Fifty-fourth Yearbook, Part I, *Modern Philosophies and Education*, Chicago: The University of Chicago Press, 1955.

Plato, *The Republic*, Book VII (any publication which presents the seventh book unabridged).

Wild, John (ed.), *The Return to Reason; Essays in Realistic Philosophy*, Chicago: Henry Regnery Company, 1953, chaps. 1–6.

CHAPTER 7

Relativistic Value-Theory

AS we have seen, if truth is assumed to be man-made, it follows that any particular formulation of truth is likely to be very human in nature and to be characterized by the frailties as well as the strengths of human thought processes. It can never be considered absolute—independent of man, final, perfect. Now we can add that the same is true of values.

Relativistically speaking, values are taken as growing out of human minds and human hearts; as representing no more and no less than human aims and aspirations; they are not of cosmic origin. I was having a talk one time on a Chicago-bound train with a man whose business was selling iron pipe to oil and gas companies. The conversation took a turn which caused him to ask the question of what constitutes value anyway. I had to ponder a moment before answering, "Well, I guess it's what you are willing to settle for." After we had talked the matter over a bit, he seemed to feel that the answer made sense.

If I really like and want oysters, more than anything else in the world, then indeed shall I be willing to trade anything for oysters. If and when I find something which I am not willing to trade for oysters, I have found something which I value more highly than I do oysters. It seems to be as simple as that. We indeed have a hierarchy of values, as what we have just said implies. But the hierarchy is not a fixed one. It is not cosmic; not absolute. It changes from time to time. There are times when oysters appear to be worth much; there are others, possibly, when we would be distressed to have them about. Thus, values are taken to be humanly determined; a function of time, place, and person. They are relativistic.

If taken to be cosmic, values are placed beyond the realm of human disposition. Goodness is goodness and justice is justice, regardless of how human beings view them. There is an Ultimate Right, and the march of human progress in the moral or ethical realm is toward progressively fuller allegiance by human beings to that Right. In such a view, man is not the "measure of all things," but must strive patiently and with humility (or is it docility?) to achieve the Revelation and then must align himself with it forever. In this way man achieves the Highest Good.

Relativistically, however, if we may never hope for final answers but only relative ones, then we must ask, relative to what? This calls again for the answer, to what we are willing to settle for.

If we are willing to settle for short-term, immediate ends, the proverbial "bird in the hand" without considering the possibilities of the two or perhaps even more in the bush, then our hierarchy of values is measured on that kind of a scale. If, on the other hand, we are inclined to judge immediate ends and present values in light of broader, deeper, carefully considered, lifelong aims, even those perhaps which extend beyond our own life spans, then our hierarchy of values is of an entirely different kind. We are not seeking the welfare of others *rather than* that of ourselves; we are looking to our own welfare, but broadly rather than narrowly; not in terms of philanthropic altruism, but of *enlightened self-interest*.

It is on this point that there is widespread misinterpretation of pragmatic or relativistic theory; some of it the result of misinformation, some of it seemingly willful. The term "selfishness" is commonly used as one of reproach. And pragmatism is frequently presented by detractors as involving a value-system which is nothing but narrow, short-sighted selfishness. The argument is that "the pragmatic way" is to seek what will make the most for one—here and now—and to disregard long-run outcomes. This, it seems, is what the word "selfishness" is commonly taken to mean. To be selfish is always to seek immediate, personal advantage, regardless of what may be a final outcome.

On the other hand, enlightened self-interest introduces a flavor of caution into one's planning. It causes one to consider not only what will be an immediate outcome but also what a given procedure will achieve in the long run. This is what, for Dewey, is discipline—disciplined action and disciplined thought. To adopt a given line of action, he says, even though it involves effort and perhaps considerable discomfiture but because it will lead to satisfaction of long-run objectives or desires, and to persist in such a line even in the face of difficulties and discouragements, is to be disciplined. This is the discipline of a person who evinces wisdom, the discipline of enlightened self-interest. To set up a philosophy which involves a value-system based on such considerations can hardly be reasonably characterized as something which would constitute "the solace of a wastrel," or the short-sighted selfishness of emotional immaturity.

The doctrine of enlightened self-interest is not claimed to be one of philanthropic altruism; of always considering others before self. It is, indeed, one of considering self before others and of expecting others to do likewise. For whom can I expect to take into account the welfare of myself and of those whom I hold dear as much as I would myself do, or as much as I should do for myself and mine? This, as we shall see, is the genius of democratic commitment; that each is fully expected, in fact considered obligated, to present and to work for his own interests to the end that they will as far as possible be incorporated in a final decision. By working *on equal terms* with others similarly motivated but all committed to abide by the collective decision, the common good will be more adequately achieved than in any other way, and the good of individuals as well. In this way minority rights *are* protected. This is democratic conviction and expectation.

The adjective "enlightened" is what makes this concept differ from what ordinarily is communicated by the term "selfishness." An *enlightened* self-interest is one which makes for a generous, outgoing self; one which takes pause in order to differentiate between the "desired" and the "desirable"; one which is disciplined to take into account more remote and more inclusive interests while reaching decisions on what to do about presently desired enjoyments; one which is able to discern whether and when the self is better served by foregoing immediate, short-term gains for the self alone in favor of longer-term gains for one's entire group.

A matter of national policy might be mentioned to illustrate the point. Should we continue to adhere to the policy of national sovereignty or self-determination of nations, or should we exert our influence in behalf of the principle of international sovereignty wherein each nation agrees to forego absolute self-determination on specified matters and to be bound by collective action on some international level, even that of "one world"? The wisdom of such action was recognized by us on an interstate level in 1789. Have changing times made it desirable, even mandatory, that we now enter into a binding agreement to settle internation conflicts peaceably? Will our own self-interests be better served by such an arrangement than by continuation of the cold-war strategy which now prevails? What would genuine enlightenment in terms of our own interests in this matter indicate that we should do? What has the funded experience of humanity shown in terms of what best serves the personal interests of individuals—individual action or group action?

As to the desired versus the desirable, this is a difference in degree; not in kind. And it, as the above, is a matter of being enlightened. Unless recourse is taken to cosmic determination, the question of whether a desired object or outcome is also desirable is to be answered in terms of two considerations. First, to what further objects or outcomes (ends) does it commit us? Second, with what other equally desirable, consummatory, or intrinsic ends is it compatible or incompatible?

In the foregoing pages of this chapter, we have been discussing *values* and have noted that they seem to represent what a person— or, we might have added, what a group of persons—is willing to settle for. This is something which is very *personal*. It is not something regarding which, as with truth, we can get help from nature by asking whether she agrees or disagrees. The two questions of the preceding paragraph, however, involve us in a theory of valua*tion* rather than a theory of value. Here is a difference between process and product. A value is one matter; the process of arriving at a value is quite another. Similarly, a theory of what constitutes a strike in a game of baseball is one matter, of vital concern to an umpire. But the theory of how to throw a strike, one which will get past the batter, is a matter quite different, of vital concern to a pitcher but of little if any concern to an umpire.

In answering the question of whether something desired is also desirable, one is involved in a *process* of *evaluation*—arrival at a value. Can this be other than completely arbitrary, "subject to individual will or judgment" alone? Seemingly, it can and doubtless should.

In dealing with the question of the further outcomes or ends to which a given object or event commits us, we are dealing with its instrumental or mediatory function. If we see it as promotive of a desired outcome or end, we regard it with favor or as having positive value. If we see it as obstructive to a desired outcome or end, we regard it with disfavor or as having negative value. Hence, this question has to do with *instrumental values*. And, as far as instrumental values are concerned, personal likes or dislikes, favor or disfavor, do not hold sway. It is in this sense that "the end justifies the means." If a given end is to be achieved, then means or instruments which further or promote that end *have* to be inaugurated—whether persons involved like it or not. And determination of means conducive to a given end under given circumstances is an epistemological—truth getting—matter, presumably to be by way of scientific investigation. Therefore, *instrumental values* are *scientifically verifiable*. To be arbitrary on a matter such as this is to court disaster.

There are, however, values of a different kind; values which in given contexts assume the status of ends in themselves, at least in the sense of the final ends in view. Note the contextual qualification; we are *not* thinking in terms of absolutes. Push a given matter back as far as you will, sooner or later an end-value is reached which, for the occasion, is consummatory, intrinsic, the stopping point beyond which (at least for the time being) one does not, possibly cannot, go. These we call *intrinsic values,* and it is these which are overpoweringly personal. It is to these that tradition applies the expression, *De gustibus non est disputandum*—there is no accounting for tastes. Therefore, intrinsic values are *not* scientifically verifiable. They are axiological, not epistemological. And in relativistic philosophy they are not determinable by epistemological pursuits.

That Dewey recognized this is attested by his eighteenth chapter of *Democracy and Education,* entitled "Educational Values," in which the following statements appear:

> . . . as long as any topic makes an immediate appeal, it is not necessary to ask what it is good for. This is a question which can be asked only about instrumental values. Some goods are not good *for* anything; they are just goods. Any other notion leads to an absurdity. For we cannot stop asking the question about an instrumental good, one whose value lies in its being good *for* something, unless there is at some point something intrinsically good for itself. . . . Contribution to immediate intrinsic values in all their variety in experience is the only criterion for determining the worth of instrumental values . . .[1]

It may be argued by students of Dewey that, between 1916 when the above was published and 1939 when his 67-page "Theory of Valuation" appeared, he underwent a change of mind. Unquestion-

[1] John Dewey, *Democracy and Education,* New York: The Macmillan Company, 1916, pp. 283, 292.

ably, it is easy to reach this conclusion, but I believe it to be unjustified. It is out of place here to consider this point exhaustively, but
I think it should be noted that in the later treatise Dewey is dealing
throughout with valua*tion* rather than with value, with process
rather than product; note the title.

So viewed, there need be no contradiction and I believe that there
is none. Recognition of the scientific verifiability of instrumental
values and recognition also that any and every "end" is "intrinsic"
only in the sense that it is a stopping point for the time being or for
the particular context under consideration (the principle of the ends-
means continuum) means that one can never think of reaching a
final intrinsic (an absolute). Therefore, as long as one is continuing
the deliberation—that is to say, as long as one is conducting an
evalua*tion*—one is dealing with matters subject to verification.

Moreover, evaluative study need not even end there. Dewey has
the following to say in *Democracy and Education*: "We may imagine a man who at one time thoroughly enjoys converse with
friends, at another the hearing of a symphony; at another the eating
of his meals; at another the reading of a book; at another the earn-
ing of money, and so on. As an appreciative realization, each of
these is an intrinsic value. It occupies a particular place in life; it
serves its own end, which cannot be supplied by a substitute. . . .
Each is the specific good which it is, and that is all that can be said.
In its own place, none is a means to anything else."[2]

Even though the mutual independence of the foregoing "goods"
may ordinarily hold, there do come times or occasions when they
become affective of one another, either promotively or obstructively,
as when a physician receives an emergency call from a patient while
attending a symphony concert. This is somewhat of a variation of
the ends-means continuum. Two or more ordinarily independent
intrinsics for some reason get tied together so that a choice has to
be made between or among them. Which will receive the nod?
Valuation has to come, either beforehand or at the time; for the
physician mentioned above, it was doubtless beforehand. First, of
course, each "intrinsic" is reëxamined to determine whether it will
turn into an instrumental. If so, to what further intrinsic does it
lead?

But when the respective intrinsics are determined, it must then
be dependably determined whether they are compatible or incom-

[2] *Ibid.,* p. 280.

patible; whether it is a case of both-and or either-or. And this would appear to be for the most part scientifically, experimentally, or experientially determinable. For the physician, the question might be whether he can first hear out the concert, then attend the patient. With sufficient information he can reach a judgment; a truth-judgment, however, not a value-judgment. If it is a case wherein the patient cannot wait, then it is *either* the concert *or* the patient; and this is a matter of heart rather than of head. The valua*tion* is at an end; the finally indicated values take over.

The principle which emerges from all this is seemingly quite simple. Instrumental values are verifiable, so one carries forward the search for instrumentality as long and as far as circumstances will permit, reaching truth-judgments all along the way. Reaching whatever relatively final intrinsics may be involved, these are then compared with one another to determine compatibility or incompatibility; also truth-judgments, hence verifiable. If no decision regarding either present or future action is required, the matter can then be dismissed. However, if a decision must be reached, a *value*-judgment then has to be made, and that is not verifiable.

When, in the summer of 1945, President Truman finally had all obtainable information before him regarding the atomic bomb and the war with Japan, he had a decision to make. He had no philosophical absolutes to rely upon; his own value-judgment had to stand. He had come to the "parting of the ways"; there was no turning back and no more time to contemplate; this was IT. Whether his decision was right or wrong can probably never be verified. That his was a considered opinion I believe few will deny; he can surely be said to have dealt with the *desirable* rather than the *desired*. Through valuation, he came to a value—a value-judgment. The final decision was arbitrary, as Webster defines the term; considered, yes; but "subject to individual will or judgment," and dependent upon that entirely.

It seems that, in Dewey's later treatise ("Theory of Evaluation"), he is desirous of making extremely clear his nonreliance upon philosophical absolutes. For this reason, he finds the expressions "intrinsic" and "an end in itself" somewhat unsatisfactory and prefers the expression, "an *end in view*." This is perhaps a justifiable corrective, for we might then speak of a *final* end in view without the absolutistic connotation of none other possible. We can always extend the view, given time, occasion, facilities, and disposition. Our own feeling is that, if a given reader is determined to read absolutistic connotations into what we have to say, there is no way to prevent him from doing it. Whatever words are used will be unjustifiably interpreted by some. Hence, our own practice is to make as large or extensive use of common terms as possible, taking reasonable care to make clear the meanings which we assume. Hence, we merely say here that in the way we use the three expressions—intrinsic, end in itself, and end in view—they are essentially the same.

The practical implications, as limitless in number as life itself, of a thorough-goingly relativistic theory of value can be exemplified by considering the question of "character education" in American public schools.

Assuming that American educational procedures should be democratic and that democracy means equality of opportunity to participate in *making* decisions and equality of obligation to abide by them after they are made and until they are changed, how can we conduct classes so as to build character? Let us think for a moment of a kindergarten class dealing with a playground situation.

There are three swings and 20 children. The first three get the swings, attempt to keep them, are pulled and tugged by others, tempers flare, and a melee ensues. Teacher could settle the matter at once by announcing rules and then enforcing them. But here is an opportunity for democratic character education. Therefore, teacher might decide to take advantage of the opportunity, call a halt, and consider the problem.

No one is having a good time. What shall we do? The first three keep the swings? Anyone who can keep a swing may have it? Certain ones only may swing? Take turns? For how long each? How shall we decide on whose turn will be when?

This is a matter not wholly, but almost, within the jurisdiction of the youngsters themselves; therefore to be decided essentially by them. Certain suggestions, such as that might shall make right, have to be ruled out by teacher at the time they are proposed, with the explanation that she cannot permit them to decide that way. She might say, for example, "We cannot use that way because your clothes will be spoiled and somebody may get hurt and your mothers will therefore object." But, whether teacher considers it good or not, any plan decided upon by the youngsters which does not conflict with regulations having to do with larger-group jurisdiction should stand until further experience causes the youngsters to reconsider.

It is important that the matter of jurisdiction be kept continually in mind. Children may not be permitted, of course, to damage or destroy school property wantonly or unnecessarily, for the reason that a larger-group concern is at stake. Children's wishes and desires should indeed, when they wish it, be expressed to the jurisdictional group and given serious consideration by that group. But there is nothing undemocratic in denying to any group within a democracy the opportunity to flout enactments of the jurisdictional group of which it is only a part. Such smaller groups should *participate* in decision-making, but not decide by and for themselves.

On matters over which they have jurisdiction, however, school children's considered decisions should stand even though a teacher may consider them wrong. Children may not be permitted to jeopardize life, health, property, or the integrity of the educational process, for those are matters of larger-group concern. Short of such, even "wrong" decisions should hold sway until experience convinces the group that a change should be made. A teacher will, of course, call the children's attention to the manner in which their decisions are working out—*good decisions as well as bad ones,* and never in an I-told-you-so manner.

In such way democratic morality is built into the characters of school children. Not only are they experiencing democratic process, they also study it as they go, seeing *whether* it enables them to live their lives as they would have them lived. The teacher does not set out to "make them like democracy." In fact, there is no absolute guarantee that they will like democracy. There is only the rather firm conviction that such experience so handled will develop progressively greater conviction that the democratic is the preferable way of life. But, *though it is anticipated that they will become partisans for democracy, the method by which they become so is distinctly nonpartisan.* Ends as well as means are recognized as humanly determined and continually subject to human redetermination. Children are brought up in that atmosphere, are given every possible opportunity to evaluate and reëvaluate it consciously and thoughtfully, and are progressively prepared for the time when they will assume the full responsibilities of adult citizenship. Thus, in the nutshell of a single example is contained the germ of relativistic character education.

Any and every absolutistic educational effort is oriented toward eventual achievement of Ultimate Right. Such Right may be near or it may be far away; clearly envisioned or only vaguely sensed; pre-emptorily demanded or patiently sought. In any and every case, Cosmic Right is the ultimate to which every head shall bow and which every heart shall desire. Humanly determined values, practical judgments, must in the end always give way to Cosmic determination. In the degree to which a teacher is convinced that he possesses knowledge of Ultimate or Cosmic Right, he is ready—even considers himself morally bound—to insist that his pupils adopt that Right. He may be patient or he may not, but he continually and doggedly strives to win adoption of his own convictions.

If, perchance, an absolutistically minded teacher should also be highly favorable to democracy, he might attempt to satisfy his democratic convictions by becoming agnostic and assuming that, although there is such a thing as absolute truth, no mortal or finite man will ever be able to grasp it. In consequence, he can logically disclaim any responsibility for knowing *The Way* and cannot be expected to point his pupils toward something about which he cannot know. But this, the agnostic, alternative implies too much. It means that a teacher, if he does not know Ultimate Truth and can therefore not know even the direction in which to seek it, is no better off than a pupil and is not logically justified to offer a pupil advice at all. This is not democracy; it is anarchy. Complete tolerance is the logical requirement; there is no basis for criticism, even of a mutual sort.

Democratic character development, in which all participants (including the teacher) are expected to accept criticism as well as to tender it, is possible only when some agreed-upon criteria for criticism are available. As with a set of adopted rules for basketball or football, any and every decision of a referee can be more or less objectively judged by the spectators in light of the rules.

But such criteria are humanly, not cosmically, determined. They are not taken to be absolute. Basketball rules are one thing, football rules another, and both ordinarily undergo changes from year to year. Whatever canons for criticism are from time to time democratically adopted in a classroom apply to teachers as well as to students, and there is genuine, democratic give-and-take in all studies on all questions.

At this point it seems that a summary may be in order. In preceding chapters we have presented the epistemology, the ontology, and the axiology of relativism. Truth is taken to be a human insight or sense of pattern—a cognitive generalization—from which practical consequences or behavior patterns can be logically deduced. The insight is considered true if, and only if, the deduced behavior pattern, when tested experientially or experimentally, produces the results which were anticipated.

It is only in this sense that that which works is true. There is only one way in which the working out of an insight demonstrates its truthfulness; it must work so as to enable its possessor to anticipate behavior with accuracy.

As to existence or being, it is assumed that objects, persons, events, and ideas do exist, regardless of whether they are known or unknown by a given knower. It is one thing to *be* and another to *be known*. Even natural orderliness—"the order of nature"—can logically be assumed, even though it cannot logically be asserted. In other words, we can plan our lives as if nature were orderly, and, if we have planned with care and on the basis of experimentally tested truths, we can reasonably expect that our plans will work out as expected. This may be called ordinary common sense, but it appears also to be pragmatic or relativistic logic. A relativist cannot logically *assert* the law of gravity, but he can *assume* it. In other words, he cannot logically say, "It *is* true," but he can say, "I seem to be fully justified in acting *as if it were* true."

With regard to what is right, what is good, or what is beautiful, relativism assumes no absolutes, God-given or otherwise. A person's ethics, values, and aesthetics—his axiology—are assumed to be his own. Recognized as such, only a consummate egotist could with reason assert (or even insist) that his own represented ultimate, final rectitude and all others should acknowledge it as such. An absolutist, on the other hand, could with reason and humility make such an assertion because, in effect, he could say, "It is not I who speak, but God who speaketh through me." To this, however, a relativist would respond, "How can you *know* this?" And no absolutistic answer to this question could logically be accepted by a relativist as bearing any semblance of truth, for no statement regarding God's sayings can possibly be tested experimentally.

Since our discussion of relativistic axiology is not yet complete, we shall pursue it only a bit further here. Chapters 8 and 9, treating respectively appreciation and religion, carry the thought forward. Perhaps we may be justified in emphasizing the attitude of deep-seated humility which relativistic theory engenders in one who holds it thoughtfully. Most human beings seem honest enough, at least with themselves, to admit on showdown cases that they could possibly be wrong. Even though they may feel strongly that they are not wrong, they are hardly willing to assert openly that they could not possibly be so. Each acknowledges human frailty, even his own, and, if he consciously assumes his truth- and value-systems to be of his own making, he is very likely to consider them also to possess the frailty of most human concoctions. The logic of his philosophical outlook encourages humility; discourages assertiveness. It encourages tough-mindedness; one reaches convictions carefully and is not turned from them without convincing evidence. But it disposes one to join with others in considering and reconsidering beliefs, convictions, and proposed courses of action, in the hope and expectation that such procedure will be conducive to betterment. And betterment is always sought; finality never assumed. Such is the attitude engendered by the logic of relativistic theory.

Previously, we have noted the assumption that both truth-systems and value-systems, as held by human beings, are human inventions or formulations. In this regard they are like one another. In other words, on this point science and morality evince kinship. But does this mean that on all matters or in all ways science and morality are the same?

A real difference comes to light when we consider how we go about testing or verifying a scientific principle as compared to a moral one. As discussed before, our test of a scientific principle is an experimental one. After the logical consequences of a given hypothesis are accurately deduced, it then is clear that under a given set of circumstances certain events should come to pass. Otherwise, the hypothesis will be demonstrated as false. Going ahead at this point, setting up the circumstances, setting the principle in motion, and observing the outcomes is what is called a scientific experiment. If the outcomes are as anticipated, the hypothesis under consideration is to this extent demonstrated as correct or true. It has anticipated events with accuracy. We do not ask a casual or disinterested observer the direct question of whether our hypothesis is correct. We merely ask, "Did this particular event occur, or did it not?" But *his answer to the latter question,* even though he may not intend it or even have any realization of it, *determines or fixes the answer to the former*. If his answer corroborates our expectations, it also corroborates our hypothesis. If his answer denies our expectations, it also denies our hypothesis. Herein is the relativistic-scientific test of truth. It is an *interactive* or *transactive* process.

Let us now turn to a moral question. Is it right to cause human beings to suffer needless pain? No experiment will answer such a question for us. We can discover experimentally or experientially what it takes to cause human pain. But whether we should or should not cause such pain is not experimentally determinable. Of course, one may contend that before the time of modern anesthesia dentists and surgeons had to cause patients intense pain, and knew on the basis of experience that they had to do it. But let us not forget that they did not have to operate or to extract at all. Yes, they knew experimentally (supposedly, at least) that, if they were to effect a cure, they would have to inflict pain. This was scientifically ascertainable. But science was mute as to whether, under such circumstances, they should try to effect a cure. Hence the moral principle that a surgeon should never operate without consent of the patient or of those responsible for him. Moreover, in certain cases society has decreed that the patient's wishes are not to be consulted; that the action shall be taken, or not taken, regardless of whether patient or surgeon wishes it.

If we were philosophical absolutists either of the realistic or the idealistic variety, we would proceed epistemologically (in that sense, "scientifically") to answer moral questions. For we would then assume that The Moral Law is written somewhere across the face of the cosmos and we must find it—find truth—in order to know what it is. For absolutists, natural law is to be discovered in the realm of physics, moral law in the realm of metaphysics. But in either case it is an epistemological process; one of finding Truth.

For relativists, although scientific or natural "law" is taken to be humanly produced, the production (the law) is *hoped* to be in conformance with whatever "natural order or orderliness" may be in existence and at work. But conformance to natural order, or correspondence with it, is a hope; *it is not a test*. For how can we apply conformance or correspondence as a test, as long as we admit that we do not and cannot know it as it "really" and "ultimately" is—*sub specie aeternitatis?* How can one *test* the true via conformance with the true, if the true itself is what is the subject of search?

For relativists, determination of a moral "law" is a very human and perhaps arbitrary matter. They see no way of making it otherwise. Moreover, they are insistent that, although idealists and realists both *claim* to be obtaining such laws in other ways, such philosophers are not really doing so at all. After all, what do we have but Moses' *word* that he received the stone tablets from the Lord, or Brigham Young's word that he *found* the principles of Mormonism inscribed upon those golden tablets? (If indeed either man ever himself made such a claim.) The very act of *belief* that either of those moral codes is a God-given one is a human act; man-disposed, not God-disposed. To believe that any conceivable pronouncement regarding morals or anything else is God-given rather than man-made is a sheer act of faith, unsupported by any sort of humanly dependable *evidence*. That any and every person who so wishes has a right to believe that way, no true relativist will deny. But that does not mean that a relativist deems him wise to do so. And it certainly does weaken the effectiveness of any demands by such persons that persons other than they should have dependable evidence for their beliefs.

How are moral laws or codes relativistically determined? Our very use of both words, moral and ethical, are tacit admission of the principle that, since antiquity, custom has been the basis for either. In Latin, the *mores* are the customs of a people, and in Greek, the *ethos* is the customary or community character. This does not mean, of course, that the ethical or moral code of a given individual is derived solely and entirely from his community. Part of it, doubtless, is so derived; but for other parts he is essentially "on his own." How much it is of each is dependent on the person.

Where do these codes or value-systems come from? And when and how were they obtained? In a really definitive way, who can tell? Contrary to widespread belief, a baby appears to have the beginning of a value-system when he is born. He gives ample evidence of assigning high value to warmth, nourishment, and protection, evincing clear signs of distress whenever he senses any of them in jeopardy. How did he get them? Early as an embryo his brain began to develop, and it probably functioned in later prenatal stages much as it does postnatal. Need we pursue this point further? Briefly stated, it appears that in general we are born with a physiological structure including a nervous system, a structure having a growth potential, and through the agencies of time and experience we learn how to use it.

As to development of a value-system, as a baby grows his original value-system also grows. He becomes aware of a variegated world about him, progressively differentiates it into persons, objects, and events, and comes to decide that certain of these are friendly and others are unfriendly. He develops allegiances to the friendly and aversions to the unfriendly. Need we complicate it more than that? This interpretation adequately accounts for known facts and accurately anticipates unknown ones. If a transcendental or metaphysical intelligence is at work, so be it. It is not denied. But, in the absence of positive evidence that it is and in light of the reasonably satisfactory functioning of the naturalistic interpretation, why invoke the transcendental? All of the advantages of the law of parsimony are lost when recourse is taken to interpretations involving the occult.

There is, however, a point which requires emphasis. As we begin to inaugurate steps toward achieving desired ends, we face the question of what steps or means will be needed if we are to accomplish what we want. Determining ends is a moral or axiological matter. But determining means is one which is scientifically epistemological. What must we do under given circumstances to achieve a given set of ends? This is a question which can only be answered scientifically, if at all.

And here is the point. We take scientific determinations of the means necessary to achieve a given end as data to be employed in further consideration of whether the end itself still merits allegiance. In other words, consideration of means necessary to achieve a given end is a significant aspect to take into account in deciding whether indeed the end is justifiable. It is a two-way deal; not only should the end justify the means but the means should also justify the end. That God-sanctioned ends are not subject to such a two-way method of justification is a matter which we treat at some length in Chapter 9, so we shall not pursue it further here.

As we note above and again at the beginning of Chapter 13, once a given end has been settled upon it is then a scientifically epistemological matter to determine suitable means. The *value* of a means —hence, an instrumental value—can therefore be verified or validated. But an end in itself—hence, an intrinsic value—cannot. Scientific aid can be adduced, as indicated in the preceding paragraph, in the process of arriving at an intrinsic value. But the decision to adopt that intrinsic rather than some other is, in final analysis, a matter of unadulterated personal decision.

One might even go a step further than the means-end comparison, in arriving at an intrinsic. One might think of other intrinsics and ascertain their compatibility one with another. If found compatible, then all can be held. But if incompatibilities become evident, then a choice has to be made. If investigation discloses that acceptance of an honor will assuredly lose me a friend, then I have a choice to make. As long as those two stand opposed as intrinsics, no amount of scientific investigation will assist in my decision. If one should turn into an instrumentality, then it could be scientifically pursued to the next intrinsic, but that merely temporarily postpones the decision. In terms of relativistic theory, intrinsic values cannot be validated or verified.

It seems to become clear, therefore, that the most promising relativistic test of moral rectitude is one which might be characterized as more logical than experimental. What would be taken as the highest moral rectitude would be that which most thoroughly harmonizes one's most comprehensive outlook on life; an outlook which consciously envisions both ends and means and, in addition, has the benefit of careful canvassing of whatever interrelationships may exist among ends which ostensibly are intrinsic. What is logical may well be what fits into and conforms with an inclusive, overall pattern. Therefore, to be monistic and strive continuously to maintain an outlook which represents a single logical pattern would seem to be preferable to being dualistic or pluralistic and being satisfied with working under the aegis of two or more separate and distinct ones. For the latter is always giving rise to conflict—if and when an irresistible force collides with an immovable object, what will happen? But, knowing all this, when one comes to the final decision as to whether to be monistic, dualistic, or pluralistic and what indeed shall be the inclusive pattern or patterns chosen, man seems to be pretty much on his own. He has a personal choice to make.

SELECTED REFERENCES

Aristotle, *Nicomachean Ethics,* Books I and II.

Berkson, I. B., *The Ideal and the Community,* New York: Harper & Brothers, 1958.

Bode, Boyd H., *Fundamentals of Education,* New York: The Macmillan Company, 1921, chaps. 2, 4, 5.

Broudy, Harry S., *Building a Philosophy of Education,* New York: Prentice-Hall, Inc., 1954, chaps. 10, 14.

Butler, J. Donald, *Four Philosophies* (rev. ed.), New York: Harper & Brothers, 1957, chaps. 8, 13.

Childs, John L., *American Pragmatism and Education*, New York: Henry Holt and Company, 1956, chap. 5.

Dewey, John, *Democracy and Education*, New York: The Macmillan Company, 1916, chaps. 10, 18, 26.

Dewey, John, *Experience and Nature*, New York: Dover Publications Inc., 1958, chap. 10.

Dewey, John, *Problems of Men*, New York: Philosophical Library, Inc., 1946, Part III.

Dewey, John, *The Quest for Certainty*, New York: Minton, Balch & Company, 1929, chap. 10.

Dewey, John, *Reconstruction in Philosophy* (enlarged ed.), Boston: The Beacon Press, chap. 7.

Dewey, John, "Theory of Valuation," in *International Encyclopedia of Unified Science*, Vol. II, No. 4, Chicago: The University of Chicago Press, 1939.

Dewey, J., and Tufts, J. H., *Ethics*, New York: Henry Holt and Company, 1908.

National Society for the Study of Education, Forty-first Yearbook, Part I, *Philosophies of Education*, Bloomington, Ill.: Public School Publishing Company, 1942.

National Society for the Study of Education, Fifty-fourth Yearbook, Part I, *Modern Philosophies and Education*, Chicago: The University of Chicago Press, 1955.

Pitcairn-Crabbe Foundation Lecture Series, Vol. I: *Modern Education and Human Values*, Pittsburgh: The University of Pittsburgh Press, 1947. (The first lecture is by Bode, the fifth by Hutchins.)

Ulich, Robert, *The Human Career*, New York: Harper & Brothers, 1955, chap. 6.

Wiener, Philip P. (ed.), *Selected Writings of Charles S. Peirce: Values in a Universe of Chance*, Garden City, N.Y.: Doubleday & Company, Inc., 1958, chap. 5.

CHAPTER 8

The Meaning of Appreciation

AT least once every six months if not oftener, in a class composed of graduate students, I raise the question, "Can you appreciate something without liking it?" Then I let the class take over. Lighting this fuse never fails to bring forth a detonation of sizable proportions. The "no" answer is always forthcoming and is usually immediate and forceful.

The argument is that, when something is really appreciated, it has had opportunity to work its full impact on one and, like an old shoe, it is therefore sort of a part of one and is liked. It is further argued that youngsters do not at first like, for instance, classical music, but, after more or less extended opportunities to become acquainted with it—to appreciate—they become "appreciative." This simply means that they have come, to a degree at least, to like it. Moreover, one does not ordinarily say, "I appreciate what you have done for me," unless he means to be complimentary or to express gratefulness or esteem.

Comments often, yes usually, continue in this vein for a time until someone—myself if no one else—asks whether there are cases in which further acquaintance leads to lessened liking or esteem. Have we not often heard it said that "familiarity breeds contempt?" Do we not occasionally reach a time when that old shoe or that old hat becomes too much "old shoe" or "old hat"? Do we not sometimes say of a person that he does not wear well?

In case of such an eventuality, has appreciation lessened? If so, then it would seem that better acquaintance does not always mean better appreciation. Consequently, though in some ways acquaintance, appreciation, and liking or esteem seem to go hand in hand, apparently they do not always do so. What then becomes of our "no" answer? Is it possible to appreciate something without liking or respecting it? A bit of perplexity now begins to show on the brows of the "no" proponents.

This issue is one which I raise in a class dealing with general teaching theory, because it opens the whole question of how to teach appreciation, or how to handle "appreciation-type" subjects. For, if to appreciate something is to hold it in relatively high esteem, then teaching has to be of one kind. But, if appreciation means "getting a thing sized up," then teaching procedure will be of a distinctly different kind. Moreover, to say that teaching should be designed and organized to make students like something would be to make teaching distinctly indoctrinative, hence undemocratic. If, therefore, a teacher hopes to be thoroughly democratic in his teaching of appreciation, he is hardly justified in defining appreciation in such a way as to equate it with liking or having respect for.

It becomes evident that our question is one which hinges upon definition of terms. In such case, it would seem advisable to consult an authoritative source in order to determine whether the matter can be settled in that way. Presumably, we should go at once to Webster's International Unabridged. Here is what we find on appreciation:

1. Act of appreciating; appraisal; estimation; full recognition of worth; recognition through the senses, esp. with delicacy of perception.
2. Expression of gratification and approval, gratitude, or of aesthetic satisfaction.
3. Rise in value—opposed to *depreciation*.
4. Favorable critical estimate.
5. Sensitive awareness or perception of worth or value, esp. aesthetic value; as, his fine *appreciation* of painting.
6. *Educ.* The study of aesthetic values (as distinguished from historical values), as in music, art, or literature.

Herein we discover a matter of considerable interest. Webster is distinctly on the fence. Definitions 1 and 5 mean evaluation, and evaluation can lead to heightened or to lessened respect or esteem, dependent entirely on whether the findings are favorable or unfavorable. On the other hand, definitions 2, 3, and 4 appear to be in accordance with the etymological derivation of the term: *ad,* meaning to; *pretium,* meaning price or preciousness—"adding to preciousness." Since adding to preciousness means heightening value, appreciate becomes the opposite of depreciate. Thus, without explaining that it does so, Webster's dictionary leaves us exactly where we were before consulting it. We have two definitions which are incompatible with one another. If we use both we shall never be clear, either to ourselves or to others, as to which meaning we are employing.

Let us try again, this time using Webster's Dictionary of Synonyms. We do not find the noun, but treatment of the verb form is suitable to our purpose. Here we run into the same difficulty, for two sets of synonyms are given; first, *comprehend* and *understand;* second, *value, prize, treasure, cherish.* Under the first set we find the comment that appreciation "implies a just judgment or the estimation of a thing's true or exact value." And even under the second set is the comment, "One appreciates that which one understands sufficiently to admire critically, or to enjoy with discrimination of its values," with the addition that only "in loose use, appreciate does not always carry this strong indication of intelligent admiration but stresses rather a response such as warm approval, keen enjoyment, or gratitude." We find it difficult to see how one can "admire critically" when critical appraisal discloses nothing admirable but, even so, it is evident that the Dictionary of Synonyms mildly favors the evaluational side. Moreover, Webster's policy is ordinarily to present a preferred definition first, and in both places Webster gives this nod to evaluation.

However, it is still clear that we shall have to make up our own minds, so let us do a little considering. It seems that both uses of the term "appreciation" carry with them a connotation of emotional warmth. A matter which is genuinely appreciated has really gotten next to (or inside of) one; it has not been viewed lightly; it has really gone home. Still, can one appreciate something without liking or respecting it? Can one warmly *disapprove* as well as warmly *approve?* The second meaning presented by Webster in both sources means definitely that one cannot; the first, that one can.

When one thinks of current usage, a persistent even though frequently elusive overtone of criticalness does appear. Casual acquaintance or snap judgment is hardly taken as conducive to appreciation —"real appreciation." And common usage, which is rather meticulous, seems to support inclusion of both criticalness and emotional warmth in whatever definition is adopted. It may be enlightening to think for a moment of how human beings behave in apprecia-

tional situations. How does acquaintance heighten appreciation?
Becoming acquainted with something means learning about it.
Let us suppose it to be a piece of furniture; say, a small table. For
some reason it attracts my attention and I take a look. It has pleasing
overall appearance, simple lines, walnut wood, good finish, drop
leaves, and perhaps is large enough to seat six persons. This I see
at a glance, and, if I should carry the matter no further, my observations could hardly be deemed appreciative or appreciational. I have
a passing acquaintance; I have developed a number of insights with
regard to the table. I am about to dismiss it from mind when my
wife remarks that that is something which we might like to have.
I ask what for, and she tells me. Then I return to look further.

Is it the right length to fit the designated spot? Is it well or cheaply
constructed? Is it solid walnut or only veneer? Is the drop-leaf construction such as to achieve solidity when the leaves are up? Is the
style such as to harmonize with the remainder of the room? Is the
finish such as to withstand the wear to which it will be subject? Is
the price satisfactory? All of these questions I ask, and more, as I
carry out the investigations necessary to obtain dependable answers.
This further investigation may be said to be appreciational. After
making it, I possess something more than merely a few added insights regarding the table. I have sized it up with reference to
whether I should obtain it as my own. I have determined to a degree
how much of a "good" it might be for me. I have evaluated it. I
have taken steps toward achieving a "real appreciation" of the table.

What I have done is to become much better acquainted with the
table than I was at first. I now know much more about it; I possess
a number of insights which I did not possess before. But it was
hardly mere procurement of additional insights which caused the
second stage of my investigation to be more appreciational than the
first. Mere addition of insights hardly seems to be appreciational.

To be appreciational, an investigation seemingly needs to produce
insight as to how the matter in question is, or might be, related to
one's purposes or goals. Viewing an object as a thing-in-itself is not
appreciational. Viewing it in terms of how it might or will affect
the viewer or someone with whom the viewer is concerned is appreciational. In other words, appreciation is evaluation; a process
of determining how a given object or phenomenon ties in with
one's value-system.

Comprehending how an object or an event will or might affect one, for good or for ill, is what imbues it with emotional quality. In this way only can one secure approval or disapproval. As long as an observer sees no way in which something will affect him, he will be neutral or noncommittal about it. As long as two Canadian football teams mean no more to me than two 11-man groups running hither and thither across a playing field, I am little concerned with the outcome. I am neither distressed nor elated with the final score, and I may not even be greatly upset if I do not get to see the game out.

If I wish to find how Canadian football compares with the U.S.A. brand, I may wish to see the game to the finish but shall be neither distressed nor elated with who wins. The only way I can become emotional about who wins or loses is to discover some way in which my own value-system is involved. With my own Alma Mater, I become highly elated or depressed at the outcome. If I make a serious prediction or place a sizable bet on the outcome, I become emotionally involved. For me to become emotional about anything, I must have some notion or conviction as to how it might or will affect myself, or someone with whom I am or might be concerned.

From the foregoing, it is quite clear that both criticalness and emotional warmth are achieved by investigations which are evaluational. Therefore, to consider appreciation as evaluation is to make it include both; to remove it from the realm of the "coldly intellectual." Appreciation thus becomes invested with the qualities both of *cognitive judgment* and of *affective commitment*. The cognitive and the affective are both included, in a simple and understandable way. An appreciational study becomes one in which a certain kind of insights is sought; insights into the way that the matter in question is or may be related to one's value-system—to the goals or purposes which one seeks to foster or to resist.

When appreciation is taken as evaluation, the procedure of an appreciational investigation becomes clear. It is cognitive or intellectual; a matter of developing certain insights or understandings. To develop "feelings" about something, one investigates its actual or possible relationships to one's allegiances or commitments; to one's "self." Therefore, in order to *alter* the affective, *we must proceed by way of the cognitive.*

In other words, the way to a man's heart is not through his stomach, but through his mind. A girl must realize that it is not *being* a good cook that makes the difference; it is *being seen as* a good cook. If the prospect sees her *as* a good cook, that is what matters. Of course, in order to be seen as such it is much simpler to be one than to have to resort to subterfuge. For in matrimony subterfuge on so obvious a matter is very hard to keep permanently hidden. But it may be effectual long enough to get the knot tied, and what to do afterwards is perhaps a bridge that may be crossed when one gets to it.

Thus, instead of being coldly intellectual, an appreciation-getting process is one which is *warmly* so. The advent of an inquiring mind in the evolutionary process did not cause human beings to become appreciably less warm-blooded than they had been. What distinguishes man from brute in this regard is the calculating way in which he arrives at commitment, not in the warmth of commitment.

Much of the current palaver about "educating the whole child" seems to be concentrated on trying to have children become more emotional. If that is what those who use the expression really mean, then they should proceed to alter the child's glandular balance, possibly with shots of adrenalin; or they might even employ properly administered doses of grain alcohol. There are probably few youngsters in our school systems who are so lethargic as to require such steps.

Obviously, what we should seek is *emotional balance;* and emotional balance is to be achieved by considered commitments, not by nonconsidered ones. And considered commitments are the outcome of studies which are appreciational in the evaluative sense.

We may possibly think of scientific investigators as a coldly calculating variety of genus *homo.* But personal acquaintance will show that most of them are very warmly humane. They are a committed group, perhaps second to none among human beings. But their commitment is to the achievement of truth, regardless of what form it may take at a particular time or place. Commitment to any particular dogma, regardless of how truthful it may at some time appear to be, always among scientists defers to commitment to the scientific way of reaching truth. One is *dis*interested but not *un*interested; committed to finding beliefs which are dependable rather than to beliefs *per se.* In such commitment, they find themselves in no wise emotionally upset when it later appears necessary, in light of further investigation, to relinquish a previously held conviction in favor of a new one. Thus they achieve emotional stability, but their emotional commitments may at times be more intense than they would have been without benefit of a calculational method of reaching them.

So, in answer to our original question we can say that, if we consider appreciation to be evaluation, we can indeed appreciate something without approving of or liking it. If investigation shows a matter to be meritorious, we like or respect it. If investigation shows it to be nonmeritorious, we do not feel respectful toward it.

To think of appreciation as evaluation is to avoid truncation, not only of the term "appreciation" but perhaps also of the term "criticism." For to think of appreciation as involving only approval is to necessitate another term which involves disapproval. The term "criticism" frequently serves this purpose. Yet repeatedly are we told that criticism should just as well result in approval as in disapproval. To consider appreciation as evaluation, leading either to approval or to disapproval depending on what is found, avoids truncation of its meaning. Likewise, to consider criticism as evaluation avoids similar but opposite truncation. Thus, these terms—appreciation and criticism—become synonymous rather than antithetical.

To consider appreciation as evaluation is diametrical denial of the psychological view held by many that the realm of insights or understandings is utterly different from, and unconnected with, the realm of values. The latter view is expressed in the following quotation: "In the science type we dealt with understandings; in the appreciation type we deal with values. Here we reach the bed rock of life. It is what men value that stamps their characters and molds their conduct. On the whole people do what they like; experience shows that they often know this to be wrong; and the inevitable educational inference is that the most basic task of home or school is to make them like, or value, what is good."[1] This quote is by Morrison, with approval, from Ruth Mary Weeks. He himself goes on to say, "The learning product attached to any particular value is a simple recognition of worth. 'Appreciation' means 'putting a value to.' It is not the outcome of any reasoning process whatever; it is not a reasoned conviction. . . . The young person in the present age of science is prone to find it hard to accept the principle. He is natively inclined to ask 'Why' and he easily carries his *hypertrophied*

---

[1] Henry Clinton Morrison, *Practice of Teaching in the Secondary School*, Chicago: University of Chicago Press, 1931, pp. 339–340.

scientific attitude over into fields which belong to an utterly different kingdom of human culture."[2]

As a rejoinder, we might ask *why* we do certain things even though we "know" them to be wrong. The answer in many cases seems to be that, although a person may be aware that certain actions are commonly considered wrong, he himself is not fully convinced and is not disposed, therefore, to conform. On the other hand, one may want something so much that he is willing to run chances of getting caught and having to undergo whatever consequences may ensue—the principle of a calculated risk. And again, one may misbehave without realizing that he is so doing even though he may have been able, were he asked, to quote verbatim the violated law. He simply did not realize that that was what the law meant, or perhaps that it meant him.

The point we wish to make is that in none of these three explanations (and there are others) is it a matter of understandings and values being utterly separate from one another. An individual, "seeing" a thing in a certain way, will assign it one value; "seeing" it in a different way, he will assign it a different value. A concrete pavement may be seen as splendid for automobile travel but very bad for travel on horseback.

Speaking psychologically, a value-conviction represents the *affective;* an insight or understanding represents the *cognitive.* And, if there is any validity to the psychological view underlying relativistic thought, a *change* in the affective can be achieved only by initiating a change in the cognitive. Conviction of value—like or dislike, respect or disrespect—is the outcome of intellectual "seeing," or insight. Change in belief or conviction or attitude can be achieved only by way of change in insight or understanding. Thus, *in learning,* the cognitive comes first and the affective follows.

On the other hand, *in an action situation* the reverse is true. A wish, want, or desire (affective) is felt, and, in consequence, insights (cognitive) are sought as to how the want may be satisfied. In such case, the affective comes first and the cognitive follows. In no case do the two—cognitive and affective, insights and values— belong to "utterly different realms of human behavior." They are inextricably connected the one to the other in human action. A given evaluation carries with it a given "feeling tone"; it cannot be avoided.

[2] *Ibid.*

Teaching theory and procedures will go awry in the degree to which they violate this principle.

What does the idea of appreciation as evaluation mean for teaching appreciation? An experience with one of my sons may be used as an example. He had always been happy with his mother's cooking, but had never been particularly impressed by it. During high school, however, he and several other boys had decided to take a home-economics course and had just been studying custard pudding when by coincidence his mother had one for lunch. He tasted it, he looked at it noting its consistency, his eyes widened, and he exclaimed, "Mother! You'd get an A on this pudding!" Many times before had he eaten his mother's custard but never before had he realized how good it was. He had liked it, yes. But he had not possessed the insights necessary to evaluate its excellence. In other words, he had not really appreciated what he was getting.

In this case, because of the excellence of the object under scrutiny, heightened appreciation led to heightened respect. Many are the times, I expect, when you have done something for, or given something to, someone and afterwards wished that he had genuinely appreciated what he was getting.

When I was a youngster I was completely happy when listening to a male quartet or the town band. But a symphony orchestra left me cold. And for more years after voting age than I care to admit, symphonic productions failed to impress me as I perhaps "knew" that they should. But, possibly vaguely realizing something of what we have been here discussing regarding appreciation and realizing that musical connoisseurs seemed to derive much enjoyment from symphonies, I began to listen to them seriously.

I sought out the purpose, and listened in light of that purpose. I noted what was done with melodic line; the endless variety in which even the simplest was expressed. I noted, not the absence, but the variety of rhythm which was employed and came to be delighted with it rather than bored. I began to give attention to individual instruments, to separate them out from the ensemble and from time to time to follow them through, to watch them as they took dominant roles and again receded into the background; and afterwards, upon again attending to the overall effects, I was amazed at the increased depth and breadth of harmonic timbre or quality which I came to feel as exquisite.

As a result of study such as this, although I continued to respect the efforts of its members, the town band quickly lost its glamour. And male quartets, even though excellent as such, progressively more and more gave me a feeling of shallowness which fell far short of the depth and breadth of emotional satisfaction which a symphony could evoke.

This is not to say that I no longer enjoy a local band or a male quartet. I cannot say that I enjoy them as much as I used to; I really do not know. I do know that I become pained with off-pitch and flat-quality notes which at one time I did not "hear." But I am now much more appreciative of and impressed by the efforts put forth. And when, on occasions, I hear productions in which much more is obtained from a given instrumentation than can ordinarily be expected, it gives me a real kick.

It might be noted that, when looking at the overall outcome of enhanced appreciation even when appreciation is taken as evaluation, heightened appreciation does lead to heightened enjoyment. But this does not gainsay, it merely emphasizes, what has previously been said. For there is much of good in even the poorest aspects of life if we can only see it and thereby enjoy it; and that is the meaning of appreciation as evaluation.

One of the very important implications of considering appreciation as evaluation is that democratic teaching of appreciation becomes a logical possibility. For teaching then does not have to be indoctrinative. It is the study itself, conducted in a democratically organized classroom, which determines commitment. If appreciation is taken to mean warm approval, then, logically, teaching appreciation means teaching warm approval. Such a process is indoctrinative, therefore undemocratic, whether the object of study merits approval or disapproval.

If democracy is considered as equality of opportunity to participate in the process of reaching decisions and equality of obligation to live in accordance with such decisions until they may be democratically reconsidered and altered, then no predetermined decisions or commitments may democratically be presented to a group for unconsidered or unquestioning acceptance. Any and all proposals, whether in class or out, which are presented to a group for possible adoption must be subjected to consideration if the group so desires. If it does not so desire, that is its choice; it has had opportunity to do its own evaluating.

What mystifies most teachers is how they can give children opportunities to make their own choices, yet give the guidance and training in making the wise choices teachers know they are obligated to give. This dilemma is avoided democratically only if and when the group overtly adopts criteria for rightness, truthfulness, or wisdom on the basis of which criticism will be made and judgment reached (see Chapter 11). Thus, in order to determine whether a piece of music is good, it will first be necessary to decide what it is to be good for. If good for dancing, then the means for determining is more or less obvious. One has to decide what constitutes good dancing and choose music which promotes it.

The democratic obligation of living up to adopted decisions is satisfied, in a reflective study, by living up to the adopted criteria. Each proposal, regardless of who proposed it, must stand criticism on the basis of those criteria. Hence, whatever is necessary should be done to make pupils criticize the teacher's answers or suggestions as freely as they do their own.

However, no individual student is to be in any way coerced into liking the adopted criteria or the conclusions which those criteria require. What he likes or dislikes is a pupil's own business. He must only differentiate clearly between criticism on the basis of the adopted criteria and expression of his personal preferences. Adopted criteria—and conclusions based upon them—must be respected, in the sense of being followed for the purpose of the study. But they need not be liked, or considered as the ones which should have been adopted, any more than an individual voter should be required to believe that the majority which elected a president was right. An evaluational basis adopted at one time must be employed for that time. But it may later be changed. And it is discontent with a previous decision which promotes change.

Nevertheless, while a given evaluational basis is in force, it not only makes evaluational or appreciational study possible but also makes it possible to be democratic, because teacher and pupil alike can be required to use it and be subject to it as the basis for evaluation or criticism.

Thus, in myriad ways which are only suggested by these examples, teachers of appreciation-type subjects may in a thoroughly democratic, nonindoctrinative but highly effectual way help students to make great strides toward heightened enjoyment of that which is good. But such enjoyment must be real, not simulated. Youngsters will come to like good stuff because they see why it is good, not because teacher said so. A teacher is, in effect, letting nature take her course; giving good stuff an opportunity to hoe its own row; not trying weakly to uphold the arms of something which needs no upholding. And does this not mean, in the mind of a teacher, high respect for that which he deems good; a feeling that the matter at hand can carry its own load?

And one further point. The foregoing outlook on the teaching of appreciation means that no subjects in the curriculum are exclusively appreciation-type, and vice versa. There is much appreciation to be gained in mathematics, science, woodwork, and commercial courses. For mathematical or scientific principles may be as much a work of art as a bronze statue, and as much an object of appreciation. A teacher in woodwork who fails—before, during, and after execution—to have a student consider carefully and ably the overall as well as the detailed design of a piece which he is making, will fail to teach appreciation, will probably achieve a low-quality product, and will doubtless fail to help this student gain the independence which will enable him to carry on after school is over.

So it would seem that to consider appreciation as evaluation enables a teacher to accomplish all that the other definition implies, and considerably more. Is there any question, then, as to which definition should be adopted?

SELECTED REFERENCES

Aristotle, *Poetics.*

Broudy, Harry A., *Building a Philosophy of Education,* New York: Prentice-Hall, Inc., 1954, chap. 13.

Buswell, G. T., *How People Look at Pictures,* Chicago: The University of Chicago Press, 1935.
   A study of eye movements in viewing pictures.

Dewey, John, *Art as Experience,* New York: Minton, Balch & Company, 1934.
   The entire book is pertinent, but especially chap. 13.

Feibleman, J. K., *Aesthetics,* New York: Duell, Sloan and Pearce, 1949, chap. 7.
   For contrast, both to Dewey and to this chapter.

Plato, *The Republic,* Book X.

Scheffler, Israel (ed.), *Philosophy and Education,* Boston: Allyn and Bacon, 1958, pp. 219–236.

CHAPTER 9

Religion and Character Education

A Relativistic Religion

THE philosophy of relativism may conveniently be said to take its start in recognition of the proposition that an object or event can neither be perceived nor conceived as a thing-in-itself; that it can be humanly dealt with only as a figure against a background and viewed by an observer from a given vantage point and in light of the ideals or insights which he possesses. In other words, in light of experiential and experimental knowledge available today, human observations cannot be taken as thoroughly passive, mirrorlike reflections of the light waves and other sensory stimuli which come to an observer, as John Locke and Isaac Newton took them to be. On the contrary, human perception never gets beyond the status of *human interpretation of* what comes to the perceiver in the form of light rays, sound waves, etc. Perception as well as conception is a coöperative affair, dependent both upon the view*er* and the view*ee*. This is the *principle of interaction* as applied to the perceptual process.

Perceptual interaction means that nothing can be taken by human beings as existing in and unto itself alone; as self-dependent or autonomous; as separate or absolved from all else; as absolute. This is not an explicit denial that some or many things in the universe may be that way. It is merely assumption that human beings have no warrant for taking them to be that way—for assuming absolutes— and that it therefore behooves human beings to plan and execute their lives on the basis of refusal to assume absolutes.

A philosophic absolute is an entity which is completely and totally not subject to, nor affected by, anything other than itself. Hence,

132

philosophic absolutes have to be taken as utterly beyond human contrivance of any kind. For example, if a moral code such as the Ten Commandments is so considered, then it must be taken as sacrosanct, to be altered by human convictions in no way, shape, nor form. The Sixth Commandment, "Thou shalt not kill," is then an absolute right; any shading or modification whatever represents wrong, utter and absolute. In absoluteness there are no degrees. Perfect is perfect, than which there can be none more nor less.

Perhaps someone wishes to say that no one nowadays thinks of the Ten Commandments in this manner. With that I thoroughly agree, for I have yet to find anyone, even among the strictest of fundamentalists, who does not repeatedly look with equanimity upon the taking of life. Even Ghandi considered the taking of plant life not objectionable nor was he inclined, I suspect, to consider accidental slaying as bad as that which is intentional.

But that is exactly the point of relativization. Any exceptions whatever represent human intervention and destroy any claim to absoluteness. Yet one can hardly read with care the account in Exodus of the deliverance of the Ten Commandments and fail to catch the thorough intention that they be considered God-given absolutes. The whole pattern of thought underlying the principle of cosmic rectitude and of truth which can be ascertained by man only through revelation from on high is an absolutistic one. Right is right and true is true, whether man likes it or not. One cannot go half way with absolutes; it is either all or none. That is what relativistic thinkers realize and, frankly recognizing that it is humanly impossible to be genuinely absolutistic on any proposition, set out consciously to erect a program for living which is overtly and unapologetically relativistic.

Such a purpose means adoption of the proposition that all human plans are based on what the planners *take* the world to be; not on what it "really is." And this applies whether we are concerned with the realm of truths or the realm of values. Justification both for what is taken as true and for what is taken as right is to be found in human experience; not in some "higher deliverance." To say that something is true or is right because God made it so is, therefore, merely an excuse to justify one's unwillingness to subject one's beliefs and convictions to open and rational consideration. To put it bluntly, a relativist is unwilling to use God as a shield behind which to hide because he is either unwilling or unable to fight his own battles. Any and all propositions are taken to be true or false, right or wrong, because human experience has shown them to be so; not because God made them so.

It should be noted, however, that a relativist is required by the logic of his philosophical premises neither to assert nor to deny that God created the universe, that God created the truths of the universe, that God created the orderliness of nature, or that God determined what is right and what is wrong. For the very nature of our assumptions regarding God place Him beyond the realm of human knowing, and a relativist considers it unjustifiable to say that he knows when indeed he does not and cannot. A relativist may believe, or disbelieve, in God. That is a strictly personal matter. For it is quite my right as a person to believe or to disbelieve in something, even though I may have for it no rational or valid justification. Difficulty arises only when I go further and say, "I know." Believing is one thing; knowing is quite another.

Relativistic philosophy makes belief distinctly personal. It may be well, or poorly, grounded; whichever the individual wishes it to be. On the other hand, knowing is taken as something distinctly beyond personal whim. The one and only sanction for saying, "I know," is *anticipatory accuracy*—the accuracy in anticipating or predicting future events which the proposition in question enables a user to achieve (see Chapter 4).

In noting that relativistic premises logically require neither assertion nor denial of the existence of God, we bring out the point that the relativistic position is neither theistic nor atheistic. For theism represents adherence to the proposition that God exists, whereas atheism represents adherence to the proposition that God does not exist. Nor, contrary to statements frequently made, does the relativistic position represent agnosticism. For agnosticism is basically theistic: it adheres to the proposition that God and absolute truth do indeed exist but, being infinite, are quite beyond the reach of finite minds.

Herein is located a point of high significance. For if we are theistic we cannot consider as really within our ranks anyone who is atheistic, and vice versa. In fact, for many theists even agnostics are not to be tolerated, though these same theists, when really pushed, fall easily and without qualms into the agnostic position.

On the other hand, when one feels that he has no reasonable assurance of either God's existence or nonexistence and feels in consequence that he is not justified in casting his influence one way or the other, he can join ranks with either theists or atheists on matters of mutual concern and will become unhappy only when they become insistent that he also join them in their theistic or atheistic credo. And such action promotes in him no feelings of guilt nor twinges of conscience. And it goes even further. He may harbor a private suspicion or conviction either that God does or does not exist, as long perhaps as he keeps it private and refrains from trying to foist it upon someone else.

It is much as if, three-quarters of a century ago, one might have said, "Yes, I am aware that all available evidence seems to show clearly that there is no such thing as transmutation of elements. I still am convinced, however, that within a hundred years we shall witness even man-made transmutations." To such a statement no consistent relativist could have offered the slightest objection. He might have considered the person "slightly touched" for harboring such a conviction, with the evidence at the time so overpoweringly to the contrary. But that, in turn, would have been a private conviction and neither person would, relativistically, have been justified in saying to the other, "I *know* that you are wrong and that I am right."

But what, if not personal belief, do relativistic premises logically require? Seemingly, it is a working agreement to plan actions and live lives on the basis of the *assumption*—not the assertion—of self-dependency. Even though harboring a conviction of the existence of God, a relativist may not with consistency use such faith as a workaday principle. Such faith may be a luxury; the luxury is not denied. But do not the hard facts of life seem to indicate that man's own intelligence and wisdom comprise the best means which mankind now possesses for determining the ends, ways, and means of planning and achieving his destiny? Even Oliver Cromwell seems to have been of this persuasion when, in an address to troops before crossing a river to attack an enemy, he advised, "Put your trust in God; but mind to keep your powder dry!"

If it appears that we cannot really depend on God to extricate us from our difficulties, we had perhaps better make the assumption that we have to depend upon ourselves, and set up a program for living in accordance therewith. In this way we secure the advantage of whatever we can do for ourselves and, in addition, of whatever help God may be able or willing to give. For, if God possesses the attri-

butes of love and forgiveness and of more than common human de-
cency which are attributed to Him, He can hardly be else than grati-
fied with us for doing what we can for ourselves. And was it not
Poor Richard's Almanac which assured us that "God helps them
who help themselves"?

What we have been saying seems to add up to a position which
can be characterized, neither as theistic nor as atheistic nor even agnostic, but as *nontheistic*. As to assertions regarding God, there is
none to be made. But, as to assumptions, we have to assume self-
dependence. We have to deal with a world which is not of our making except as we participate directly in such making. But we have
to deal with it on moral-ethical bases and with truths which we can
hardly think as other than homemade. Can we, with sound justification, either credit or blame God for them? Perhaps it is something
like an author's statement in the preface of a book wherein he gen-
erously acknowledges help from various sources, but assures his
readers that he himself must take the rap for what the book con-
tains.

It would seem that we are now ready to consider the question, "Is
a nontheistic religion possible, and, if so, what might be some of its
salient points?" With reference to this question, we can let Dewey
do much of the ball-carrying, because it is to this question that he has
addressed himself in *A Common Faith*.

First, in attempting to reach a working definition of religion or
religious, he indulges in several pages of speculation as to what articles or article of faith might be found common to all religions or
religionists. And, as might be expected, he finds no specific article
of creed or belief regarding which there is consensus or agreement.
As to the immaculate conception or even the divinity of Jesus Christ,
there is great divergence even among Christian faiths. As to the vehi-
cle for God's revelation, divergence is multifarious. As to the nature
of God Himself, there seem to be almost as many different beliefs as
there are believers. Even insistence on the principle of the supernatural or of supernatural sanction to truth or morality or creed seems,
especially today, not to receive universal approval even among those
who are official representatives of the many religions of the world.
There are those, of course, who argue that no one is religious who
fails to subscribe to their particular credos. But so chauvinistic a view
can hardly be taken seriously.

There are those also who argue that, no matter how the term "religion" is defined, every human being has one. But this comment, if taken as valid, simply serves to emphasize the need for determining the nature of this something which everyone is claimed to have. That is the question, not the answer.

The upshot of Dewey's thinking may be roughly expressed by saying that, if there is anything common to the aims, aspirations, or convictions of mankind which may be called religious, it must be the human wish, desire, or hope to make things better. As to what it is that requires betterment or what indeed constitutes betterment, there is little agreement. Only the desire for it seems common. Many seem not even to hope for it in this world; only in the world to come.

Some see betterment as achievable by carrying out certain rituals; some by undergoing emotional crises which they call conversion; some by professing faith in God and resolving to be amenable to His will; some by setting up 5-, 10-, or 15-year plans and working toward their achievement; some by looking toward programs for socioeconomic reform; some by getting more money than they now have.

Our point is that, if we can take the desire to achieve human betterment (either for ourselves or for others) as a characterization of that which we deem religious, then a religion which is nontheistic is indeed a possibility. For human sanctions can be employed in determining ways and means to achieve such a purpose as well as can sanctions which are taken to be cosmic. In fact, does hardheaded examination of the events of human history show that such sanctions have ever been other than human? It is often claimed that God sanctions this or that, but each claim invariably turns out to be one made by a human being and one based solely upon human conviction.

What might be the nature of a religion based on the assumption of humanly derived ideals and humanly derived truths? An ideal is something to hope for; an end or goal to attain if at all possible, or to strive toward, if attainment seems impossible; a good which we would like sometime to possess. A truth is a principle which indicates the action necessary to achieve an end; dependable means to an end.

If ideals or ends are taken as God-sanctioned, then man must not tamper with them. Therein lies sacrilege. Man has merely to determine what means are necessary for their achievement. In other words, God-sanctioned ends (which are absolute) are complete justification for any means necessary to attain them; "the ends justify the means." Need I enumerate the kinds of deeds which this principle has evoked during the course of human history?

If, on the other hand, ideals or ends are taken as man-sanctioned, then whenever man sees that certain ends are not working out as he anticipated—when he sees certain ends requiring or leading to means which seem inhumane or indecent—he has no hesitation in reconsidering his ideals or purposes to see whether indeed they are not in need of renovation. Thus, we arrive at Dewey's proposal that an act or an effort which is to be considered religious is one in which ends and means—"the ideal and the actual"—are, either or both, so modified as to be brought more nearly in keeping with one another. It may be that ideals require alteration; it may be that procedures need to be changed; or reciprocal adjustment may be indicated. In any case, it is man's judgment which is the court of last resort; collective judgment, of course, whenever collective wrongs require adjudication. And it is not a kingdom which is indicated, but a democracy in which all participate on equal terms in arriving at decisions and all are equally obligated to abide by the decisions. Democratic governance is *the* means for achieving relativization of human social values. Democracy is a foe of absolutes.

Thus, what is it that represents divinity if not mankind's perennial and indefatigable struggle toward something which he deems better than what he now has? And what has placed him above the beasts of the field and even the fowls of the air, making him little lower than the angels, if not a human mind which can abstract particularized qualities from concrete situations, transfer them in imagination to other situations, and thereby create something new under the sun? What higher respect can we show man than this? And, if we wish to go further and assume God to be man's creator, what more than this has been said of the greatness of God's creation?

Moreover, there is place in a faith such as this for what, if not supernatural, is at least superhuman. That represents recognition of the oft-demonstrated principle that in union there is strength. In working together, on the basis of democratic governance and of employing the scientific way to attain truth (which is indeed a democratic way), men can and do achieve far more than any or all of them can or could possibly achieve by working each to himself alone. The idea that a group can rise no higher than its greatest member is doubtless a false one, hardly to be taken seriously by anyone who has had opportunity to witness the tremendous achievements of modern, coöperative, scientific endeavor. Yes, by working freely and amicably together, man is in a real sense able to transcend himself, to achieve superhumanity. What more is divinity?

A relativistic philosophy is one in which faith is freely and frankly placed in man himself. Man has to deal with a world which is not of his own choosing. But he does so on the basis of truths for which he himself is responsible, formulated by means of an inductive-deductive method which we call scientific, and on the basis of a value-system for which he is disposed to blame no one but himself. Whatever may be the assistance he has received from other sources, man's truth-system and value-system are taken to be his own responsibility. He may take them or leave them as he sees fit. Faith, ideals, truth, and commitment all play a real part in a relativistic system of thought.

Yet, though affording man tremendous freedom in ordering his way of life, relativistic philosophy is in no wise completely subjectivist, solipsistic, or based on the doctrine of absolute free will. Dewey's principle of perceptual interaction—that what I make of the world before me has to be agreeable to that world—is a thorough denial of solipsism, the "solace of a wastrel." In the degree to which I enjoy freedom in concocting my truth-and-value system, to that degree do I shoulder the responsibility for adopting a truth-and-value system which is competent and noble. Competence and nobility are not forced upon me, nor is there any guarantee that I shall evince them. But, when I recognize that competence and nobility will be mine only if and when I choose and achieve a way of life which will display these virtues, then indeed I see that I must work at the job; that I must employ my own resources to their fullest; that I must be a disciplined person, one who, though taking my full measure of enjoyment of life, nevertheless must bestir myself in ways not always agreeable or enjoyable to do my just part in ordering and carrying on the affairs of the world.

EDUCATIONAL IMPLICATIONS

Although principles to be given fuller development in later chapters will now have to be drawn upon, it seems that this is a strategic place to consider the question of what constitutes proper mode and function of religious instruction in the schools. However, since it is only in the public schools of a democratic nation that this question precipitates any great problem in basic educational theory, a reader might find it desirable first to read our chapters on democratic theory and its meaning for education (Chapters 10 and 11).

No question seems likely to arise with reference to the proposition that a school which is legally and openly organized and conducted for the purpose of promoting a given religious faith or creed (credo) is, at least within that context, thoroughly justified in "teaching" that faith or creed openly, effectually, and unapologetically. What may be done to children by so doing is not a part of present context; that is another question, important though it may be.

But a question so grave as to constitute a major problem immediately arises when the principle of separation of Church and State is in operation, together with the assumption that education lies essentially within the domain of State. This is the situation in the United States, and it is one which appears to be receiving full support by both Jews and Protestants. American public schools are faced, may even be said to be plagued, with this problem, and a satisfactory principle for solving it seems not yet to have been adopted.

Moreover, there is an aspect of the problem which is not widely recognized as being so; that is character education. Character is commonly recognized as the ability not only to know what is right but also to do what is right. Possibly a more precise way to say this is that one must desire to do right as well as know what is right before he actually will behave with rectitude. Since there is widespread support for the conviction that rectitude in behavior is primarily a concern of Church, there is therefore widespread conviction that character education is essentially within the domain of the religious and, in consequence, should receive minimal, if any, treatment in public schools.

Since this is a matter of great confusion in American thought, public school teachers have sought to avoid becoming enmeshed in it and have tended to "stay safe" by holding themselves strictly to the impartation of information and the avoidance of instruction as to what to do about it. This has worked out splendidly, but only to a certain point. It accomplishes avoidance of conflict with religious groups or agencies. But it also tends to make public school instruction an ivory-tower affair. It has led directly, I believe, to the not infrequent comment that public school instruction furnishes very little help when young people are faced with the necessity of making crucial decisions in life. In other words, it does not help to mold character. Character building is left, therefore, to the hit-and-miss effects of forces not held publicly accountable for their impact upon the character of American youth, and a matter of vital public concern goes by default. The deleterious influences of numerous agencies—including comics, movies, television, youth gangs, monopolistic newspapers, popular magazines, misleading though legal advertisements, to name only a few—are widely decried, though this is not to say that all, or even a majority of, the influences of the agencies just named fall into the category of deleterious.

Thus it can be seen that the problems of religious instruction in the schools, of character education, and of the teaching of moral and spiritual values are not three separate and discrete ones, mutually unrelated, but instead are slightly varying aspects of one and the same problem—that of education which deals with values as well as with truths; with hearts as well as with heads. And, since the question of religious instruction in public schools is current as well as is typical of the whole problem, we shall give it some attention. Let us look at several generalized patterns by which the problem might be solved, each one arising out of a distinctive philosophical orientation.

Pattern one might be the parochial school principle in which there is no problem. Such a school is permitted by our nation and our various states to conduct religious or moral instruction as it sees fit. That such instruction represents indoctrination, in the sense of being designed to promote loyalty to a given doctrine, creed, or life outlook, is a statement not likely to invoke disagreement.

Pattern two might be to conduct moral or religious instruction in public schools by releasing pupils for church instruction or by having interested church representatives come to the schools and each be assigned a separate room to which pupils go of their own free will and choice. What to do with those who choose not to attend at all is an administrative problem which is not exactly pertinent here. The instruction conducted in such separate gatherings would differ in no significant way from that conducted in a parochial school. It would be freely and forthrightly indoctrinative. But its constitutionality or legality would probably be questioned by the Supreme Court.

Pattern three might be to make instruction in morals and religion, particularly the latter, purely a matter of *acquainting* pupils with the various religions of the community, or even of the world; with their histories and their doctrines or creeds. This, however, would really not be religious instruction at all; not of the kind which seemingly is wanted by those who are distressed that public schools give no place for religious instruction. This is essentially social-studies instruction, making religious aspects of a culture as much a matter of public-school study as political, economic, sociological, and other aspects. No change from ordinary school policy is involved in this pattern, for it is teaching *about* religion, not "teaching religion."

For many religious groups, this appears to be as much as public schools are asked to do. Moreover, it might be noted parenthetically that the same treatment is being actively requested or desired by educationists for education itself—to acquaint schoolroom youth with educational history, purpose, and process as an aspect of human culture. Both religion and education are such vital aspects of the life of which today's young people are a part that it seems surprising, to say the least, that they do not appear somewhere in public-school curricula.

But this pattern, not being really a case of "teaching religion," is hardly to be considered as a genuine solution to our problem. Even if religious teaching of this kind were inaugurated—and it surely appears that it should be—the problem of teaching religion would remain; certainly that of character education in general. Moreover, a mere acquainting process, such as is pattern three, may easily become merely memorization of isolated informational details, thus merely extending the ivory-tower type of instruction and further cluttering an already overflowing hodgepodge of mutually isolated, nonintegrated items of intellectual lumber to be stored away for some remote future which may never come or which, if and when occasion finally beckons, has been forgotten.

Pattern four might be a modification of pattern two except that, instead of having the instruction conducted in separate places and with separate groups, it would be done with all together in one group. In such case, different instructors would be employed, each a proponent for his own doctrine or creed, and all heard in succession. Thus, each proponent would be entirely free to promote his own cause to the extent of his ability and be as indoctrinative, at least in effort and intent, as he wished. The institution maintains neutrality, but no individual instructor has to be so. In fact, if he were neutral, it might even tend to be detrimental to the entire program, for his outlook might not be as vigorously presented as the others and be weakened on that account. This is essentially the principle of debate, and for such purpose there ordinarily must be a presiding officer who is responsible for maintaining a fair and equal field. This function the regular, public-school teacher might be envisioned as performing. And for pattern four, we might consider that the process would be terminated after all presentations have been made and perhaps each given an additional opportunity for rebuttal. Thus, in this way all pupils would be presented with the various alternatives and left, each and everyone, to decide for himself.

Pattern five might come closer to a practical solution by having the regular teacher himself take the successive roles of the various doctrinal proponents or promulgators and thereby get all views before the pupils. This would, of course, require a very capable and highly trained teacher, but the task should not be an impossible one; at least, it should be close to possible. What would be lost in minor unfairnesses would be gained in greater workability and perhaps lower overall cost. And, since thoroughly equal individuals in terms of indoctrinative power is perhaps not achievable anyway, there might be little loss in presentational fairness. That the teacher's own personal convictions would be likely always to have a slight advantage would have to be faced, for a person capable of performing such a role would hardly be one who did not have pretty firm or positive convictions of his own. But he could exercise care, and his pupils could be warned that such advantage should be normally expected and that they should use care to identify and guard against it. This, as with pattern four, means termination of instruction with the presentation of various possibilities, leaving each student free to make his own choice or choices once he has become acquainted with the possibilities.

Pattern six would be to carry either pattern four or five a step further by inaugurating group study of the relative tenability of each doctrine or creed in light of the others; study designed to supply to young persons the assistance of a mature mind in the process of making their own choices. This assistance could be of more than one kind. For pattern six, we may assume it to be that in which the teacher adroitly but firmly "guides" the pupils along the lines of his own convictions and leads them to arrive at his own conclusions. To do this, he must perhaps be a kindly person, one who is attractive and likable, one who can use humor and other entertaining devices effectually, who is scholarly in the sense of knowing the strengths of his own position and especially the weaknesses of others, who can and does sense the mind-workings of his pupils and can gauge his own reactions accordingly; in short, a teacher who possesses and ably employs all the arts of a persuader. Above all, he must appear never to be attempting that kind of thing. This pattern, of course, is not a democratic one. It is propagandic or indoctrinative, but perhaps far more effectual than either patterns one or two. For it prepares pupils ahead of time, while they are still under the influence of the teacher, to meet the countervailing influences of other views or convictions which in a free society they are bound to meet sooner or later. This is the method of effectual salesmanship, in which a prospective customer's thinking is cleverly manipulated along a desired line.

Pattern seven might employ any or all of the methods, outlined in patterns three through six, for getting the various views before the pupils. And, as with pattern six, there would be the further step of studying the relative tenability of the various views so that a mature mind is at hand, actively assisting the immature ones in the process of forming their own convictions. However, contrary to pattern six, there would be a subtle but real difference in the teacher's purpose. Now, the purpose would be expressed if the teacher should address the pupils by saying, "I'm not trying to make you *good;* I'm trying only to help you become more discerning, or wiser, as a result of our study than you were before it." In other words, it would be like trying to help a batter know "what's on the ball" which is pitched to him so that he may be better able to do with it what he wishes. The meaning of the word "good," as italicized above, is that a pupil should act or feel as the teacher might believe he should. Instead, the purpose would be to help pupils reach considered convictions, which might or might not be exactly those which the teacher envisions at the outset.

To help students toward an end such as this, at least in a planned and organized way, is a process rarely achieved even in schools in the United States. It is a process which must be clearly understood, carefully planned, and masterfully executed. It is perhaps fostered by our national culture to a degree equaled nowhere else in the world. But it is far from clearly understood, if at all, by the American teaching profession.

To conduct a study, the end of which is not even known at the beginning yet is one in which the teacher is to be of real and significant help to the pupils, is what may be sought in what has been called "the workshop way of learning." The group-process or group-dynamics movement is doubtless aimed in this direction. Yet we have to admit a considerable degree of skepticism that via those movements much headway has been made. In order to avoid pattern six, the leader—be he teacher, resource person, or what—has to be so careful to avoid taking an unjustifiably dominant role that he is usually forced to "hide his light under a bushel," and the process tends to become one of "the blind leading the blind." In its worse forms, it is even deemed preferable that the leader not even know what outcomes should be expected, so that he will assuredly avoid a dominating or indoctrinative role.

Thus, we are faced with the problem of achieving thought *guidance* without "thought control," seemingly one of the knottiest problems of American education today and one which we shall not pursue further in this chapter. We shall return to it in chapter 11, after consideration of the nature of democracy. For pattern seven, in its possible variety of forms, seems to be the only one of the foregoing which can be deemed genuinely democratic. Patterns one and two are openly and unapologetically indoctrinative or dogmatic; pattern six not as openly so, but certainly subtly indoctrinative. Patterns three, four, and five are anarchistically permissive in form. Ideally, a teacher would avoid influencing pupil convictions at all, though this is practically a human impossibility and is ordinarily less achievable when pupils are not aware of the problem and of the teacher's convictions than when they are.

Pattern seven, by focusing the attention of classroom study upon arrival at personal convictions or beliefs, hence values, causes such study to become axiological as well as epistemological; to affect the heart as well as the head. And the reader is advised, after reading chapter 11, to recall what is said at the end of the first part of this chapter about the close kinship among democracy, philosophic relativism, and a religious outlook which may justifiably be called nontheistic, all leading with seemingly high logicality to an educational program which is genuinely promotive of the development of character.

SELECTED REFERENCES

Broudy, Harry A., *Building a Philosophy of Education,* New York: Prentice-Hall, Inc., 1954, chap. 15.

Brubacher, John S., *Eclectic Philosophy of Education* (rev. ed.), New York: Prentice-Hall, Inc., 1951, chap. 30.

Brubacher, John S., *Modern Philosophies of Education,* New York: McGraw-Hill Book Company, Inc., 1950, chap. 13.

Butler, J. Donald, *Four Philosophies* (rev. ed.), New York: Harper & Brothers, 1957, chaps. 10, 16, 23, 24.

Butts, R. Freeman, *The American Tradition in Religion and Education,* Boston: The Beacon Press, 1950.

Childs, John L., *American Pragmatism and Education,* New York: Henry Holt and Company, 1956, chap. 11.

Dewey, John, *A Common Faith,* New Haven: Yale University Press, 1934.

John Dewey Society, The, Seventh Yearbook, *The Public Schools and Spiritual Values,* New York: Harper & Brothers, 1944.

National Society for the Study of Education, Fifty-fourth Yearbook, *Modern Philosophies and Education,* Chicago: The University of Chicago Press, 1955.

Park, Joe, *Selected Readings in the Philosophy of Education,* New York: The Macmillan Company, 1958, Parts V, VI.

Scheffler, Israel (ed.), *Philosophy and Education,* Boston: Allyn and Bacon, 1958, pp. 244–258.

CHAPTER 10

A Definition
of Democracy

ALTHOUGH since 1930 the literature of professional education has indicated widespread recognition of the proposition that all public educational policy in this nation should be based on the assumption of democratic commitment, there has been little tendency to carry the thought much further. What to do about it or how it should make educational practice differ from what it would be under antidemocratic commitment has, to say the least, not received the attention it deserves. Yet, if there is any point in bringing up democracy at all, it would seem that we ought to become clear as to what to do about it.

One may wonder why such a situation should exist. It would seem as if a nation, approaching two centuries of democratic commitment, would by now have clearly worked out the major aspects of democratic educational policy. In many ways great headway has been made. The percentage of persons of school age who are in school, especially at secondary and collegiate levels, is amazingly high when compared with other nations. Dictation by central governmental authority is conspicuous for its absence. School personnel enjoys great freedom in carrying on educational practices which it deems wise and in inaugurating new practices which it is convinced that it should. Yet thoughtful persons who are thoroughly informed as to the way classes are handled in the United States are far from happy with what is being done. They are distressed with the many ways in which such practices are little, if any, different from what they would be under dictatorial auspices.

To the present writer it seems that the reason for such a situation is not hard to find. Experience with professional groups, large or small, shows a clear tendency to shy away from the question, "What does democracy mean for teaching?" And that condition holds, seemingly, because we in educational circles are far from clear or agreed as to what we mean by democracy. We are not alone to blame, because our population as a whole seems little better off. But it would seem that the problem of making ourselves clear on the meaning of democracy, and what to do about it educationally, is one of the first-line problems in educational theory, if not the most pressing one. With leadership in world affairs almost forced upon this nation today, it behooves us to understand matters of national policy, and the very meaning of the democratic ideal is surely one of these.

This writer makes no apologies for repeatedly speaking and writing on the matter of democracy. His feeling is that, if any apology is due, it is for not doing more of it. The extensive literature on democracy, both within education and without, is rife with glittering generalities and half-thoughts. To say that democracy cannot be defined is doubtless absurd, but to say that it is not being clearly defined is stating the case mildly.

Before considering possible definitions, I would like to make a proposal which I believe would, if followed, do much toward securing agreement as to what we mean by democracy. I wish to propose a set of criteria which might, and I believe should, be adopted to determine the adequacy, the suitability, or the propriety of any proposed definition. Until we agree on what a definition should do, we can hardly agree on a definition. My proposal is that a definition should: (1) indicate with clarity any line of action which may be involved; (2) differentiate sharply among alternatives; (3) avoid self-contradiction; (4) be as precise as feasible; and (5) in light of the foregoing, represent as much of consensus among probable users as is possible.

These criteria are formulated on the assumption that the purpose of having a term at all is to use it for communication among human beings. The fifth criterion is proposed, therefore, so as to take advantage of whatever common usage or understanding has already been achieved, thereby reducing to a minimum the necessity of learning and using new terms and new meanings. But full consensus is rarely achieved, even among our most commonly used words, so we hope only to work toward it rather than to achieve it. Moreover, consensus on a definition which would violate one or more of the first four criteria would hardly prove satisfactory.

Clarity of a meaning can hardly be expressed other than in terms of possible lines of action; hence criterion 1. That is Charles Sanders Peirce's proposal as to the only way in which meanings may be made clear, and it is ordinarily taken as the historical starting-point for the Peirce-James-Dewey line of pragmatic thought. According to Peirce, if between two ideas or thoughts there is no appreciable difference in terms of consequent action, there is no appreciable difference between the ideas.

Criterion 2 seems highly important because in common practice it is so often overlooked. In defining terms, we commonly confine ourselves to the positive side alone. Does the term express what I want it to express? We fail to turn it about and consciously consider whether it denies what we wish denied. That is the difficulty, for example, with saying that democracy means freedom, which indeed it does. But anarchy also means freedom, and, even in dictatorship, freedom is never completely absent. Thus, to speak of democracy as freedom or liberty and nothing more represents gross failure to differentiate among alternatives.

Criterion 3 is also highly important. For self-contradictions cause one to be one's own enemy—probably one of the worst—and, in communication, to foster frequent confusion or misunderstanding on the part of communicatee, if not of communicator.

Criterion 4 may not be as important as the others, but it would seem highly desirable. For to speak with simplicity is promotive of understanding and it would seem that, if one should ever speak understandably, it would be in the definition of terms.

With the foregoing as preliminary, let us give thought to what we *should* take as the meaning of democracy. And the word "should" is used here intentionally, with the idea that, if we agree to be bound by the five above criteria, we shall be required to reject certain definitions and to accept others, possibly only one.

We have already noted a major obstacle in the way of defining democracy as freedom and saying nothing more. Freedom is unquestionably involved, but, on freedom, democracy seems to hold no monopoly. Indeed, complete and unlimited freedom is expressed by the term anarchy (without rule) rather than democracy (power in the hands of a people). It seems, however, that there are two major usages in which democracy and anarchy—freedom, unlimited—are thoroughly confused with one another. One is to say that, if we would have democracy in our schools, we shall have to let children do what they want to do. To leave the members of any group entirely free to do what they, each and all, want to do is *anarchy;* and anarchy breeds chaos. No democratic people has ever tried to dispense with properly enacted law nor with the requirement of conformance to such law, enforced if necessary. The coercive function of democratically enacted law is a concept which seems to involve no self-contradiction; yet, if democracy were to mean complete freedom, it would indeed be self-contradictory.

An aspect of this view, when applied outside of classrooms, is the insistence by press, radio, and chambers of commerce that democracy means freedom from governmental restraint. Moreover, nonschool personnel are far from alone in this insistence. Thousands of American educators are thoroughly imbued with the conviction that any form of governmental regulation, particularly at the federal level, is a breeder of totalitarianism, if it does not constitute totalitarianism itself. Some persons even go so far as to argue that, because coercion is always present in one form or another, no court action can possibly be democratic. Usually such an argument can be brought up short by asking whether one would not rather be tried in an American court than in one in Russia. When careful thought prevails, there is little question that coercion is an aspect of democracy; coercion needed to promote compliance with duly enacted law.

A second way in which democracy and anarchy are commonly confused is in the contention that "pure democracy" is an impossibility because not all men are angels. The thought apparently is that, if everyone were angelic, then everyone would not only *want* what is right but also *know* what is right. But the everyday world is not made up that way; many are those who fall short, either by not knowing what is right or by preferring not to do right. Since in such cases coercion has to be practiced in order that chaos may be avoided, then democracy is practical only to a limited extent. Moreover, if complete democracy is not possible anyway, then why be serious about democracy at all? The pessimism engendered by such thought is far too prevalent today for comfort. Such confused thinking cries out for clarification.

→ A view which requires particular attention here, because of its high incidence in sophisticated educational literature, is that democracy can be defined in terms of some form of the expression, *respect for individuality*. The following quotations, all from recent publications, are indicative.

The distinctive quality of the democratic principle seems to reside in the emphasis that is given to individual freedom.[1]

. . . the fostering and development of distinctive personalities . . .[2]

The heart of the American value-system is faith in and respect for the common man—that is, for the individual irrespective of his religion, color, occupation, political views, or social position.[3]

This [a democratic environment] means an atmosphere in which the supreme worth of each individual personality is recognized.[4]

Democracy is a form of social organization which holds that the optimal development of the individual, of *all* individuals, represents the highest good.[5]

Our argument is not that, for all authors quoted, the above excerpts are fully representative. We merely wish to indicate the prevalence of the expression. It is true, however, that employment of the expression is seldom accompanied by adequate elaboration or clarification. Repeatedly, it is asserted that respect for individuality does not mean unbridled individualism or anarchism, but how to make sure that such an implication will not be drawn from the expression is seldom, if ever, made clear.

The point which we wish to emphasize is that to define democracy ←
in terms of respect for individuality (or of concern for the general welfare, or of anything similar) leads one away from democracy rather than toward it. We do not question that ends such as these are a major concern of democratic-minded persons. Democracy is desired because it is sensed or seen as the most likely way to attain such ends. But to define a process in terms of ends to be achieved is to make ends justify means. Therefore, any and all means (processes) are justifiable in the degree to which they promote the end. In other words, any process which promotes the end receives approval. Logically then, benevolent despotism might be even more democratic than democracy itself. For it is conceivable that an action might be democratic yet be such as to promote *dis*respect for individuality or

[1] I. N. Thut and J. Raymond Gerberich, *Foundations of Methods for Secondary Schools*, New York: *McGraw-Hill Book Company*, 1949, p. 12.

[2] Progressive Education Association, *Science in General Education*, New York: Appleton-Century-Crofts, 1938, p. 35.

[3] B. Othanel Smith, William O. Stanley, and J. Harlan Shores, *Fundamentals of Curriculum Development*, Yonkers-on-Hudson, N.Y.: World Book Company, 1950, p. 106.

[4] Harold O. Rugg and B. Marian Brooks, *The Teacher in School and Society*, Yonkers-on-Hudson, N.Y.: World Book Company, 1950, p. 426.

[5] John Dewey Society, Tenth Yearbook, *Democracy in the Administration of Higher Education*, New York: Harper & Brothers, 1950, p. 63.

lack of concern for the general welfare, whereas despotic action could hardly be termed benevolent if such should be the case. Hence, equating democracy with respect for individuality does violence to our third criterion for a satisfactory definition; it promotes self-contradiction.

Democracy is widely recognized as a way—perhaps the only way —in which people may get what they themselves want, rather than get what someone else believes they should want. It is not a question of whether what they get is good or bad, helpful or harmful. If what a people has decided it wants turns out later to fall short of anticipations, the way is open for a new decision. Whether the decision was good or bad, whether it represented respect for individuality or not, had no bearing on whether it was a democratic or an undemocratic decision. The mere fact that a person elected to public office turns out afterwards to have been a poor choice does not, of itself, cause us to characterize the election as undemocratic. We may have chosen unwisely, even though we may have been thoroughly democratic in so doing. Democracy makes no guarantee against errors in judgment.

Evidently, many of us are so convinced that democratic decisions will assuredly be good ones that we think it in no way amiss to define the one in terms of the other. We have seen or believe we have seen, during the course of human history, that peoples have tended to fare poorly under autocratic rule and better under democratic. In consequence, we have come to believe that democratic organization is more likely to achieve desired ends, such as general welfare and respect for individuality, than governmental organization of any other kind. But we should not confuse the anticipated or desired end with means of achieving it. The latter should not be defined in terms of the former.

Whenever we define democracy in terms of product rather than of process, we defeat the very end we are seeking. If, in effect, we say to a people that it may make its own decisions only as long as they do not encroach upon respect for individuality, we limit its sovereignty. In each case of presumed encroachment, human judgment in some form or other has to be invoked to say whether encroachment exists, and this means that the decision of the judging group takes precedence over the previous decision of the people as a whole. To that degree the people is not sovereign.

If we argue that such a situation is desirable because a people is likely at times to overstep itself, to be hasty, or in some other way to evince poor judgment, we are merely saying that we do not believe in democracy; we do not believe that a people will, in the long run, conduct its affairs more wisely if it makes its own decisions than if decisions are made for it. This point is crucial. Either we believe in democracy or we do not. If we do not believe in it, then let us not employ the subterfuge of talking as if we do.

This is a point which must be emphasized. When we identify democracy with any commitment other than to a way in which further commitments shall be reached, we merely say that we, the people, are not sovereign. If, for example, democracy is equated with private enterprise, we are estopped from making decisions which may have anything to do with modification of private enterprise. The same goes for democracy itself. If we put beyond the jurisdiction of a people the question of whether to continue democracy, that is limitation of sovereignty even though the limitation may be such as to keep that people from putting further limitations upon itself. It is not *un*democratic to enable a people to put limitations upon itself; most laws represent some form of limitation. It is not democratic to deny them the opportunity so to do, whenever and in whatever way they may wish. If sovereignty means anything, this is it.

That this is dangerous doctrine is readily admitted. Democracy is not a haven for the fearful. It is dangerous to be free; one may do either bad things or good. If we are unwilling to trust ourselves, then we do not desire democracy. Writers who speak disparagingly of "tyranny of the masses" have almost surely shown their hand. And the cards are not those of democratic commitment.

Process? or product? If governmental power and authority are to be of a people and by a people, then the *process* of governance has to take precedence over any particular product of that process, be it considered or hasty, good or bad, wise or unwise. Our third criterion for a definition—avoidance of self-contradiction—is violated if we say that a government of a people and by that people must also be *for* (the good of) that people. If democracy is to mean popular sovereignty, then it is self-contradiction to establish limitations. Hence, whatever formal definition we reach has to be one of *process;* not product.

With popular sovereignty or power in the hands of a people taken as an essential aspect of what is commonly understood to be democratic, need anything more be said? Perhaps there is, because of the equally persistent idea of majority rule. Somehow or other, we seem unable to think of democracy without the majority-rule stipulation. On the other hand, is there any way in which majority rule might conceivably become undemocratic? Seemingly, there is.

A basic purpose of democratic organization is doubtless to hold open the way for continual making and remaking of the way of life of a people; to guarantee that orderly change shall be possible whenever that people desires it. And, since ideas for change always originate with a minority—usually a very small one—, this means continuous protection of the right of any minority to speak of change and to labor for its effectuation. Hence, if ever a majority should become so solidified in its thinking and in its possession of the power necessary to carry out its thought as to prevent expression of minority dissent, it would indeed become dictatorial. This is widely recognized as a grave threat to a democratic nation when it embarks upon a major war. The very danger of any threat to all-out wartime effort may cause the majority which demands the effort to require that no expression of opposition to such effort shall be tolerated. Thus, any and all minorities may be prohibited from attempting to change the majority will.

Yet it seems equally clear that any expression which is taken to be the popular will has to be the expression of a simple majority. Whenever an American stops to think that a two-thirds majority makes it possible for one vote in opposition to a proposal to balance two votes in favor, he gets the feeling that it is "not quite fair."

A person brought up in the United States of America is pretty well inured to the idea of "equal rights," "no special privileges," "all men created equal," and the like. If I am fined for overparking or exceeding a speed limit, I may not like it. But, unless I believe that others have done likewise without fines, I do not think it unfair. When I vote for a losing cause, I feel that my loss is unfair only if and when the winners won because their votes counted more than did those of the losers. For us, *equality* is a revered concept.

Yet, if we call it "equalitarianism," we are not sure. Between equality and equalitarianism there seems to be a difference. Whatever difference there may be is, of course, in terms of our own usage. What is that usage? Equality may be achieved in many ways. Being supposedly "created equal" is only one way, and even this expression has different meanings for different persons. Equalitarianism is often used as an expression of reproach and, even when not, it seems commonly to designate some form or degree of equal distribution of goods; the produce of a culture is to be distributed equally among the people.

If democracy were taken to mean equalitarianism in this sense, it would indeed mean a socialistic economy and would be logically opposed to capitalistic *laissez faire*. This appears to be the basis for the claim by Russian Communists that theirs is a democratically oriented nation. But equality in this sense is an economic rather than a political term. Either Russia or the United States, politically diverse as they are, could decide from time to time to become more or less equalitarian in terms of distribution of the nation's goods. In fact, both nations have made significant changes of this kind during the past half-century. Yet these changes have only indirectly, if at all, changed their basic political patterns. In fact, it may be easier for a dictator-dominated nation to become economically more equalitarian than for a nation which is predominantly democratic, because fewer persons have to become convinced of the advisability of the change. It is to be granted, of course, that economic or financial power may be and often is used for political purposes. In such case, a democratic nation might well become less democratic, slowly or quickly, depending upon circumstances. But to say that two aspects of a culture are causally related to one another does not mean that these aspects are identical.

On the other hand, in this nation and elsewhere are many who are firmly convinced that democracy means capitalistic *laissez faire*. Democracy and freedom, they argue, go hand in hand, and, if a man is not free to conduct his business as he chooses, he has been bereft of his democratic rights. This argument is directly opposite to that with which the preceding paragraph began, and the later comments in that paragraph would seem to apply equally here. In fact, it may even be noted that during the past quarter-century dictatorial Russia's major moves may have been toward capitalism, whereas those in the United States have been in the other direction. Yet Russia has seemingly not become less dictatorial, nor the United States less democratic.

Evidently, whenever a definition of democracy is in terms of a particular economic system, it does violence to our second criterion—that a definition should "differentiate sharply among alternatives"—

and, perhaps even more, it violates our third criterion by failing to avoid self-contradiction. In the first place, as we have shown, either political form can inaugurate economic changes in either direction and not, by virtue of that act itself, change its own political character. In the second place, if the original meaning of democracy (*demos,* the people; *kratos,* authority) is to be preserved, it is self-contradictory to designate certain areas or ways in which a people may not be in authority. Democratically, a people may on its own authority decide to limit itself—to delegate authority temporarily to some other group or person. But to make such action permanent or final, as incorporating it in the definition certainly would do, would, as far as that action is concerned, deny the very point of the idea or concept. What is this, if not self-contradiction?

Just what kind of equality is it that we feel is democracy itself? Seemingly, it is *political* equality—equality in terms of *governance.* Even though the practice may have been spearheaded by both Dewey and Bode, it appears misleading to say that democracy is a "way of life" *rather than* a form of government. The "rather than" seems to be inadvisedly used. Democracy may well be considered a way of life, in the sense of being applicable whenever two or more persons are gathered together in a mutual enterprise. If rules of governance are to be set up, then whether to have democracy is a pertinent question. But democracy always pertains to government, whether it be national politics, organized athletics, a business enterprise, a bridge club, or a sand-lot baseball game.

It may seem obvious almost to the point of a cliché to say that democracy means equality in terms of voting. However, to make it focus upon this point *to the exclusion* of anything else is perhaps not so obvious. Let us be explicit. Voting has to do with making decisions; decisions on matters of group concern. On many matters, of course, the group at a given time feels it unnecessary to express concern. Such failure does not mean that the group does not have jurisdiction. It simply means that under the circumstances it deems that no action is necessary. As often is done by legislative bodies, certain legislative action may arise for consideration but not receive an affirmative vote and not be taken. The point is that the people as a whole is sovereign and, on whatever matters it decides that action should be taken, such action stands. Matters on which it takes no action remain in the realm of individual decision; but only because the group as a whole considers it better that way, not because the group does not have the right to take action should it choose to do so. If popular sovereignty—sovereignty by a people—means anything, this is it. To argue that a law may not democratically be passed if it "infringes on personal liberty" is a specious argument; convincing on first thought but with further consideration found to be untenable. Few, if any, laws on statute books anywhere fail in one way or another to infringe upon personal liberties. The *hope* is that greater liberty will thereby be obtained, but greater liberties are possible only as lesser ones are curtailed.

We recognize that this principle constitutes logical denial of the principle of "inalienable rights," on which our nation supposedly was founded. But that was seventeenth century political doctrine and, in point of fact, was no more the actual basis for political or legislative enactments then than it is now. Moreover, after the tremendous twentieth century advances in speed of transportation, communication, and other means of tying the peoples of the world together, the need for explicit statements of more and more rules for living together grows continually. For example, legal enactments to limit highway speeds to 80 miles per hour would have been the height of absurdity, even when I was a child; but are hardly so now.

In light of the foregoing considerations as well as perhaps of many others equally cogent, we come to our proposal as to a definition of democracy. We propose that democracy should be defined as *equality of opportunity to participate in making group decisions and equality of obligation to abide by them,* once they are made and until they are revised or rescinded.

Let us at once make explicit certain points.

1. Voting is not an absolute necessity. If a given proposal receives "common consent," no vote is necessary. Present practice requires the casting of a vote only when dissent is expressed. Voting is a last, not a first, resort. Moreover, it is conceivable that in the foreseeable future casting ballots will be as antiquated as is riding in two-horse carriages today. In obtaining an expression of popular will, it has even today been demonstrated that the method of taking public-opinion polls achieves results which are very close to those obtained from balloting, either on national or on subnational levels. Moreover, how do we know that the results of such polls are not, even today, the more accurate measures of public opinion? This is only a suggestion as to

what the future may bring. The point is that the above definition leaves wide open the way for improvement in expression of the "will of a people."

2. No person is required to participate in the making of a decision, if he wishes to refrain. The definition requires for him only the *opportunity* to participate. He should be acutely aware, therefore, that whenever he does not actively participate he is, in effect, approving whatever decision is reached. He has no right to maintain that he was left out; that a vote should be retaken because he did not originally participate. He must, of course, be given due notice of what will be considered, and when; and time and place must be chosen to equalize as nearly as possible the convenience of all. But, after a decision is reached, it must stand until changed by further, regularly channeled action.

3. All are equally bound to live and act in accordance with the decision. The definition requires no one to be in favor of a given decision if his personal convictions are to the contrary. Nor does it require that he refrain from voicing disapproval. Herein is where minority rights are protected. The minority right is to disapprove; but not to disobey. Minority disapproval may in time lead to revision or rescission but, until such takes place, obedience is a democratic requirement. Hence, police action against legal offenders, as long as it itself maintains legality, is in no wise undemocratic.

Since we have rejected a number of current definitions of democracy on the basis of violation of one or more of the criteria which we have proposed, we are obligated to subject our above definition to the same tests. Although, in light of the foregoing discussion, it may be more or less clear that these criteria have been actively functioning in the entire process of arriving at the definition, it may be well now to make their application explicit.

1. The line of action required by the definition should be clear. To make our way of life democratic, two requirements must be satisfied and two only. When decisions are to be made as to that way of life, all members of the sovereign or jurisdictional group must be guaranteed equal opportunity to participate, and, after any decision is made, all are equally obligated to abide by it. Whether a given decision is wise or unwise, good or bad, conducive to the furtherance of democracy or otherwise, is not to be considered when we are asked the question, "Is it democratic?" That we might democratically decide to eliminate democracy entirely is exactly what the defi-

nition means. That would mean an end to democracy, but the very genius of the democratic idea is that the process itself can be terminated in just as orderly a fashion as can any other enactment. It is obvious that herein lies danger, but what goods in this life are achievable without some very real likelihood of danger?

2. There is sharp differentiation between the alternative of anarchy on the one hand and of autocracy on the other. *Anarchy,* as contrasted with the limited freedom of democracy, is to be taken as *un*limited freedom—freedom to do as one chooses, regardless of group wishes or requirements. This is evidently what those have in mind who argue that democracy would be fine "if men were all angels," or that democracy is all right as long as it is kept within reasonable bounds. The underlying thought seems to be that people should do as they want as long as they not only want, but also know how, to do right; in other words, as long as they behave angelically. But this, with certain checks and balances presumably attributable to "perfect competition," is the rationale of anarchy—known in the field of economics as *laissez faire*—and not of democracy. It is vital to the success of democratic organization that this distinction between democracy and anarchy be clearly understood and consistently employed. Our definition makes this possible.

On the other hand, *autocracy* is in agreement with democracy in placing limitations on personal freedom. However, the limitations of autocracy are *un*equal, whereas those of democracy are equal. Autocratically, favored persons or groups are favored either in law-making or in law abidance or in both. A democratic people may democratically decide to designate certain areas for special treatment, as when ambulances on emergency runs are given right-of-way along busy streets. But such decisions require discriminating judgment. Care must be taken that the fundamental democratic process —equality in law-making and law abidance—is not jeopardized. For example, our national decision to permit wide variations in personal financial incomes is fraught with the danger that those with high income may use it to control votes or to purchase special dispensations and thereby violate democratic process. In consequence, many safeguards, such as the Sherman Anti-trust Law, are set up. Although it may frequently be difficult to determine whether a given decision may be wise or unwise in terms of the welfare of a people, our definition makes it fairly easy to determine whether it is or was democratic. Regardless of what comes from it, a decision is democratic if, and only if, it is democratically reached and democratically applied.

3. Self-contradiction is avoided. In this connection, our entire previous discussion of democracy as decision-making is in point and need not be repeated here. The same is true of the section dealing with democracy as process or product. Only by making clear which, in case of diametric opposition, is to be precedent—process, or product—can this criterion be satisfied. A sovereign people is one whose will stands even though it may be a mistaken or ill-advised will.

This is a matter on which so many writers and speakers appear to be confused that it may be the most controversial aspect of the whole question of what democracy means. The criterion, for example, of respect for individuals as such is certainly vital to the very life of democracy. As soon as individuals must, in decision-making, bow to some form of statism, democracy is on the way out. But this is what equality in law-making and law abidance actually means, so it is written into the definition as we have it. The point need not, as well as must not, be repeated. It must not be repeated because that would fence off an area and place it outside of the realm of decision-making, thereby limiting the sovereignty of the people. This is self-contradiction. It is not questioned that, if a people passes or permits to be passed regulations which are disrespectful of individuality, democracy will to that extent be limited. But the very genius of democracy, as we have said already, is that democracy can be voluntarily and in orderly fashion terminated, if and when a people decides that it should be. And if, in the definition itself, this very point of genius is denied even on a single matter, then this very point of genius is nonexistent from the start. If this is not self-contradiction, what is it?

4. As to preciseness, if there are still parts of the definition which can be deleted without loss of what is vital, we shall welcome such deletion. But we do not now see the possibility, and we do feel that a high degree of preciseness has already been achieved.

5. Finally, as over many years we have read treatises, listened to lectures, participated in discussions, and talked with all manner of persons, we have been impressed with three points of agreement on the American way, at least as far as the United States people is concerned. Those are that the people shall be sovereign, that equal rights shall be maintained, and that there shall be equal responsibil-

ity before the law. These points, we believe, are clearly written into the definition.

After the above is said, popular agreement seems to reach an abrupt end. The reason seems to be that then we come to detailed implementation. The matter seems to have been succinctly stated one time by a friend of mine, after one of our numerous disagreements. He said, "E_____, you and I always seem to agree on the kind of thing we want, but we never seem able to agree on how to go about getting it." My response, of course, was, "Well, R_____, I think you are entirely correct on that. But, after all, isn't whether you get what you want almost entirely dependent on the way you go about getting it?"

Admitting this, however, we must proceed to further realization that our wants are never single or even simple; that the multifarious wants or purposes which we embrace at any given moment are likely in many ways to be at odds or in conflict with one another. Hence, in order to avoid continually working toward the defeat of our own selves, we need to give attention first to harmonization of ends, then to harmonization of means with ends; and it is seemingly at this stage that we as a people fall apart.

The advantage, seemingly, of arriving at clear-cut and workable definitions of key concepts in our philosophy of life, such as the concept of democracy, is that this is a necessary step toward harmonization both among ends and of means with ends. Until we agree on what we mean by democracy, we can hardly hope to agree on how to get it, or even on whether we really want it. Once we reach a working agreement (or at least clarity) on definition, then we can make headway in determining what else is in keeping with what is defined and, if what is defined should in a given context become an end, what means are necessary for its achievement.

We feel that our definition of democracy does indeed go a long way toward catching the spirit of what James Truslow Adams has called "The American Dream," and that acceptance of this definition, even if it should be only for a limited period of time, will be a great aid toward enabling us to reach agreement on many next-steps to be taken in terms of democratic educational practice. To indicate what some of those next-steps might be will be the purpose of the next chapter.

There are those, however, who are unhappy with our definition, insisting that it is too narrow, that it does not protect minority rights, and that it opens wide the door for undemocratic outcomes. It is evident that these are persons who are highly committed to democracy; dedicated to its continued expansion and refinement. We are certainly in league with them; they are on our side and we on theirs. But we feel that their sentiments may be getting a bit out of hand.

There is a Midwestern expression, "He wants it so bad, he can taste it." One whose die may be cast with a minority group may become so sensitive to the necessity for protection of minority rights that he overlooks the possibility that the rights of the remainder may thereby be overridden. Is this not exactly what the right to filibuster has achieved in the United States Senate? And are there not many Senators who deplore it, yet hesitate to support its abolition because they sense that there might come a time when they themselves would wish to use it; when there was something at stake so dear to them that they would be unwilling to run the risk of a majority vote to the contrary?

In our discussion of process versus product (see pp. 151–153), we already met this point squarely. We shall not repeat what has been said. Our point of insistence is that here resides the crux of the whole democratic process. If a people's will is not to be taken, for a given occasion, as final, then we do not have democracy; regardless of how right or how wrong, how good or how bad, that will may be. If we do not trust a people's judgment, we are not democratically committed. If the rights of a minority are protected beyond guaranteeing the persons who compose it opportunity to participate in making and remaking decisions equal to all other persons in the jurisdictional group, then protection of minority rights has overreached the democratic principle.

It is not easy at first to see how it could be democratic for a majority to hold a group disenfranchised because of skin color or sex. Yet that seems to be exactly what one must accept if self-contradiction is to be avoided—if sovereignty by an overall jurisdictional group is not to be placed under limitations. It is easy to comprehend how *expansion* of membership in a jurisdictional group would be democratic, but not so easy if it is contraction. Yet if sovereignty includes the one, it must include the other also; else it is not sovereignty.

I was much helped in my thinking about democracy by association with Dr. H. Clay Jent in his doctoral study of the meaning of democracy.[6] It may have been then that I caught the full impact of what democracy requires of the expression, "equality of opportunity." It is equality of opportunity for *one thing only*—to participate in decision-making—together with the necessary sequel, equality of *obligation* to abide by the decisions. To set up any other stipulation establishes divided allegiance, and there always come times when one has to choose which allegiance shall take precedence. Possibly this is what prompted Lincoln to proclaim that "a house divided against itself cannot stand." To settle such precedence ahead of time makes for consistency and dependability in policy and in action; one knows where he himself stands, and others also have the opportunity to know.

As for minority rights, it seems entirely clear that they are given full democratic protection as long as the stipulations of the definition are maintained. This is all that can be required of a definition. If a given people has not the wisdom or discernment necessary to realize that any further curtailment of minority rights will definitely curtail democracy itself, any such action actually taken may indeed be taken democratically, but its *effects* (product) will be undemocratic in the sense of working toward curtailment of democracy. This, of course, is merely to say that by way of democratic process a people may indeed terminate democracy—the door is wide open and held open as long as the definition holds. That criticism is indeed a just one. But the only democratic remedy is to be continually on guard not to adopt policies which, either rapidly or slowly, work toward the demise of democracy. This is why democratic *policy* calls for a nation-wide educational program which improves the reflective capacity and the wisdom of every citizen and prospective citizen to the highest degree possible. The definition does not require it, but policy does.

Finally, to claim, as some do, that our definition thoroughly justifies a subgroup to gainsay the registered will of a larger group of which it is only a part, can hardly be done without entirely missing the meaning of the definition. Although this matter is rather thoroughly covered in our next chapter, where we discuss *jurisdic-*

[6] H. Clay Jent, "A Study of the Meaning of Democracy and of Its Salient Implications for Teaching," unpublished doctoral dissertation, School of Education, the University of Kansas, 1951.

tion, it may be profitable to put down a few comments here. An entire sovereign group, say the enfranchised citizens of a democratic nation, is taken as the jurisdictional source; at least as long as the peoples of Planet Earth operate on the principle of national sovereignty. Our national group is not "Washington," but is our entire people voicing its wishes via the machinery which we have adopted for the purpose.

Having overall jurisdiction, the national group may take whatever action it deems advisable. A "constitutionalist" will deny this, but he is to be reminded that the people can change the Constitution at any time that it makes up its collective mind to do so, even though certain undemocratic obstacles such as two-thirds-or-three-fourths-majority requirements have been placed in its way. Delegation of jurisdictional authority is also within its power, and it is only by delegation that any subgroup, be it large or small, derives jurisdictional authority.[7] This is democratic theory as it seemingly has to be if our definition has any meaning at all.

Delegated authority may, in turn, be further delegated to sub-subgroups at the discretion of any subjurisdictional group which may be named. Moreover, whatever is delegated may later be withdrawn by the delegating group. It follows, therefore, that no subgroup may deny the will of any higher group from which it derives its authority. It may legislate only as long as it does not violate enactments of a higher jurisdictional group. Hence, a state, even though called upon to do so by its own qualified voters, may not democratically repudiate national enactments.

All in all, it certainly does not look as if our definition can with justification be criticized as too narrow. That it is simple and easy to understand seems to be true. It furnishes a clear basis for judging what is democratic and what is not, and it certainly seems to represent the spirit of the American people. Like a Bikini bathing suit, it may not include unnecessary material but it does seem to cover essential points.

[7] I am fully aware of the legalistic principle, under which this nation has presumably functioned, of ultimate authority residing in the separate states and federal authority being only that specifically delegated to it by the states. But this was adopted at a stress time, to make possible our getting started as a nation and to have a constitution at all. In the form of Nullification, it was directly challenged, and was presumably denied by the outcome of the Civil War though not in a sufficiently clear-cut manner to keep it from plaguing us in the form of states-rights claims even to the present time. Yet the practical point remains that, when the issue cannot be avoided and there is a showdown, national concern takes precedence.

SELECTED REFERENCES

Bayles, Ernest E., *The Theory and Practice of Teaching,* New York: Harper & Brothers, 1950, chap. 3.

Bode, Boyd H., *Democracy as a Way of Life,* New York: The Macmillan Company, 1937.

Bode, Boyd H., *Modern Educational Theories,* New York: The Macmillan Company, 1927, chaps. 1, 10, 11.

Brubacher, John S., *Eclectic Philosophy of Education,* New York: Prentice-Hall, Inc., 1951, chaps. 11, 12.

Bruce, William, *Principles of Democratic Education,* New York: Prentice-Hall, Inc., 1939, chaps. 12, 15.

Childs, John L., *American Pragmatism and Education,* New York: Henry Holt and Company, 1956, chap. 5.

Childs, John L., *Education and Morals,* New York: Appleton-Century-Crofts, Inc., 1950, pp. 27–28, chap. 9.

Dewey, John, *Democracy and Education,* New York: The Macmillan Company, 1916, chap. 7.

Dewey, John, *Problems of Men,* New York: Philosophical Library, 1946, Part I.

Dewey, John, *The Public and Its Problems,* Chicago: Gateway Books, 1946, chap. 5.

Gabriel, Ralph Henry, *The Course of American Democratic Thought,* New York: The Ronald Press Company, 1940.

Hobbes, Thomas, *Leviathan.*

John Dewey Society, Second Yearbook, *Educational Freedom and Democracy,* New York: Appleton-Century-Crofts, Inc., 1938, chap. 1.

Kilpatrick, W. H., et al., *The Educational Frontier,* New York: The Century Company, 1933, chaps. 2, 9.

Locke, John, *Of Civil Government,* New York: E. P. Dutton & Co., Inc., 1936.

Rousseau, J. J., *The Social Contract,* New York: E. P. Dutton & Co., Inc., 1913.

Smith, T. V., and Lindeman, E. C., *The Democratic Way of Life,* New York: The New American Library of World Literature, Inc. (Mentor Book), 1951.

Tocqueville, Alexis de, *Democracy in America,* New York: Vintage Books, 1954, 2 vols.

CHAPTER 11

Democracy and
Keeping School

WHETHER our proposed definition of democracy will be found acceptable or not will definitely depend on what it implies in terms of logically deduced procedures. This is merely another way of saying that "the proof of the pudding is the eating." If, on the other hand, the definition is already deemed acceptable, then we shall also wish to know what it implies in terms of logically deduced procedures. This twofold purpose is, therefore, served by the present chapter.

Moreover, since the major concern of this book is educational, this chapter will be focused mainly on educational matters. Before proceeding to these, however, a bit of attention may well be paid to points noneducational.

That what we now have nationally represents thorough-going democracy is neither claimed nor implied. Indeed, the very fact that we sense a need for formulation of a definition signifies at least a suspicion that what we have does not quite live up to what we would like to have. By clarifying our ideal, we take a necessary step toward becoming discerningly critical of what we have and in turn becoming more able to know what adjustments or corrections are needed to attain the ideal.

Formulation of a standard which for the time being will serve as a frame of reference or a point of fixity is a *sine qua non* for determining whether we are moving, how fast, and in what direction. If that standard is a goal or end which we are seeking to achieve, then and then alone can we tell whether we are making progress and how much. By clearly defining democracy, we gain two advantages:

(1) we become better able to tell whether we really want it, and (2) we become better able to tell whether we have it and, if not, what we must do to get it.

Another general point is the intricate question of power structure necessary to enable a people to maintain democratic political structure. It indeed is a point of first importance, but it is beyond the scope of this work. It is the question of how a people which seriously desires democracy will be able to withstand the onslaughts of forces which would deny it the opportunity to have its way once it knows what way it wants. For instance, how will it make sure that its chief executive officer, its army, or its police force will act as its servants and carry out its wishes? How will it make sure that its judicial structure will adjudicate in terms of enacted law and not take liberties which will have the effect of writing its own laws? How will it make sure that its legislative representatives will legislate in terms of its wishes, and not be unduly or unfairly influenced by the special interests which are prone to bring high pressures to bear in behalf of enactments in their favor? How will it make sure that private control of large accumulations of wealth will not be effectual in securing special privileges of various and sundry kinds? How will it make sure that current channels of information necessary for reaching wise decisions will make available such information when decisions must be made? And how will a people make sure that its educational system will indeed function in such a way as to do what democracy requires of it?[1]

Questions such as these are pertinent, and of prime importance, in a study of democracy. But this chapter can deal with only a portion of the problem; not with all of it. The question before us in this section is what democracy requires of its educational system. That covers none but the last of the questions stated above, except indirectly, and, of course, that last one cannot itself be exhaustively handled in the following pages. But we can indicate some of the educational implications which logically grow out of our adopted definition, and this we shall proceed to do.

---

[1] For an extended treatment of this whole problem, see Lewis A. Bayles, "Freedom and Power in a Multigroup Society as Related to the Control of Education," unpublished doctoral dissertation, the Ohio State University, Columbus, 1957. Dealing also with extensions of this problem is Myron Lieberman, *Education as a Profession,* New York: Prentice-Hall, Inc., 1956.

Control of Student Behavior

It may not always be the case, but it usually is, that, if and when teachers come to deliberate on the meaning of democracy for education, an early question will be what to do about school discipline or the control of student behavior. And widespread feeling is that democracy in schoolrooms means letting students or pupils do largely as they please or, at least, letting them decide what shall be the rules of behavior.

A rational, as well as realistic, answer to this question can perhaps best be reached through consideration of the matter of *jurisdiction*. Since, as noted in Chapter 10, our definition places supreme authority in a people as a whole, it follows that any assignment of that authority lies with the people as a whole. Whatever enactment the whole people deems desirable, and whenever it deems so, it has authority to enact. If it chooses not to act, that is its prerogative. This also holds if and when it should desire to assign authority to some other group to handle designated enactments, both to make and to enforce them. Such designated group may be either within or without the people as a whole. Whether such designations later prove to be wise or unwise is not the point; only that the whole people is sovereign, democratically justified in making such designations or reaching such decisions as this paragraph includes. This is what our definition means if it means anything.

If, therefore, a given group (other than the whole) is assigned by the whole the task of handling certain matters, then on those matters it has jurisdiction and continues to have it as long, and only as long, as the whole people lets the assignment stand. This practice is so common that it almost seems superfluous to write it down. Yet its very commonness makes conscious recognition important. We often forget that this is an essential aspect of our system, and many are the groups or persons which seemingly do not realize that their jurisdiction or authority is only a derived one and may be withdrawn by the authority which established it.

"Freedom of the press" is a common expression, and is indeed a principle held dear by the rank and file of democratic peoples as well as by those directly connected with or part of the industry itself. Let us not forget, however, that such freedom is only an assigned one; that it may democratically be modified or rescinded just as readily as it was originally established. This may be a danger for us all to guard against, or, on the other hand, it may be a reminder to the industry that abuse of the principle could justifiably lead to its withdrawal.

Members of Boards of Education sometimes become obsessed with their powers over school personnel, insisting upon their right to make or break teachers as they choose. Such members quite forget that they are merely representatives, first, of their own local electorate (in as far as that electorate has jurisdiction over schoolroom practices) and, second, of whatever other jurisdictional bodies may have concern for their actions. The latter may include state boards of control, and even national policy. In this nation it may be argued that the principle of "unstated powers" residing within the separate states includes educational matters; hence, federal enactments may not gainsay the states. But even in this case there is probably more weight to the argument that in matters of serious and significant federal concern the national policy does take precedence. Witness the case of federal action in 1957 at Little Rock, in the "sovereign" state of Arkansas.

Bringing the matter down to student behavior in individual classrooms, our definition clearly implies that only on issues definitely considered subject to student opinion do students themselves have jurisdiction. On all other issues it is the assigned group which is jurisdictional, not the student body. Of course, the right of appeal and petition to the jurisdictional body is always implied and should assuredly be protected as well as encouraged by school personnel. Such is an aspect of "learning the ways of democracy." But it is equally important to learn that democratically enacted laws are to be obeyed, whether one approves or not.

It is thoroughly fallacious to argue that, in order to be democratic, we must let children do as they wish, or even enact whatever rules and regulations they wish. Because a community decrees that damaging school property shall be a penal offense does not at all mean that the democratic rights of students have been denied. Nor does refusal by a college or university president to legalize a holiday in honor of victory in a crucial football game. Only on matters over which a student body has specifically been given jurisdiction by a responsible group, or on those over which no action to the contrary has been taken or implied, are student wishes to be taken as final. Such matters are numerous, and presently are likely to include orderly behavior on school premises at off times during a school day; certain choices among extracurricular and curricular electives; many of the forms which school social gatherings may take; within wide limitations, clothing to be worn at school; many choices having to do with projects and other activities within classrooms; generalized lines of study in upper levels where specialization is possible; incumbents of numerous school offices held by students; much of what goes into student newspapers, annuals, and other publications; etc., etc.

At one point above we mention "student wishes to be taken as final." This is a point of importance, and one which in principle is many times violated. On all matters over which students are given to understand that they have jurisdiction, their own expressed wishes must be taken as final; of course, until some change is made. Violations often take the form of permitting or asking students to vote on something, then becoming distressed, even at times to the point of rescinding the action, if and when the vote goes the wrong way. Usually, perhaps, students are aware of when a certain vote which they might take would be found unacceptable, and circumspectly refrain from taking it. But they usually resent being pushed into such a situation, and the educational outcomes are far from wholesome. No person, young or old, relishes being asked to make a serious judgment when he knows that he will be gainsaid if his judgment turns out "wrong." He is inclined to retort, "If my judgment will not stand should you consider it wrong, then don't ask me to make it."

Student councils sometimes are asked by principals to vote on whether halls should be policed between classes, when the members know that they will be "in bad" if they vote in the negative. Then, after what is essentially a duress vote, the principal follows with, "Now that you have voted for this measure, you will be expected to enforce it." This is almost a sure-fire way to develop student resentment. And who can blame the students? Moreover, it is not democracy.

Permission to vote only on matters over which there is jurisdiction implies that each vote shall be the real choice of the voter. Whether considered good or bad by some school officer, student decisions should stand on any matter put to them for decision. If such cannot be, then they should be so apprised, shown what choices are genuinely available to them, and asked whether they wish to choose among those. As to policing halls after a principal deems such procedure necessary, the Council may be informed of the necessity, why it appears necessary, and asked whether they themselves wish to do the policing or have it done by others. This could then be a free choice and, if a vote to police were forthcoming, the task would be undertaken with alacrity.

After a decision has been democratically made, it must be democratically enforced. Enforcement means coercion, at least for recalcitrants, and coercion is democratic if applied equally to all such without fear or favor. Democracy is a *working* governmental system; any feature which experience demonstrates as unworkable becomes a candidate for alteration into a workable one. Human beings, including children in schools, have to be worked with as they are here and now. Unneeded rules and regulations should indeed be avoided, out of school as well as in. But needed regulatory measures, if democratically enacted, require enforcement even though they may be distasteful to certain members of a body politic.

RELATIONSHIPS BETWEEN THE EDUCATIONAL PROFESSION AND THE BODY POLITIC

A distinctly uncharted realm of jurisdictional relationships is that involving the degree of autonomy to be exercised by educational personnel in the pursuit of their professional duties. For example, is what is to be included in schoolroom curricula—what is to be taught in our schools—something to be decided by the body politic or by the profession? Let us think of this question for the present on national terms, so as to keep it as simple as possible by avoiding the complication of federal versus local control. The question is one of how much the profession is obligated to follow the wishes of the body politic on matters which call for professional judgment as to how national policy can best be carried out.

To state the question in the latter way is to go far toward answering it. National policy, of course, is to be determined by the nation as a whole, by the entire citizenry, the body politic. But on innumerable matters good judgment on the details necessary to carry out basic national policy is not possible on the part of the citizenry as a whole, for reasons so obvious as not to require enumeration. Hence, specially trained commissions or professions have to be allotted the tasks of deciding on such necessary details and given (or delegated) the power to take the necessary action. The procedure is quite similar to a private citizen's relations with his physician. Jonh Q.

Citizen decides to put his case in the hands of Dr. X. In consequence, he asks Dr. X what he should do and proceeds to do it. He is not under the autocratic dictation of Dr. X even though he is fully obedient. He is hiring professional advice and is using it. But all the while Mr. Citizen is watching results and judging for himself whether Dr. X is justifying the trust placed in him. The moment Mr. Citizen loses confidence in the capacity of Dr. X to serve him as Mr. Citizen desires, the services of Dr. X are terminated and those of some other presumed expert are sought. Dr. X is serving while he prescribes; he is not dictating.

It would seem that the educational profession is in exactly the same position as the physician in the above illustration when it comes to matters of curriculum. Though professional curriculum makers, whether teachers or some more specialized personnel, may deem it profitable to consult with various citizen groups on various and sundry curriculum matters, all decisions which determine curriculum action actually to be taken in the schools are the responsibility of the profession and not of the citizen groups. A citizen group would be tying a noose around its own neck if it should try to make the situation otherwise—like a patient with his doctor— and I expect that most citizens are fully aware of this and act accordingly. School personnel are indeed badgered by many who seek to influence professional decisions to serve their own (usually shortsighted) ends; but in each case these individuals unquestionably represent a minority, usually a small one even though annoying and in some cases sufficiently powerful to achieve dismissal or other reprisal against a few professionally unprotected individuals who oppose them. A significant point to note is that, if and when the action sought by some non-professional pressure group should backfire after being adopted, that group would likely be among the first to deny responsibility and to accuse those professionally responsible of professional incompetence or malpractice.

It would seem that at this point organizations of professional personnel should be performing a major function: taking steps necessary to protect their members against such group pressures as above described and thereby enabling the profession as a whole to discharge honestly and to the full extent of its capacity its obligations to the body politic. This seems to be a central tenet of Myron J. Lieberman in his recent book, *Education as a Profession* (Prentice-Hall, 1956), and in other recent and forthcoming writings. His basic position would seem to be a valid one and one which needs to be taken seriously by the educational profession.

In broad principle, it would appear that the American public-educational profession is assigned by the American public the task of carrying forward the educational enterprise in a thoroughly American (presumably democratic) way. Failure to do so is, therefore, the mark of professional incompetence. Professional incompetence is what the body politic is not wise to tolerate. But the body politic is wise to judge incompetence only in terms of results, not in terms of procedures. As to steps to be taken in carrying out major public educational policy, the professional organization should be autonomous; it should rely on its own judgment, and not be influenced here or there by small-group pressures, not even, as is most often the case, by local boards of education. "By their fruits ye shall know them," is a principle which the lay public should employ and which the profession should stand firm to defend.

This principle should seemingly hold within the profession as well as in its relations with the public. Teachers, for example, are presumably chosen on the assumption of competence to handle what goes on in their respective classrooms. Hence, those held responsible for determining whether the required competence is evinced are obligated to judge in terms of results, *not* in terms of procedures. For a superintendent or a principal to go into a classroom and tell a teacher how to conduct the class would be as much of a violation of professional ethics as it would be for a private citizen to enter the superintendent's or principal's office to tell him how to conduct his affairs.

In American public elementary and secondary schools, it would seem that the line-of-command principle—from Board to superintendent to principal to teacher to pupil—has been greatly overworked. It has its place, as we shall indicate presently. But first let us deal with the principle of professional obligation or responsibility. A superintendent is presumably responsible for the proper functioning of a school system as a whole, be it a large one or a small one. For this he is responsible, basically, to the *nation as a whole,* and to the state and local boards of education only as they pass judgment as to how well he carries out national policy, together with whatever modifications or additions such state and local groups have within their respective jurisdictions. For example, since local school boards are ordinarily (within limits) responsible for local-district budgets, the superintendent (the executive officer) has the task of allocation and the obligation to stay within the budget. Expenditures by principals or teachers are subject to his approval.

A building principal is responsible for the portion of the total enterprise which is connected with his building. That is his specialty; relative to that he presumably is competent and not subject to dictation by some person "higher up." But the principal's responsibility is with his building as a unit, to keep its overall functions in proper working order. Scheduling of classes, enrolling of pupils, coördination of the curriculum, oversight of custodial services, oversight of inter-classroom and extra-classroom aspects of student behavior, and a host of other matters which make for unified orderliness of the educative process as carried on in his building *as a whole*—these are his domain.

Insofar as what goes on within a given classroom affects that classroom alone, the teacher of that classroom is responsible, not to the principal or the superintendent or the board of education, but to the citizenry of the nation as a whole. He is far from free to do as he pleases, but the limitations are established by the obligation to carry forward the national educational commitment, not the particular whims of some "higher-up." If a teacher is to be told by a principal or a superintendent how he is to do his job, he falls short of professional status or stature and becomes only a menial whose thinking is done for him by someone else. This, in a broad sense, is slavery.

It is only if and when incompetence on a teacher's part is evident, suspected, or anticipated that a principal is in any way justified to enter a classroom for the purpose of effecting changes in classroom procedures. If both teacher and principal are competent within their respective areas of service to the educational enterprise, there is no more justification for a principal to tell a teacher how to do his job than for the teacher to tell the principal. In terms of democratic educational theory, there must be no feeling of "higher-up" between teachers and principal, either one way or the other, as long as each is competently doing his job. In such matters, the principle of "line of command" is thoroughly and completely out of place. Only when incompetence appears should steps toward correction be taken, and then it would appear to be just as justifiable for the teaching staff of a given building to apply corrective measures for an incompetent principal as for a principal to apply corrective measures for an incompetent teacher. That this is revolutionary doctrine, as far as elementary and secondary schools are concerned, is not denied; but it would seem that nothing short of this doctrine is democratically professional.

This principle is, in fact, widely accepted and is traditional practice at the university level, even though possibly in some of the smaller colleges it may not be so. A university faculty member, who has passed his "apprenticeship" and achieved permanent status, would be simply astonished to have a dean or a president (or chancellor) presume to tell him what or how he should teach. To protect faculty members from such encroachment is one of the major purposes of the American Association of University Professors (AAUP, organized in 1916), and a faculty member who would permit himself to be taken to task in this manner would lose the respect of his colleagues. I would very much like to go into detail regarding this situation, but to do so is not justifiable here. Readers may be inclined to feel that the principle may be all right for university faculties, but it should not hold for secondary and elementary faculties. Why? Simply because university faculty members are considered competent—whether justifiedly or not—and the others not. Well, isn't that exactly what we have been saying? And, in the interests of democratic education, is it not essential that our goal be to secure personnel which represents competence at all levels and in all aspects rather than to settle for anything less? Moreover, it may be added that corrections in attitude in this regard on the part of the profession itself will do much toward raising the level of competence of personnel, and both in turn will alter public attitude and lead to further improvement. I am convinced that professors of educational administration and supervision have been highly remiss in this area of professional instruction and would do well to look critically at what they are teaching.

But we promised to take a further look at the line-of-command principle. This principle, it would seem, is democratically justified as long as it is limited in each case to the professional domain of the personnel in question. For example, when the ventilation-system of a school building requires that all outside windows be kept closed, it is certainly the business of the principal to see that the requirement is fulfilled and it is reasonable to expect each and every teacher to carry it out. Again, for one teacher to make demands on students such as to interfere with their work in other classes is an intolerable situation and certainly the business of the principal to rectify, even if it means interference with the way the offending teacher handles his own classes.

In this sense there is a line of command from principal to teacher to pupil, because the problem has to do with building-wide matters and is therefore within the domain of the building principal. However, such line of command can also work in the opposite direction, even though many principals and superintendents are prone not to recognize it. For example, whenever conditions within a classroom are adversely affected by outside factors, it is certainly the obligation of the building principal to take whatever steps he can to alleviate the situation and the teacher would certainly be professionally justified, if it became necessary, to put the matter in the form of a demand. After all is said and done, the individual classrooms are the heart of any educational system, and the only justification for the existence of any and all other aspects or parts is the service they render in making classrooms optimally contributory to the educative process. As far as school personnel are concerned, teachers are in a very real sense at the "top of the heap." And, carrying the thought further, in perhaps the most crucial context of a democratic educational program it seems justifiable to say that "the pupil is king." It is his educational needs—not his expressed whims or fancies—about which all else should revolve.

Therefore, in answer to the original query of this section, it would seem that democracy requires a wide range of freedom on the part of educational personnel in exercising and acting upon their own judgment as to how they are to carry out the requirements placed upon them by the body politic. They are to be judged, not on procedures, but on overall results, results which can reasonably be expected in light of available facilities. If, on such bases and after fair hearing, they are judged by the public to fall short, then they should be dismissed in the hope that more competent personnel may be procured. This principle should hold for intra-professional relationships, as has been discussed, as well as for those between the profession and the public at large. The line-of-command principle holds *only* insofar as a given professional person or group is carrying out the tasks for which it is specifically responsible; concerning those tasks, if and when necessary, he gives orders or directives, whereas on all others he receives them. Ideally, of course, no person is to become imperious in his issuance of orders nor servile in following those of others. Ideally, democracy is based on coöperation, with no people trying to push other people around and no people permitting themselves to be pushed around by other people, yet all willingly and gladly doing their respective parts in the collective enterprise which represents the combined will of the entire people.

Control of Student Attitudes or Beliefs

We now change the subject. We have been considering actions or behavior. But what about attitudes, beliefs, or personal convictions? What does democracy mean for the person who is unhappy with a given enactment? That he must act or behave in accordance with it has been established earlier in this chapter. Evidently, however, he is not required to like it. There is nothing in our definition which even remotely implies that any member of a democratic nation is required to approve any law, regulation, or rule enacted by that nation or any part thereof. A majority of those voting on a given proposal must indeed approve it; otherwise, it would not be enacted. But minority approval is neither required nor expected. Nor are those who disapprove expected to suffer in silence. In their disapproval they may be as vocal as they choose, as long as they maintain legal decorum.

Moreover, democracies are ordinarily very careful to protect the privacy of personal beliefs and convictions. Enter "thought control," exit democracy. In principle, the secret ballot is almost universal democratic practice. When asked how he voted on a given matter, anyone versed in the ways of democracy will be inclined to think, "Is that a legitimate question?"

However, although the foregoing applies to a citizenry as a whole, when teachers deal with students they are faced with a different situation. Though he may not be able to say exactly why, one of the things which seemingly "every teacher knows" is that he must do something about the beliefs of his pupils. He cannot with equanimity let them continue "thinking wrong thoughts." At least among thoughtful persons, there are perhaps few who are not convinced that, if a teacher cannot or does not influence the thinking of his students so as to make it better than it otherwise might have been, he has no business being a teacher.

Herein, therefore, arises a possible dilemma, and for a large majority of teachers it appears to be an actual one. Even the better writers of treatises on education are far from clear on the matter, if they face it at all. It is easy enough, of course, to *say* that we must have thought *guidance* but not thought *control*. But what is the difference? Thought guidance certainly must mean letting a student know when he is thinking poorly and when well. On the other hand, is this not tantamount to letting him know when he agrees with us and when he does not? If he agrees with us, he is thinking well and is to be encouraged along that line; if he fails so to agree, he is thinking poorly and needs to be straightened out. But is this not authoritarian dictation? Is it not "thought control"? If we are to avoid educational anarchism, we must "guide" student thinking. If we are to avoid educational dictation, we must guide on some basis other than agreement or disagreement with our own beliefs or conclusions. How can this possibly be done?

Obviously, these questions involve us in the problem of indoctrination. It may therefore be helpful to take into account what others have had to say. Varied as may be the views on indoctrination of those whose names I shall mention, in no case do I have any reason whatever to doubt the sincerity of the person's belief in democracy. As far as I have any knowledge, all of them wish to promote the democratic commitment of this nation as much as I do. Whatever differences may exist seem to be wholly in terms of what such commitment is taken to mean educationally.

It is, of course, recognized that there are persons and agencies in this country who do not favor democracy. In fact, perhaps much of the talk of too much power in the hands of "government" is plainly and simply a double-talk way of saying that "the many" have been able to impose regulations which "the few" find distasteful. Moreover, when any group—religious or otherwise—conducts an entire educational program on the basis of edicts promulgated by an autonomous source, it can hardly be, and usually is not, claimed to be democratic. One-way lines of communication make democracy impossible. Without the principle of "feedback," as it is recognized in cybernetics, democracy cannot exist.

A widely held, albeit often not clearly formulated, view is that "good indoctrination" is democratic, whereas "bad indoctrination" is not. The United States Chamber of Commerce opposed the Rugg series of social-studies textbooks on the grounds that they were indoctrinative. (And indoctrinative I am satisfied that they were.) But the Chamber and other groups of its kind were at the same time warmly supporting the use of other textbooks which were equally indoctrinative, usually in behalf of views less tenable than were those advocated by Rugg. It was clear that the Chamber was not opposed to indoctrination as such; it was against only the kind which favored views that it did not like. "Bad indoctrination" was what it found distasteful. Of course, it would have been happy for the schools to stay away from certain subjects completely because then its own channels of communicating with the public could function unimpeded. This kind of school policy should, however, not be called nonindoctrinative. It is indoctrination by omission rather than by commission. But it is indoctrination none the less, for it gives the green light to nonschool agencies which are then able to regale the public with whatever information and whatever thought-line they wish the public to adopt.

But to favor "good indoctrination" and to oppose only that which is "bad" is the position taken by many within the ranks of professional school men. I have heard it expressed by liberal arts college professors. Moreover, one time about 1940, before a class of mine to which he was invited to speak, George S. Counts said, "I am opposed to indoctrination which is bad and in favor of that which is good." To the class it was obvious that Counts opposed only indoctrination for a view which he opposed.

In *The Education of Free Men in American Democracy,* Counts asserts that "democracy must be presented to the young as a way of life and a social faith immeasurably superior to all others."[2] His conviction was that undemocratic groups should not be permitted to use democratic means to further undemocratic ends. Can it be that he was forgetful of Voltaire? In *Education for Democracy in Our Time,* Jesse Newlon insisted that "a democracy must foster in its members loyalty to the principles of a free society"; and that "it will foster those values that the race has found good."[3]

What seemingly touched off the hot controversy of the late 1930's was the final volume of the *Report of the Social Studies Commission* of the American Historical Association sponsored and perhaps mostly written by Counts and Newlon. Schools are not to be neutral on matters of broad social policy. They must stand for something. They must "dare to build a new social order." In this volume was

[2] George S. Counts, *The Education of Free Men in American Democracy,* Washington, D.C.: Educational Policies Commission of the National Education Association, 1941, p. 79.

[3] Jesse Newlon, *Education for Democracy in Our Time,* New York: McGraw-Hill Book Company, Inc., p. 87.

introduced the expression, "a frame of reference," and, although at no place was there an explicit statement, it was rather overpoweringly evident that the frame of reference presented in the second chapter was the one on which the new social order was to be built. That the kind of social order presented and obviously advocated was an improvement over the one we then had is not the issue raised here. The point is that the impact of the proposal was indoctrinative; *advocacy* of one view over others.

The same position was anticipated by Harold Rugg in his "frontier-thinkers" concept (*Culture and Education in America,* 1931), on which he based his social-studies series of textbooks. By means of tabulations of the writings of "frontier thinkers," chosen of course by Rugg or on the basis of criteria determined by him, a "description of society" was derived. This description was what was to be taught to students. In his social-studies series, Rugg presented alternative views only meagerly, if at all, and then only in derogatory fashion or as something which may have been good for the country at one stage in history but as now out of date.

B. F. Pittenger, in *Indoctrination for American Democracy,* presented exactly the same theme with only two slight variations. First, he was explicit that the preferred view—he employed the in-quotes expression, "eternal verities"—be frankly and unapologetically indoctrinated. Second, his way of obtaining the list of supposed verities was to gather lists of formulated educational objectives from the widest variety of sources obtainable, separate out from the lists the objectives common to all, and see that those are put over. Needless to say, his final list was made up entirely of items which were either highly innocuous or too vague to pin down to anything. And he reminded his readers that the list was only tentative anyway.

All the writers in the Forty-first and Fifty-fourth Yearbooks who are overtly presenting absolutistic philosophies of education show rather clearly that their position on indoctrination is much like the foregoing. Wild wishes not to be "harsh and authoritarian," but the absolutes when known are to be taught with "deep conviction, rhetoric, and persuasive force." He chooses a UNESCO list as the best now available.

Greene wants an educational institution as a whole to be neutral. To that end, each view recognized in a given community is to be represented by a separate instructor. But each instructor is to present his own view as convincingly as he can. Therefore, each can without qualms of conscience be as indoctrinative as he pleases, because he is assured that all other representative views will be presented likewise.

Not explicitly stated in the Forty-first Yearbook but definitely so elsewhere, Frederick S. Breed's position was, in almost his own words, "What I know I shall teach; what I do not know I shall teach as such." In other words, what a teacher is satisfied is a true replica of the absolute is to be pressed in no uncertain terms, but what he is not sure about he will present in terms of the various alternatives and leave students to their own untrammeled and undirected choices. In the former category he placed the natural sciences and mathematics and in the latter the social sciences.

Like Greene, Herman H. Horne was very mild in his convictions of his own rectitude. Hence, he tended to bend backward against efforts to bring students to his way of thinking. His personal humility led him continually to indicate the limitations of his own knowledge of the ultimate and the continual need for him in his teaching to be basically permissive. In fact, his functional position was essentially agnostic—ultimate truth is there but while I remain mortal I shall never encompass it. Hence, he said, there will always be plenty of leeway for the practice of democracy in teaching. To him, evidently, democracy meant permissiveness. Let each student, as long as he showed himself competent (whatever that meant), come to his own conclusions and convictions without interference by a teacher.

I am rather sure that all of the foregoing writers (perhaps with the exception of Pittenger) do find or have found it objectionable to be classed as indoctrinative. Their feeling seems to be nicely expressed by Newlon when he wrote, "Indoctrination or, better, propaganda has come to mean distortion, withholding of information, evasion, imposing upon the individual; propaganda is often plain lying. Techniques such as these have no place in education for democracy. But deliberately and consciously to teach democracy is in no sense either propaganda or indoctrination. For intellectual freedom is an essential of democracy."[4]

But this is merely another way of saying that one is opposed to bad indoctrination and in favor of good. Like Newlon, we are opposed to evasion and distortion. Unlike Newlon, however, we are equally and for essentially the same reasons opposed to advocacy on

[4] *Ibid.*, p. 103.

the part of teachers of views or principles which can be justified *without* distortion or evasion. If equality of opportunity to participate in decision-making means anything, it means that a teacher may not justifiably use eloquence and position to secure acceptance of the views for which he stands; even if democracy itself is at stake. *Let us not confuse education with politics.* Advocacy is doubtless justified in democratic politics, but not in democratic education.

Since what I have just said will doubtless be about as distasteful to Brameld as it would have been to Newlon, I am forced to place Reconstructionism in the same category as the views of Newlon, Counts, and Rugg. All of these have been united in upbraiding Bode for what they consider his nonconcern for action. If there is any significant difference between Brameld and Bode—and Brameld is insistent that there is—it is on the matter of indoctrination; of advocacy as part of a teacher's business. Brameld wants a group which is properly representative of a citizenry at large to assemble and, through the benign and mellowing process of group dynamics, arrive at a consensus which, in turn, will become the "myth" and will serve as the banner around which school children will be marshaled. Twenty years or more ago, Bode characterized a fundamentally similar plan as taking advantage of defenseless childhood. And those whom he was accusing seemed to have no idea of what he meant.

Somewhat, perhaps decidedly, different from all the foregoing is the stand taken by Kilpatrick that there shall be no indoctrination whatever, but that school children all along the way and as they become maturationally ready shall be given opportunity to face the problems of mankind and *think out the answers.* In full accord do I accompany Kilpatrick to this point. But he stops there, and that seems to be too soon. What constitutes thinking? And how do we know when the outcomes of our thought processes are good and when they are not? In other words, what constitutes able thought, and when is our thinking not so? All of us do some thinking once in a while. Sometimes we do well and sometimes not so well. How can we know when we are doing which? To that question I find no answer in Kilpatrick. And Kilpatrick is far from alone in that regard.

Thus, we reach the crux of the problem of indoctrination, one of the most vital problems in democratic education. *How can a teacher criticize and guide pupil thinking, yet avoid indoctrination?* If we are to teach children *how* to think, we simply have to make them aware of when they are thinking well and when poorly. However, when we have nothing more than agreement with our own thought processes as the criterion for judgment on what is good thinking and what is bad, then we are being as authoritarian and dictatorial as the least benign of despots. The real question is, how can we judge, when a pupil's conclusions are not in agreement with ours, whether he is thinking *not* as well as we, or *whether he is outdoing us?* The latter is indeed a possibility. Moreover, although we seldom think of it, the same question should arise in our minds when pupils come to agreement with us. Are we all thinking as well as we should, or should we stay at it until we all do better? Just how, anyway, shall we know when we have done well enough?

An absolutist will answer, "When our conclusions are in agreement with, or correspond to, the thoughts of God or the laws of the universe." But, if we do not know for sure what those thoughts or laws are, how can we know when we have secured agreement or correspondence? All of you can well see, I expect, in what kind of predicament we would place a basketball referee if we would speak similarly to him as to his basis for refereeing a game.

What we must do to avoid complete chaos in connection with something no more complex than a game of basketball is, and has been, entirely clear to all of us. We simply decide beforehand on a set of rules—criteria which shall be used by a referee in judging right and wrong—and agree for the time being to be governed by them, coercively if necessary. They are taken, until further consideration, as the basis for determining good or bad; right or wrong. Thus, they are axiological. In like manner, we can set up rules or criteria for determining truth or falsity, and in this way deal with matters epistemological. And with it all we are satisfying the democratic principle—a principle which sets up what shall be considered proper relations among persons—of equality of opportunity to participate in making decisions and equality of obligation to abide by them.

If our definition of democracy means anything, it means that in democratic classrooms neither teacher nor pupils shall be entirely free to think as they themselves choose or wish to think. All are equally bound to abide by previously established criteria, determined either by their own agreements or by those of a jurisdictional group of which they are a part. If the jurisdictional group (in many cases it will be the class itself) decides that t-h-r-o-u-g-h shall be taken as the correct way to spell "through," that a drawing ought to look like what is being drawn, or that three plus five equal eight, then that has to be the basis for judging correctness or incorrectness of answers which involve these relationships. If, on the other hand, other relationships are previously determined as correct, then those shall hold, and teacher and pupils alike shall be judged correct or incorrect as they follow or fail to follow such relationships. If to some of you this sounds chaotic, please be reminded that that is the way it is being done, and has long been done, whether you like it or not. Actually, it is our only way to avoid chaos, as our illustration from basketball has shown. Not always are we democratic in determining what the rules shall be, but in all cases the rules are set up by human agencies. It is very true that, in myriads of particular cases, the human participants deemed that they were setting up criteria or rules in accordance with those of God or of universal law. But, as is often said, that is what *they* thought.

What has just been said, it should be noted, has dealt only with requirements which have to do with actions, even though many of the actions may be essentially mental. Following out a given thought-line and reaching the conclusion which it entails is a form of action. But it is also highly important to note that *no participant*—no one required to follow a particular line of action, be it mental or otherwise—*is required to like it.* Even though a given thought-line may, under given circumstances, be decided upon as a correct one and the one which must be followed, no one is required democratically to believe that it is what should have been adopted. For heretics, the way is always open to seek adherents for their heresy and to labor for reopening the question. This the teacher of a democratic classroom should always keep in mind and keep before the minds of his pupils. Hence, always in order is the question of whether, when, and how previously adopted criteria for criticism or rectitude should be modified or rescinded. As time goes on, both criteria and the fruits of those criteria may be constructed and reconstructed. Stability is thus achieved—relative stability—but the way is continually open, and pertinaciously held open, for change; change to a new basis upon which, until further change, a new stability can be maintained.

Those who have insisted that Bode (and likewise Dewey) stood for nothing definite and tangible simply did not, it would seem, give either Bode or Dewey the credit which was due them. Although neither, to my knowledge, overtly defined democracy as I have defined it, they certainly did in a functional way understand it as such;

and stand for it four-square. The persons concerned in a given matter and having jurisdiction over it shall be the ones to decide how it is to be handled and shall be bound by the decision until a change is inaugurated. May I ask, "What more stable basis is available to man for determining his welfare or his destiny?"

I would like to point out that I have refrained from saying at this time what criteria I believe should be adopted for distinguishing between good and bad, right and wrong, or true and false. Such criteria, it seems, would depend on time, place, and circumstance. Moreover, I have found that to introduce the further question at this point confuses the issue. I want here to make it emphatic that it is *not what* criteria are adopted that make guidance and criticism democratic. It is the fact of *adoption of* criteria, whatever they may be, and *agreement to be bound* by them. This is what makes criticism work in all ways, including teacher as well as pupils, and thereby fulfills our definition of democracy. Whether a decision is democratically achieved and democratically followed is one thing. Whether it is wise, just, or right is quite another. The latter is a matter which in this chapter we have chosen not to consider.

How Much Education Does Democracy Require?

The question of how much education democracy requires for a people is important, and is so frequently raised that we may give it a bit of attention. Since our definition requires only that a people shall make its own decisions, not that the decisions be wise or promotive of its own good, what basis is there for expectation or hope that so necessary an end may be realized? Obviously, the people must be widely and thoroughly educated. If a people is unwise, its decisions will be unwise, except perhaps when chance or luck may operate in its favor.

However, possession of wisdom is not by itself a guarantee of its employment. One must also be *disposed* to employ it. How does democracy promote such disposition? If a person is asked to make a decision when he knows that any he makes will undergo scrutiny by some higher authority and will be corrected if found wanting, he may go ahead and make it but is likely to be rather careless or offhand about it. He may even resent being asked to make it. On the other hand, if for good or for ill he knows that his decision will stand, he is likely to be thoroughly disposed to bring to bear whatever wisdom or discernment he may be able to marshal. Thus, the latter part of our definition—the requirement of having to live with whatever decisions we make—furnishes the incentive, not only to use whatever wisdom we may possess but also to gain as much more as we can. The disposition to decide as best we can inheres in the very nature of democracy as we have defined it.

There remains, therefore, only the question of *how much* education democracy requires. Is it elementary education for all, secondary education for all, college education for all? This seems to be a two-pronged question which, if not recognized as such, becomes unanswerable. If the question is how much popular education our *definition* of democracy requires, the answer is, "None." As previously noted, if we limit the sovereignty of a people we deny the principle of popular sovereignty—a self-contradiction which our definition avoids. Hence, by definition, if a democratically functioning people decides that it will support no educational system at all, that is its decision. We can easily argue that such a decision would be a prelude to the demise of democracy itself, but the democratic process does not preclude it. Only our own discernment as a people will protect us from making so catastrophic a decision. This is a point for application of eternal vigilance.

If, on the other hand, the question is how much popular education democratic *policy* requires, the answer is doubtless, "As much as the people feels that it can possibly afford." Then the facts as to how much we are willing to pay for public highways, for private automobiles, for liquor, tobacco, or chewing gum, as compared with the amount we are paying for public education, are indeed pertinent. Which, if necessary, had we better go without, chewing gum or democracy? This is the kind of question we must first answer if we are to be wise in answering the question of this paragraph. When out of total national income of almost 400 billions of dollars annually we spend 45 billions for armaments and only 15 billions (federal, state, and local) for education, is it educational expenditures which are pauperizing us?

Thus it is that in democracy the general welfare, including education, is achieved only through the discernment of the people. It is not guaranteed by democracy. Democracy furnishes only the opportunity. That whatever discernment a people may possess actually will be employed in decision making is strongly promoted by the definitional requirement of having to live with its decisions. That the great advantages of collective effort will be realized is promoted by the requirement that all participate on equal terms; any and all of the various interests of a people are given fair hearing and receive consideration. The sought-after ends of respect for individuality, of concern for the general welfare, of enhancing the wisdom of all, though in no way guaranteed, are more likely to be promoted than with any other governmental form. These are the *hopes* and the *expectations* of a democratically organized people. They do not serve as part of the definition.

SELECTED REFERENCES

Bode, Boyd H., *Progressive Education at the Crossroads,* New York: Newson, 1938.

Brameld, Theodore, *Ends and Means in Education,* New York: Harper & Brothers, 1950, chaps. 7, 10, 13, 19, 24.

Brameld, Theodore, *Toward a Reconstructed Philosophy of Education,* New York: The Dryden Press, 1956.

Childs, John L., *American Pragmatism and Education,* New York: Henry Holt and Company, 1956, chap. 10.

Childs, John L., *Education and Morals,* New York: Appleton-Century-Crofts, Inc., 1950, chaps. 1, 9.

Counts, G. S., *The Education of Free Men in American Democracy,* Washington, D.C.: Educational Policies Commission of the National Education Association, 1941.

Hunt, Maurice P., and Metcalf, Lawrence E., *Teaching High School Social Studies,* New York: Harper & Brothers, 1955, chaps. 1, 7.

Kilpatrick, William H., *Philosophy of Education,* New York: The Macmillan Company, 1951, chap. 22, especially pp. 307–310.

National Society for the Study of Education, Forty-first Yearbook, Part I, *Philosophies of Education,* Bloomington, Ind.: Public School Publishing Company, 1942.

National Society for the Study of Education, Fifty-fourth Yearbook, Part I, *Modern Philosophies and Education,* Chicago: The University of Chicago Press, 1955.

Newlon, Jesse H., *Education for Democracy in Our Time,* New York: McGraw-Hill Book Company, Inc., 1939.

Pittenger, Benjamin F., *Indoctrination for American Democracy,* New York: The Macmillan Company, 1941.

Raup, R. B.; Axtelle, G. E.; Benne, K. D.; and Smith, B. O.; *The Improvement of Practical Judgment,* New York: Harper & Brothers, 1950.

Rugg, Harold, *Culture and Education in America,* New York: Harcourt, Brace and Company, 1931, pp. 269–282.

Social Studies Commission, Report of the, *Conclusions and Recommendations of the Commission,* New York: Charles Scribner's Sons, 1934.

CHAPTER 12

Reflective Teaching

IT has often been said that democracy requires teaching pupils not *what* to think, but *how* to think. The present writer has more than once made this statement, both in speaking and in writing. However, perhaps the statement had better be to teach pupils *not only* what to think, *but also* how to think. For indeed it is widely recognized that one can hardly help pupils learn to think better or more ably without paying careful attention to the outcomes of their thinking; without looking closely at the conclusions which they reach as well as at how they reach them. Consideration of the nature of democratic teaching, therefore, leads two ways—both into the nature of the process and into the nature of the product. The former involves the topic of this chapter, *reflective teaching*. The latter leads almost unavoidably into the question of *indoctrination,* which has been treated in the preceding chapter.

What is meant by reflective teaching? To be reflective is to be thoughtful; to be considered rather than impulsive in coming to conclusions. Competent, discerning, or wise conclusions or decisions may indeed be reached quickly or impulsively. Snap judgments may be either excellent or poor. In fact, perhaps most of our living is under the guidance of quick or snap judgments, a vast majority of which prove to be highly satisfactory. Whenever a situation and its meaning—that is, realization of what should be done about the situation—occur simultaneously in experience, immediate action can be taken and the course of life progresses smoothly and competently. This we call habit—habit-level behavior.

It is only when what should be done about a situation is not immediately clear that we are confronted by the necessity of being thoughtful or reflective. Only when we meet a problem—a forked-road or no-road situation—do we need to be reflective. We can, of course, even then avoid actually becoming reflective either by walking out on the problem or by consulting the most likely person or informational source available and merely taking his word for it. But, when we are not sure what to plan or do and are disposed to exercise at least a degree of ingenuity or self-reliance in finding out, then are we faced with the necessity of being reflective or of embarking upon the business of problem-solving. Moreover, if our teaching is to be promotive of self-reliance on the part of our students—as we have assumed democratic teaching to be—it must be such as to promote competence in the art of reflection or problem-solving.

In Chapter 5 we have dealt with the generalized nature of the scientific-reflective process. But this is only one kind of reflective procedure. One does not have to be scientific, at least in the narrower sense, in order to be thoughtful. For example, assuming Euclidian postulates, I may consider the question of how many degrees are comprised by the interior angles of a plane triangle and whether the number is always the same. For one who does not already know the answer and the proof, this question certainly calls for thought, as will the further question of what differences, if any, are indicated for a triangle on a curved surface. The thought processes required by questions such as these should probably be designated as logical rather than scientific, even though logical processes are an important ingredient of scientific problem-solving.

Again, one might wish to determine what, if anything, Queen Elizabeth or Francis Bacon had to say about Shakespeare. This could well require a great deal of "research," whether one would call it scientific or not. Whatever may be the personal feelings of scholars from various fields, this kind of investigation is widely accepted as meritorious for conferment of the doctor-of-philosophy degree. It is certainly thoughtful in the sense of requiring one to "use his head."

In reflective teaching, classroom procedure follows the general form of reflective study. The class is first maneuvered into a problem, an I-don't-know situation. Unless a group of students is faced with a question whose answer is to them unknown, no reflection is for them possible. It makes no difference who else knows the answer, the teacher or the whole outside world; if the answer to a given question is unknown to the members of the group involved, for them the question is "food for thought." In the words of one of the investigators on whom we reported in our first chapter,

> In most cases the children come to us with the opinion that the teacher's word is final; she knows the answers. I found them amazed when, after we had discussed a problem, they turned to me for the final answer and I said, "I don't know." A problem had arisen when we were discussing what plants we need and one little girl mentioned flowers. A few scoffed at the idea, but she defended herself by saying, "You have to have prettiness and flowers are pretty." Naturally, the question was whether we had to have pretty things in order to live. After some discussion, they turned to me for the answer but were told, "I don't know." They paused, then asked how they could find out. The problem had been raised and we were ready and wanting to find a solution.[1]

Thus, the first step in reflective teaching is problem-raising. Then follows problem-solving. Continuing the above quotation, "Of course, we had first to decide what we meant by living. They finally reached the conclusion that we might "exist" without pretty things, but we couldn't really "live" without them. They had solved the problem to their own satisfaction, and they had learned much about plants and about living conditions in the process."[2]

A problem-solving process may be short and simple, as it may seem in the case just described. Others may be long and involved. But, whether short, long, or in-between, it is reflective teaching only if the class members themselves are actively working and thinking the matter through to a conclusion. Of course, the teacher will give help; at times only a little, at times perhaps a great deal. Be such help little or much, however, the thought-line is that of the pupils and the conclusion is theirs. In fact, each pupil is encouraged—in extreme cases, perhaps, almost impelled—to come to his own conclusions, even though they may differ from the ones which represent majority agreement. In stating a conclusion, the teacher should persistently use the form of expression, "In light of our study, the conclusion seems to be that . . ." This provides an open way for later modification and for differences in personal conviction among the group members, but, at the same time, provides a tangible and concise outcome—something to show for the effort.

---

[1] Quoted from a typewritten report to the present writer and approximately repeated in, Reader, Edna C. L., "An Experimental Study of Reflective Teaching in a Fifth-Grade Classroom for a Two-Year Period," unpublished Master's thesis, University of Kansas, 1953, pp. 36–37.

[2] *Ibid.*

To ask a class in American history what were the battles which led up to Lee's surrender to Grant at Appomattox Courthouse could well stump the class and produce an I-don't-know situation. It could even send the members to their books to find the answer or answers. But, after The Wilderness, Spotsylvania, Cold Harbor, Petersburg, and Five Forks were named and identified, the matter would be pretty well closed and little else would come of it.

On the other hand, after having followed the adverse fortunes of the Union forces through 1862–1863, particularly of the Army of the Potomac and Lincoln's troubles with his commanding generals in opposing the brilliance of Lee, and coming finally to Grant, the stage might be well enough set for suddenly posing the question, "What might we have done if we had been in Grant's place and had had his job to do?" With proper dramatic build-up and timing, this could well provide the challenge necessary to take hold of the imaginations of the class members, cause them to listen intently to the teacher's description of the geographical difficulties of the terrain, locations of the various forces, the necessity of really bottling-up Lee's army and taking it out of the war for good; then send them to find what Grant did, what Lincoln and Jefferson Davis were doing in light of what each was trying to do, and how events in the whole nation built up to the culmination of Appomattox. Then could come the problem of Reconstruction—of Lincoln's policy of malice toward none and charity for all, of his assassination, of Johnson's continuation of his policy in opposition to Thaddeus Stevens and his fellow Radical Reconstructionists, of Johnson's avoidance of impeachment by a single vote, and consideration of what might have come had Stevens' side really had its way.

This example is chosen because it is not a black-and-white kind but sufficiently "iffy" to challenge the imagination (if artfully handled) and provoke breadth of outlook and research. We wish to show how information is gathered, not to satisfy teacher, but to contribute to solution of a problem. Hence, the example may show something of the interruption of a thought-line which makes for a problem-situation, but also the kind of procedure following the interruption which represents problem-solving. For reflective procedure involves, first, problem-raising, then problem-solving. The answer comes after, and as a result of, the testing of the various possible answers which are proposed for consideration.

Problem-solving may be thought of as encompassing two aspects: formulation of hypotheses and verification of hypotheses.

Thus, in our example we would consider, of course, what Grant did and how that worked out in terms of recorded history. But in addition we would want contrasted with that the kind of campaign which McClellan had been conducting, how he might have conducted this one had he been left in command, and what might have come of that. The class members, too, would be encouraged to do some conjecturing of their own and their various suggestions considered as to how they might have worked in terms of defeating Lee as well as of affecting national policy. Thus, in the end the class not only is acquainted with what did happen, but also has an appreciation of the events as products of human thoughts and plans, and of how they worked out when translated into actions and deeds. History comes to life and study of the past takes on significance for the light it may possibly throw upon the future.

The problem-solving aspect of reflective-*scientific* study takes the general pattern of formulating and testing hypotheses. Guesses are made as to what the solution might be; then deductions are drawn from the various guesses. Available data are studied in light of the various sets of deductions and the guess (or hypothesis) whose deductive pattern best fits the data is taken to be best. Further tailoring may perhaps be in order, to secure a better fit.

Next, deductions are made, looking toward data not already available, and steps are taken *to secure or to produce* those data, the latter representing experimentation. If such data turn out to be as predicted, the final step in scientific-reflective study has been taken and the guess or hypothesis responsible for such outcome is taken as the solution to the problem, or the conclusion. Such a conclusion, of course, although subsequently serving as the basis for designing whatever action or behavior may be within its domain, retains its tentative or hypothetical status; the conclusion to be held as long as it continues to satisfy the foregoing conditions but to be rejected as soon as it fails to do so.

Reflective teaching, then, is the name which we give to classroom procedures which follow the general form just indicated. A question is raised whose answer is unknown, study follows looking toward an answer, and finding the answer marks the culmination or conclusion of the study. The teacher is not giving silver-platter handouts. She or he is acting essentially as chairman of a group of investigators who are thoughtfully carrying out their investigations and, by so doing, are progressively learning how to be self-reliant or independent in arriving at answers to questions which concern them.

Some readers may have become a bit concerned with our previous averment that not all reflective studies are necessarily scientific. They may feel that the two-stage procedure of problem-raising and problem-solving, characteristic of all the foregoing examples, possesses the basic earmarks of scientific procedure and might as well be so termed. Our feeling is that, although for many contexts this may be justified, there are others for which it may not. In the narrower sense of "scientific," conclusions to be found acceptable have to satisfy the criteria of adequacy and harmony in light of obtainable data (see Chapter 5). Yet conclusions which represent highly acceptable culminations for many types or kinds of investigations do not satisfy these criteria at all. Scientific investigations have to do with the ascertainment of truth; they are epistemological. But, as we develop elsewhere (see Chapter 7), there is the whole realm of intrinsic values which is axiological and not to be judged on the basis of epistemological criteria. On the basis of what data am I to judge whether I should, or should not, experience gustatory delight upon eating French-fried snails? Our investigation (Chapter 10) of the definition of democracy which we *ought* to adopt could not be a scientific one, yet, as a result of our adoption of criteria by which to judge a definition, we were able to arrive at a thoughtful conclusion. Thus, we find it advisable to recognize cases of reflective study and teaching which are not, in the narrow sense, scientific.

Nonreflective Teaching

For the purpose of achieving greater clarity and deeper understanding by the use of contrast, we might give a little attention to certain forms of teaching which are *nonreflective*. First, there is that which is basically *rote* or *memoriter*. Although these may not be synonymous terms, they do designate essentially the same kind of teaching. Actually, Webster recognizes *rote* only as a noun, not as an adjective, and calls it "a fixed course or routine, as of study or speech; hence, repetition of forms of speech, often implying want of attention to the meaning; memorizing through repetition or repeating solely from memory."

Teaching, then, which is concerned merely with words themselves, with only meager attention (if any) to meaning, may be termed memoriter, memory-level, or rote (following Webster strictly, we would have to say, *by* rote). This is the familiar, long decried but still widely practiced, traditional form which gives rise to the term "recitation"—to put in motion again, to repeat. It is verbalistic; barren; yet discouragingly common. It is the way out, for those who know nothing better. To disparage it is merely to join the herd; to depart from it is to do the unusual.

There is another form, however, of nonreflective teaching. That we may call *understanding-level*. To understand is to do something other than remember. To understand means to be able to *use* what we know, rather than merely repeat it. Getting the sense or meaning of a matter, one can move forward into what is, at least for him, new and unexplored territory. And this, in consequence, is precisely the kind of test which must be applied in order to determine presence or absence of understanding: can the individual correctly resolve situations which are novel or new to him—such as he has never actually thought out before (see Chapter 14)? Since novelty precludes repetition, what one knows has to be used, not repeated.

The word "meaning" is another which may be used in this context. Teaching which makes life meaningful is teaching which gets at the roots of things, ascertains "what makes them click," and enables its beneficiaries to become persons of discernment. They are the ones whose judgment is sought when serious and important plans are being made for the future. For meaning means pointing—*sign, sign*ify, *sign*ification—anticipation of what is to come. And, since accuracy in anticipation (see Chapter 4) is the relativistic test for truth, an important philosophical link is established.

Furthermore, understandings and meanings are the outcome of *generalization* of experience; of extracting from many particular (or single) experiences those *principles* which are common, general, or universal. Thus, we establish another philosophical link, this time with our theory of transfer of training (see Chapter 3). And, since principle, tentatively adopted and in process of subjection to the test of experience and experiment, is what is commonly called *theory,* understanding-level teaching is promotive of respect and concern for that which is theoretical and is opposed to the widespread, seemingly thoughtless or unconsidered attitude that teaching should deal with the practical, not the theoretical.

In reality, preference for understanding-level over memory-level teaching means belief in the proposition that *the only way to make teaching genuinely practical is to make it basically theoretical.*

For basic theory or principle is the only kind of mental accomplishment which has wide usability. A *fact,* in the sense of a human interpretation of a single event or experience, is limited to that event or experience. To have wide usability, the interpretation must be tested to see whether it holds for a variety of apparently similar experiences; if so, it becomes a generality or a principle, it becomes theoretical. Transfer of training means exactly this, and if training is not transferable it is usable, if at all, only in most limited fashion.

What does this mean for teaching a school subject, such as spelling? Prior to the 1910's, spelling was taught by learning first a rule and then a list, or lists, of words which followed the rule. Ordinarily, the teaching was such as to cause pupils to learn *by rote* both the rule and the words. Hence, it was only occasionally and by chance that a pupil would really comprehend or appreciate the connection between the rule and the way the words were to be spelled, and a lot of rules were learned but never used or applied in the spelling of new or unfamiliar words. Under the circumstances, the rules became useless impedimenta. During the later 1910's when the criterion of usefulness came to be rather stringently applied, rules all but disappeared from spelling textbooks, as also did grouping by rules, phonetic or otherwise. The attitude then became that, since the English language is so largely nonphonetic, rules of spelling not only are unused but are unusable. This practice and attitude persisted until well past the mid-1930's, and it is yet far from eliminated.

With the advent of Henry Clinton Morrison's emphasis on understanding-level teaching,[3] slow recovery began to be observable and teachers here and there perhaps rather hesitantly began to let rules and rules-groupings of similarly spelled words slip back into their classes. But such recovery will be of minimum benefit unless pupils are made acutely aware of how rules can help them to make good guesses at how words *ought* to be spelled, even before they become aware of how they actually are spelled.

If English spelling were essentially phonetic, as are Italian and Japanese Romaji, then spelling instruction could be confined to developing working understandings of the phonetic relationships and the job would soon be over. What hours of school time could be saved for more important matters! Since English falls considerably short of being wholly phonetic, the teaching problem is compli-

[3] Henry Clinton Morrison, *Practice of Teaching in the Secondary School,* Chicago, The University of Chicago Press; 1926.

cated. But it is hardly, as often claimed during the 1920's, nonphonetic in its entirety. In fact, actual counting of phonetic and nonphonetic letters in paragraphs of ordinary publications in English will probably show that between 80 and 90 percent are phonetic, depending on how stringent is the definition of phonetic. Is it not better that children be required to learn only 15 per cent by rote than 100 percent? Moreover, since much of even the nonphonetic parts are amenable to degrees of generalization (or rule), the 15-percent figure is doubtless too large.

The upshot of our discussion is that the advantages of understanding-level teaching over memory-level strongly indicate the desirability of return to spelling rules, to rules-groupings of words for spelling lessons, and, in addition, to testing which places emphasis on words which have not been studied beforehand. Tests over previously studied words may possibly show something more than memory-level achievement, but not dependably so. Teaching of this kind will necessarily foster greatly heightened attention to care and precision in pronunciation, for that is probably a major cause of misspelling even now. And, after all, might we not just as well become a little more tolerant of "creativity" in spelling, as were our Puritan forefathers? We might even come to like "Masachusits" better than the conventional rendition; and who would not know what is meant?

Reflective Teaching Versus Understanding Level

If, with subject matters such as spelling, we not only seek understanding-level achievement but also develop understandings reflectively, we derive, as a "fringe benefit," considerably heightened accomplishment. For understandings, reflectively developed, are much more thorough than are those taught nonreflectively.

It is what goes on in pupils' heads that is important educationally. What is said by teachers may, or may not, register in the minds of children, to say nothing of older aspirants to an education. A principle may be explained ever so well by a teacher and even be followed carefully and seem entirely clear to a student, yet be found later not to be possessed in usable form by the student. This has happened many times to the writer, as student, and he is confident that in this regard he is not exceptional. This is a finding of psychological experimentation.

On the other hand, when a student is first maneuvered into a problem situation in such a way as really to comprehend it as a problem—to have an ongoing thought-line actually brought to a halt and to sense the cause of the stoppage—then he is in a state of intellectual "readiness" to consider proposed ways to surmount the difficulty and to sense the relative potentialities of the various proposals. Can one, from reading a few closing pages, really appreciate, or perhaps even remember, the solution for a detective story unless he first becomes pretty thoroughly conversant with the circumstances which led to the solution?

Moreover, only after one has examined a greater or lesser variety of possible or likely explanations for a given phenomenon does he "deeply" understand any one of them. The very fact of contrast—to see not only what a thing is but also what it is not—is conducive to clarity and depth of comprehension. This is an aspect of the psychological principle of configuration (of figure and ground); nothing appears to be seeable as a thing-in-itself, but only as a figure against a background, and, at least within limits, the sharper the contrast the clearer the figure.

Both of the foregoing conditions are present and functional in the reflective development of understandings. Hence, understandings so achieved are of higher quality than those not so. Returning to spelling, after a group of beginners has pretty well mastered the -*at* words, such as "cat," "bat," and "fat," the teacher might then introduce the -*ate* words and explain how the terminal silent-*e* lengthens the preceding vowel and how spelling and pronunciation are both affected. But how much greater will be the accomplishment, both group and individual, if the pupils themselves are led to work out the rule! After working with a carefully expurgated set of -*at* words and mastering the spelling principle, exceptional -*ate* words are permitted to slip in and teacher sees to it that their exceptionality is sooner or later noted. Well, what shall we do now? How shall we decide? Yes, let's see whether we can find other exceptions. Let's write them on the blackboard and compare them with the -*at* words. Anyone who has studied young children will perhaps readily see that it will not be long before the working principle will be uncovered and become clear. And what a good time the youngsters will have had in working it out! This is what Raymond Holder Wheeler meant when he said, "The life of learning is discovery of plan." By "life" he indeed meant the vivacity or fun of it, as well as the very nature of it. Our first chapter was devoted to a report of a number of studies of the efficacy of reflective teaching, studies which seem to show rather convincingly the truth of what we are saying.

So we close this rather brief discussion of reflective teaching by noting that democracy appears to require us to teach pupils not only what to think but also how to think. And, if our thought-line is logically defensible, this requires reflective teaching, at least as an overall or dominant procedure. It means making life meaningful rather than occupying the time memorizing words. But meanings are to be worked out by pupils and teacher, coöperating as a team. They are not to be teacher handouts, even though meanings or understandings so taught may represent vast improvement over the memory-level recitations of what we hope will soon be yesteryear. And finally, when the reflective method is employed rather than either memory-level or understanding-level handouts, the meanings of life are much more effectually gained and appreciatively grasped, and much more enjoyment is experienced in the process.

THE PSYCHOLOGICAL VERSUS THE LOGICAL

Before closing the chapter, we need to deal specifically with a matter which heretofore has only been indirectly implied. That is the question of the *psychological* versus the *logical* in the handling of subject matter. In looking over what we wrote regarding this matter in a previous book,[4] it seems that we now have little to add, so with the publisher's permission we repeat that discussion here:

Certain writers and speakers on educational affairs, all of whom are desirous of improving the quality of American teaching, have been inclined to lay the blame for many of the shortcomings of traditional teaching on the fact that it was logical and not psychological. At times, the line-up on this controversy has appeared to place professors of education on the side of the psychological and experts in the various subject-matter fields, usually members of liberal-arts-college faculties, on the side of the logical. Actually, the line-up was by no means 100 percent either way.

Should subject matter be logical or psychological? That is to say, should its arrangement or organization for teaching purposes be logical or psychological? Roughly, the argument for logical organization has been that if we are going to teach youngsters to think logically we need to arrange their learning in logical form. On the other hand, the proponents of psychological organization have argued that if the material for study is not made interesting to youngsters they will not think, or learn to think, at all.

[4] Ernest E. Bayles, *The Theory and Practice of Teaching*, New York: Harper & Brothers, 1950, pp. 127–131.

Without going further into the arguments, many of which tended to generate more heat than light, we might suggest that, since logicality and psychologicality both seem to be highly desirable qualities, we may do well to assume that subject matter should be both logical and psychological. But how can it be both, when the two qualities have appeared to be so oppositional in nature? Perhaps it will be well first to define terms.

There appear to be as many different forms of logical organization as there are purposes for making organizations. A grocer arranges, or organizes, the goods on his shelves in such a way as to make them attractive and readily available for serving customers. An engineer organizes his knowledge of the characteristics of materials in such a way as to make them easily available for aid in constructing buildings, bridges, or whatever it may be. But the kind of logical organization which is usually referred to by those who would employ it for teaching purposes is that of an expert in the subject-matter field.

According to Dewey, logical organization of an expert in science is "of a nature to exhibit to one who understands it the premises from which it follows and the conclusions to which it points."[5] Elsewhere he says that "scientific subject matter is organized with specific reference to the successful conduct of the enterprise of discovery, to knowing as a specialized undertaking." And again, "The ideal of scientific organization is that every conception and statement shall be of such a kind as to follow from others and to lead to others."[6]

Logical organization from the point of view of a scientific expert in any subject-matter field—chemistry, geometry, music, literature, or whatever it may be—is the kind of organization that is needed for scientific purposes, for research. Known facts are assembled and organized into principles and principles in turn are used to predict new facts.

Because the logical organization of a scientific expert represents a wide field of factual information arranged in such a way as to serve, for those who understand it, as a perfected tool for research, such a form of organization is hardly suitable for beginners. Says Dewey, "There is a strong temptation to assume that presenting subject matter in its perfected form provides a royal road to learning. . . . From the standpoint of the learner scientific form is an ideal to be achieved, not a starting point from which to set out."[7]

A beginner cannot possibly appreciate, or understand, such presentation because he does not have sufficient experience in the field to make understanding possible. An understanding might be said to be an interpretation of a group of known facts such as will enable an individual to deal successfully with those facts and with others like them. Understanding is therefore im-

[5] John Dewey, *Democracy and Education,* New York: The Macmillan Company, 1916, p. 256.
[6] *Ibid.,* p. 224.
[7] *Ibid.,* p. 257.

possible until after a considerable number of the facts in a field have been experienced and are known. One cannot organize something one does not have.

It would seem, therefore, that the starting point in a process of learning is with the knowledge and experiences which the learner actually possesses. Moreover, this knowledge and these experiences must be organized in such a way as to achieve some purpose which the learner understands and wishes to achieve. "The chronological method," says Dewey, "which begins with the experience of the learner and develops from that the proper modes of scientific treatment is called the 'psychological' method in distinction from the logical method of the expert or specialist."[8] He then goes on to say, "Moreover by following, in connection with problems selected from the material of ordinary acquaintance, the methods by which scientific men have reached their perfected knowledge, he gains independent power to deal with material within his range and avoids the mental confusion and intellectual distaste attendant upon studying matter whose meaning is only symbolic."[9]

Our definition of psychological organization is that it is the type which *follows the logic of a growing mind*. Psychological organization is achieved when the organizer steps down from the rostrum of the expert and looks at the world through the eyes of a learner. An ongoing, or easily evoked, interest is chosen as a starting point. It may be suggested by a pupil or by the teacher. It makes little difference who actually offers the suggestion originally, as long as it genuinely represents an ongoing or easily evoked interest.

With discussion started, it is adroitly guided so as sooner or later to culminate in a problem. But it must be a pupil's problem and one which really challenges him, not a problem which concerns only a teacher or an expert. The study and solution of this problem are followed into the consequences or implications of the solution, until soon another problem is opened and the process repeats. So it goes, one problem leading into another as the learner's outlook broadens and deepens. This type of organization we would call *psychological*.

Nothing is taken up which does not have the active interest of the class, but it is expected that a teacher's influence will have much to do, though by no means all, with molding pupil interests. What we want is in reality pupil-teacher planning—neither pupil planning nor teacher planning alone, the one to the exclusion of the other. We would expect the original plans of the teacher to be distinctly modified by pupil contributions as each study progresses.

The process of solving a problem requires that data be gathered and organized. As previously noted, the accepted solution is the one which enables the data to be arranged in a thoroughly harmonious, or logical, pattern. Thus,

[8] *Ibid.*, pp. 257–258.
[9] *Ibid.*, p. 258.

the solution of a given problem means that an organization of the materials of study has been reached which is logical in as far as the participators in the study have been able to make it. Therefore, through a *psychological* approach a *logical* organization is reached. In this way organization of the subject matter of teaching becomes simultaneously logical and psychological.

"Rome was not built in a day," and we do not try to bring youngsters to the logical organization of experts in a single bound. As a learner progresses, step by step, his outlook broadens and deepens with the addition of new insights and the modification of old ones. But the teacher must see that, with the additions and modifications of insight, each learner also continually considers how well the new and the old agree. Failure to agree may require modification of the old or of the new, or perhaps of both. But the question of consistency of total outlook should be an important consideration at every step of the way. Consistency is the essence of logical organization.

In this way the further a learner progresses along the highway of learning, the further does he progress toward the logical organization of experts. This is Dewey's meaning when he says, as already quoted, that "scientific form is an ideal to be achieved, not a starting point from which to set out."

Furthermore, we may mention in passing that our own experience has shown that, in organizing teaching units and courses of study, we find some of the best suggestions for a "psychological approach to logical organization" in the historical development of the subject in question. This should not be surprising because the growth of any field of intellectual endeavor has been the product of mankind collectively laboring with pressing, practical problems of one kind or another. The characteristic pattern of development has seemed to follow, first, practical problems of everyday living until a broad, unifying principle has been formulated. Then, interest has turned to theoretical outworkings of the principle until, after a while, new practical applications have become evident. Thus, we have gone from the practical to the theoretical and back again, always reaching broader and higher levels of insight. This too is psychological approach to logical organization, and an individual "mind in the making" can often with profit follow the collective "mind in the making," because both naturally and more or less inevitably follow the same generalized pattern.

It will probably become evident to the reader as he peruses the next chapter that what has just been said about the logicalizing of subject matter in learner's minds as a result, we hope, of reflective study fits exactly into the overall educational purpose of developing enhanced and more harmonious outlooks on the life of which students are a part. Harmonization might almost be thought as synonymous with logicalization. Once, when preparing a chapter of a previous book, I asked a colleague—an expert in the field—to read it for scientific accuracy. One of the first remarks he made in a follow-up conference was, "That is one of the most logically developed treatments of the field I have ever seen." I smiled and replied, "Well, that's interesting, because it was planned to be psychological—to follow the logic of a growing mind." Thus, it seems that being logical is to handle harmoniously what is to be handled. An *approach* to a solution, to be logical, has to be in keeping with the processes of a mind at that stage of development; that is the psychological. The culmination of the study of the problem calls also for a logic, but then it is the logic of solution and is different from the logic of approach. To foist either logic upon the other aspect of the study process is to violate the principle of logicality itself.

SELECTED REFERENCES

(See also references listed at close of Chapter 5.)

Bayles, Ernest E., *The Theory and Practice of Teaching*, New York: Harper & Brothers, 1950, chap. 7.

　　Also, in Chapters 10, 11, 12, 13, and 14 will be found numerous examples of how classroom units might be taught reflectively, representative of a wide variety of subject matters from kindergarten through college.

Bode, Boyd H., *Fundamentals of Education*, New York: The Macmillan Company, 1921, chaps. 6, 7.

Bode, Boyd H., *Modern Educational Theories*, New York: The Macmillan Company, 1927, chap. 9.

Dewey, John, *Democracy and Education*, New York: The Macmillan Company, 1916, chaps. 11, 12, 13, 17.

Hunt, Maurice P., and Metcalf, Lawrence E., *Teaching High School Social Studies*, New York: Harper & Brothers, 1955, chaps. 3–8.

Morrison, Henry C., *Practice of Teaching in the Secondary School* (rev. ed.), Chicago: The University of Chicago Press, 1931, chaps. 2, 3, 4, 6, 11, 12, 13.

CHAPTER 13

American Educational Purpose and Program

OF unquestioned first-line significance, yet something from which most investigators seemingly try to maintain safe distance, is the matter of what ought to be the fundamental purpose or purposes of American education. Determining what these *are* is a sizable task, but it appears to be much less formidable or forbidding than that of considering what they *ought* to be. The latter, however, is the matter of crucial importance since, until it is relatively settled, we are in no position to tell whether those which now obtain should continue or should be changed. It is to the question of what American education should be designed to accomplish that we wish to address this chapter.

Investigational methods for determining what *is* are fairly well established. Not so for determining what ought to be. Yet we are continually faced with the stark necessity of deciding what ought to be, and we seem pretty well convinced that by "using our heads" we can reach better decisions than we can in any other way. Consideration of ends, goals, or purposes which merit adoption involves values and value-theory. And values seem highly personal, maybe dreadfully so; humanly subjective. You may be fully convinced that what I want or like is not what I ought to, but I doubt that you will go so far as to say you *know* it to be so. This about adds up to saying that, on values, our hearts determine rather than our heads.

But in Chapter 7 we noted that in arriving at values—in *evaluation*—heads may be very helpful, especially so since the whole realm of instrumental values is subject to scientific verification and even intrinsic values have a way of continually shifting from intrinsic to extrinsic (or instrumental) and back again. Furthermore, even among intrinsics there seems to be for everyone a flexible though fairly stable "order of precedence"; one which evinces itself whenever conflicts arise, as they seem to be continually doing, among intrinsics. And, although when such conflicts arise it seems that hearts are determinative rather than heads, nevertheless determination of whether conflicts actually do exist is a scientifically verifiable matter, so heads can be helpful even then. Since all this has been previously discussed at length, we merely review the points here and shall neither illustrate nor elaborate.

With the foregoing in mind, we return to the question for this chapter, "What ought to be the fundamental purpose or purposes of American education?" Obviously, for the educational enterprise itself, our question is one of an intrinsic or end-value. However, education is not the sole-and-only concern of this nation; in fact, as an aspect of national policy it is perhaps a means or instrument for achieving something still more inclusive; some further end. This further something to which we as a nation seemingly are committed is *democracy*. For educational purposes it does not seem immediately pertinent that we examine why we are democratically committed. Sooner or later, that question doubtless needs to be met consciously and squarely, but for this chapter (and maybe even for this book) that seems unnecessary.

A more immediate question is what we shall take democracy to mean, and that is dealt with in Chapter 10. There we show why we assume democracy to be governmental organization which represents equality of opportunity to participate in the making of decisions and equality of obligation to abide by them. Since this places responsibility for the wisdom or nonwisdom of governmental enactments squarely upon the shoulders of the governed, it behooves a democratic citizenry first, to exercise as much wisdom as it can, and, second, to enhance the wisdom of each and every member as much as possible.

To achieve the first behoof, education for democracy should continually strive to sensitize the citizenry, present and prospective, to the fact of personal responsibility: decisions will be wise or foolish as they make them, each and every one. This indeed is a very sobering principle, once it is really comprehended. And perhaps a serious failure of American education today is that the population in general and teachers in particular are not sufficiently clear and emphatic on this point. The common attitude, that politics is a dirty, nasty racket with which respectable and intelligent persons should not soil themselves, would certainly seem to be one which a democratic people would, for its own good, not dare to tolerate. Shall this be other than a matter of primary concern in a democratic educational program? This does not mean indoctrination; it does mean that democratic teaching has an *obligation* to see that all for whom it is responsible have repeated opportunities to study with care how decisions are affected by the application or lack of application of this principle.

To achieve the second behoof, to develop as discerning a citizenry as possible, education for democracy seems obligated to promote reflective teaching (see Chapters 1 and 12); teaching which, while promoting arrival at present decisions or conclusions, simultaneously reveals (through practice) how to arrive at future ones; teaching which helps students learn *how* to think *as well as what* to think. Although in this regard American education is, on the whole, at least abreast (perhaps a little ahead) of the world at large, it is certainly not accomplishing what it should. Classes are overwhelmingly conducted as promulgators of information to be stored for possible future use, mainly in passing final examinations. (This situation is particularly evident from upper elementary school through college; it is seemingly aggravated as the students mount the ladder.) It is true that our overarching culture does seem to promote a degree of intellectual independence among the citizenry and that our schools contribute somewhat. But a great deal more seemingly could be done and surely should be done. Is it not high time to dispense with factual examinations, in which students are called upon merely to *repeat* what they know, and go all-out for examinations which test understanding and promote reflection, in which students are called upon to *use* what they know? This would mean large use of open-book examinations, in which students would be permitted to bring class notes and books of reference to the examinations and use them as desired.

Thus, it appears that, if we adopt the premise that American education should carry out the democratic commitment and that democracy should be defined as above, we are logically committed to foster *intellectual independence* among our people and, therefore, to promote reflective teaching. Independent learning capacity, then, *ought* to be a fundamental and functional part or aspect of our overall educational purpose. Is anything else required?

Although intellectual independence or independent learning capacity can be an educational objective, hence representing subject matter or curriculum content, its achievement seems to be essentially a matter of method. What is affected is mainly *how* we teach, regardless of *what* we teach. In other words, every teaching unit should derive its basic methodological pattern from the reflective process. This is not to say that a teacher should never "tell" a student anything. Far from it. Without information, high-quality thought is impossible, and surely information should be obtained wherever and however feasible. If needed and not conveniently available otherwise, why should a teacher not tell it? Much information is unobtainable by "thinking," and certainly obtaining information should not *per se* be thought of as thinking. This is to say, however, that a major *source* of information and experience which students gain regarding the *process* of reflective thought should be their own procedures as, with the help of an able teacher, they make progress in the attainment of wisdom and discernment.

But what are the basic "whats" of democratic teaching? What *ought* to constitute curriculum content? Or, to look at it another way, what should be our *criteria for choice of subject matter?* Up to this point, we have been making deductions which grow logically out of our original premises—of democracy as accepted governmental pattern and of the definition which we have found it necessary to employ. Now, however, we seem to have reached a stopping point and must regroup our forces. As we have noted in Chapter 11, the only requirement which *democracy* makes as to the *outcomes* of the thinking which is done in classrooms is that they shall satisfy whatever criteria—bases for judgment—have been adopted for the purpose. What those criteria shall be is a matter subject to time, place, and circumstance; each new occasion calling for redetermination. Thus, we have come to what may be called a "logical breakpoint," wherein deductions from a given proposition terminate and those from a new one begin.

What kind of thought patterns should we seek to promote in the minds of those who are preparing for full-fledged democratic citizenship? This is a tricky problem since, though "guidance" is required, indoctrination must be avoided. The configuration of thought patterns possessed by a given individual at a given time may be called his "outlook on life," something which is very tangible and very real even though, because it is often very complicated, it is often very elusive. What kind of *outlooks on life* should democratic education seek to develop?

Perhaps the first stipulation is that they should be outlooks "on the life *of which the students are a part.*" This was for long a matter of insistence by Dewey. The future he was far from ignoring; likewise, the past. In fact, the future was for him a major concern; the past must be examined for the light it may possibly shed upon what steps should presently be taken in order to promote a desirable or desired future. Thus, it is assumed that by dealing reflectively with the present—problems and issues of the here and now—we shall likely be doing the best we can, first, to lay the groundwork for a desirable future and, second, to develop the competence necessary to deal with future problems and issues as and when they arise.

But what kind of outlooks shall be considered *good* and what not good? This, obviously, is a value-problem, and, for the present purpose, one which is largely intrinsic, hence, distinctly personal or arbitrary—a matter on which a people has to make up its own mind. To this question we want an answer which is as thoroughly American as possible. And we reach our answer in the following way.

In seeking solutions to our hard, practical problems of the here-and-now, the American people seems pretty well convinced of, and highly dependent upon, the scientific method; broadly viewed, of course, but that in essence or spirit. Even though many of us may be theoretically insistent upon the efficacy of dependence upon "higher authority" for solution of the bigger, more fundamental problems of life, still, such persons are seemingly never happy with other than scientific, practical solutions to the smaller ones. And, as with Eddie Cantor's observation on the outcome of an early agreement with his wife that he would settle the bigger problems and she the smaller ones, actual occasions for settlement of bigger problems never seem to arise. Actual settlements always seem to involve the smaller problems; never the larger ones. Who among us are willing to settle on a charge for gas, water, or electricity on any basis other than the reading of a tested meter?

A scientific solution to a problem should perhaps be taken to be a thought pattern which, first, takes into account all obtainable information (data) pertinent to the problem and, second, causes those data to become apparently harmonious or compatible with one another. After all data, which pertain and can possibly be obtained, have been obtained, then only the thought pattern which causes *all* such data, without exception, to fit together in apparent harmony is accepted as the "good" solution—the one which settles the matter "beyond *reasonable* doubt." Thus, a thought pattern (or outlook) which is scientifically satisfactory is one which satisfies the criterion of *"adequacy and harmony of outlook or conclusion in light of obtainable data."* Careful analysis of any competently performed and reported investigation of a crime, whether from book, magazine, radio, or television, will reveal this principle at work.

Although the above method is one which ordinarily is taken as applicable to problems involving truth, it also seems to suggest a criterion which can be useful in settling problems of value. We have been referring to it as a "good" way to achieve a "good" solution; and "good" is a value-adjective. Our proposal—a personal decision, of course, as it has to be—is that a truly American criterion for judging a "good" outlook on life is *one which is adequate and harmonious in light of obtainable data.* While granting that this is an arbitrary or personal judgment as to what is truly American, we insist that it is a judgment which fulfils its own requirements —it lives up to, or is in keeping with, itself. It covers, harmoniously, a very wide expanse of American ideals and aims. Especially is it thoroughly in keeping with democratic educational requirements, for it provides teachers with a workable instrument for *guiding* pupil thinking yet at the same time avoids indoctrination. This is a principle which does not *have* to be adopted, but we have yet to discover one which better satisfies requirements.

To summarize the conclusion which our thinking has so far reached, we can say that American education *ought* seemingly to *promote development of more adequate and more harmonious student outlooks on the life of which they are a part, and heightened capacity to reconstruct outlooks independently.* This conclusion seems to be the one to which we are logically committed if we assume, first, the democratic commitment and take that to mean equality of opportunity to participate in the making of decisions and equality of obligation to abide by them and, second, the scientific commitment as an axiological or value-principle and take such commitment to mean adequacy and harmony of outlook in light of obtainable data. It is *democracy* which requires *independent* capacity to construct and reconstruct outlooks, and *scientific* commitment which requires *adequacy and harmony* of outlook. But, in keeping with both democracy and the method of science, neither requirement is a static one. As the world grows and as people grow, previously adequate outlooks become inadequate, and harmony achieved on old bases sometimes becomes disharmonious when the new also has to be encompassed. Hence, the capacity for progressive and continuous "reconstruction of experience" (Dewey's own expression) is the keystone of the arch of habits whose formation is a requirement of democratic education.

Although we have reached a conclusion which represents an answer to the question which opens this chapter, we are by no means through. In fact, it might be said that we are just now ready to begin; that is, to begin operations, or to work at the operational level. However, from this point for a long way ahead, each next step is logically deducible. Few, if any, logical break-points will be met or new premises required.

Our next step is to state the educational *program* which seemingly grows out of our statement of *purpose*. It is to *promote reflective studies of problems which represent not only inadequacies but also disharmonies in student outlooks on the life of which they are a part.* For to promote *adequacy* of outlook, we must begin with *inadequacies;* to promote *harmony* of outlook, we must begin with *disharmonies;* and to promote *reflective capacity,* we must provide students with repeated opportunities to *study problems reflectively.*

Teaching method can be disposed of quickly. It must be basically reflective, whatever the curricular field. This means *reflective teaching;* hence the reader is reminded both of Chapter 12 and also of Chapter 1, "Experiments with Reflective Teaching." To be *scientifically* reflective will be far from always required, as this chapter has shown regarding our derivation of American educational purpose, and as does Chapter 10 on derivation of a definition of democracy. We do not claim to have reached a scientific answer in either case; nor in Chapter 11 wherein we deal with the implications of democracy for keeping school. But do we not have justification for claiming those treatments to be reflective or thoughtful? We have done what was proposed near the close of Chapter 11 as a democratic educational requirement: we have adopted criteria and have tried to be bound by them. We do not claim to have reached the "only" answer, in the sense of a philosophical absolute. But we do insist that we have reached a rather binding one, bound first by the deductive logic we have tried to follow, second by the premises from which the deductions are made. Seemingly, to "get out of the bind," we must either find a flaw in the logic or challenge the premises.

What, now, of curriculum? To what criteria for choice of subject matter does our educational purpose commit us? Obviously, we are to study "problems which represent not only inadequacies but also disharmonies in student outlooks on the life of which they are a part." Thus, we have a substitute for Dewey's principle—long a subject of criticism because of its seeming vagueness—of "growth which leads to more growth." (On this it might be noted that Bode was one of the leading critics.) That our criterion will indeed promote "growth which leads to more growth," I believe can be demonstrated. But it is hoped that our substitute is more explicit and may be more understandable than Dewey's.

In the first place, the life of which students are a part is to be taken as an inclusive expression, at least as broad as the terms "heritage" or "culture." It is meant to include everything—objects, persons, and events—which pushes or pulls them about; everything which affects them either immediately or remotely. Hence, we call it the students' *world of effect*. Moreover, it includes past as well as present, and, in the sense in which the future exerts a pull upon the present, future is also involved. Thus, a student's world of effect represents a space-time continuum which is far-flung and inclusive.

On the other hand, student outlooks represent another world—a *world of insight*. A student's outlook, representing a compendium or configuration of the insights which he possesses, represents what he knows of his world of effect. Hence, his "world of insight" is an expression which signifies what he knows of his world of effect. This may be needless multiplication of terms, but my experience is that it tends to be helpful. Simply stated, one's world of insight is merely what one knows of one's world of effect, that is, of what pushes and pulls one about. And, since a person ordinarily is concerned to know progressively more and more of what is pushing and pulling him about, the growth principle in this regard is to expand (enhance) one's world of insight toward further encompassment of his world of effect. Of course, if and when one's world of effect also keeps expanding, this is a continuing pursuit, and growth is leading ever to more growth.

But our criterion is not confined to expansion alone, and the second aspect—harmonization—is fully as important as the first. The only difference is that, although the first has been a functioning criterion in education of the young perhaps as long as such education has been practiced, the second has for the most part been functionally nonexistent. When something has appeared to be unsatisfactory about existing curricula, the almost universally adopted remedy has been to add a new course, or new items within courses. Seldom has the question been asked, "Does what we have hang together?"

It is at this juncture that Boyd Henry Bode brought pressure to bear. It might well be said that he spent a professional lifetime inveighing against our seeming unawareness that numerous significant aspects of our heritage or culture simply do not hang together. Following is a sampling of his thought:

If we note . . . how the schools adapted themselves to this rising tide of demands, we are in a position to see both how our educational system has become needlessly cumbersome and how it has become involved in a sorry confusion of purposes or aims.

Whenever something is found to be lacking, the favorite remedy is to start an agitation for an extension of the curriculum. . . .

The result of this general tendency has naturally been to produce a curriculum containing a bewildering variety of more or less unrelated "subjects.". . .

Our educational practice of compartmentalization not only keeps basic problems out of sight, but adds to the difficulty of locating them. . . .

The consequence of such education is that we acquire an insensitiveness to contradictions in beliefs and practices which would otherwise be quite unintelligible. . . .

The belief in anything is apparently not regarded as a bar to the belief in its opposite. . . .

Logically it is impossible to believe that a thing is round and also that it is square, but psychologically there does not seem to be any particular difficulty about it. All that is needed is to keep these beliefs in separate compartments and to use them in turn as may be convenient. . . .

Our notion of democracy is in part a hang-over from the past and in part a product of modern conditions, which means that we have no respectable philosophy of democracy at all. . . .

In brief, the basic trouble with the modern college is that, like Stephen Leacock's horseman, it rides off in all directions at once.[1]

[1] Boyd Henry Bode, *The Educational Frontier*, New York: The Century Co., 1933, pp. 3, 4, 6, 7, 8, 10, 15–16.

He finally reaches the conclusion in the chapter that "the primary concern of a democratic educational procedure is to stimulate a reconstruction of our beliefs and habits in the light of their mutual relationships."[2] Thus, by having a study begin with recognition of an incompatibility or disharmony in outlook, there then is a possibility that out of the study may come harmonization. Certainly, that is the point of the strategy.

Summing up, each study unit in the curriculum is required to focus upon a problem which represents either an inadequacy in outlook, or a disharmony, or, preferably, both. In other words, students must study *issues;* matters which, at least as far as they are concerned, are unsettled. Use the adjective "controversial" if you must, but it is redundant—to say the least, unnecessary—for, if a matter is not controversial, it is not an issue.

A study, chosen because it represents a problem (an I-don't-know situation) which involves both an inadequacy and a disharmony in outlook and beginning (through problem-raising tactics) with such, moves forward in the direction of adding or remodeling insights which serve to fill in gaps, to clarify confusions, and to harmonize disharmonies. Thus progress is made toward more adequate and more harmonious student outlooks on the life of which they are a part.

And is this not real progression in the direction of improving the mental health, not only of the students themselves but progressively of the nation as well? After all, it is not long before youths reach adulthood and become active participants in the body politic. For are not the findings of those who study mental pathology that an extremely fertile source of mental ill health is the unrealized self-contradictions which, by existing in a human personality, cause that person to be his own worst enemy? Resistance by an outside source tends sooner or later to become identified as such and has possibilities of being avoided if not overcome. But resistance within one's self cannot be avoided, because one cannot get away from one's self, and, worse yet, it is likely to go unseen and unknown. Charging the normal educational process with responsibility for systematically seeking out potential complexes (disharmonies in outlook or *intrapersonal conflicts*), bringing them into the open, and possibly ironing them out before they become pathological would surely seem

[2] *Ibid.,* p. 29.

to carry out the time-honored adage of an ounce of prevention worth a pound of cure.

As one's world of effect continues to expand, requiring expanding outlooks via added insights merely to keep pace, so does this expanding world of effect also require continual reëxamination of total outlook in the interest of continuing the degree of harmony already attained, to say nothing of increasing it. Thus, for both aspects of our criterion, growth leads to more growth, and Dewey's insistence is having its way.

That new knowledge may entirely upset an old integration is strikingly illustrated by the discovery of radioactivity during the 1890's by the Curies. One discovery led to another in rapid succession until, in what seems an incredibly short time, the two great principles of Isaac Newton, the laws of Conservation of Mass and Conservation of Energy, had to be rejected and replaced by the unified law of the Conservation of Mass-Energy.[3] Moreover, such an overturn in scientific thinking soon began to have its effect on philosophical thought, and the relativistic philosophical and psychological thinking of Dewey gained tremendous support by the scientific overturn. And it may not be too unkind to pause here for a moment and offer the suggestion to those who still cling to absolutistic philosophies that we would be more than glad to welcome them into the twentieth century. After all, straight thinking on a pre-twentieth-century basis may possibly require alteration to achieve equal straightness when the expanded knowledge-base of the twentieth century has to be considered.

Perhaps you are now wondering how to get started on setting up units for a curriculum such as here envisioned. Where do we begin? This is one advantage of the proposal; you can begin where you are and with what you are now dealing. You do not have to have a core program or anything special. You have pupils and they have outlooks on the world of which they are a part. For a given occasion, *the most important unit-topic is the intrapersonal problem-conflict (inadequacy-disharmony) which promises most in immediate expansion and harmonization of your own pupils' outlooks.* Others will open up as you move along; begin where you and your

---

[3] We hasten to add, however, that Newton's two laws appear still to hold regarding the territory for which they were originally designed—that which lies between the realms of the sub-atomic and of the astronomical.

pupils are. Let us assume both reflective method and subject matter which deals with intrapersonal problem-conflicts.

A kindergarten teacher, struggling with a roomful of little self-centered individualists, opines aloud on how the room can possibly be made to look pretty for a visit by Idamae's and Frankie's mothers while she attends to a lot of other things that must be done. Of course, the children want the room to look pretty. What needs to be done? Who can do what? For many, coming newly from homes where they have had no personal responsibilities, this can be a really impressive study in coöperation. And they will love it.

A lower-grade teacher, ready to take up multiplication, asks how many pencils the children in the first six chairs to the left have. Each indicates how many he has, and the numbers are added. Several other group totals are determined, and maybe the sum total of all. Then she might ask how many shoes or ears each group has, or, supposing each has three pencils, how many would each group have. With the prior addition context and with no previous experience in multiplication, the class is likely to determine all answers by addition. Possibly some adroitness will have to be exercized to maintain the addition context for a bit, but possibly someone will pretty soon note that they are doing an easy job a hard way. If so, the teacher can feign surprise and ask how so. If not, the teacher may have to broach it. Then it will probably rather quickly dawn on the class that multiplication is a short cut to addition, in the special case when all the numbers are the same. All they need to know is the various combinations, and, with experience, these can soon be learned. That multiplication be from the first understood in this way invests it with meaning which can easily divest it of the fear and drudgery which so often make it a bugbear for youngsters.

A high school social-studies class is noting the events in the Little Rock, Arkansas, school segregation issue. Since education is an unstated power which constitutionally resides with the separate states, it seems clear that federal intervention is unjustified. Yet it was Supreme Court action which precipitated the issue, and President Eisenhower seemed to have convincing precedents for his action. Moreover, if a people as a whole wants something, is it democratic justice to permit a group within it to block satisfaction of that want? Does this not set up the problem in a way that would be comprehended by an eleventh- or twelfth-grade class? And does it not give promise for a thoughtful study which would not need to be indoctrinative, which might indeed not settle the matter in the minds of all class members, but which would promote progress toward an enhanced and much more harmonious outlook on the whole problem of states rights and federal control, on the part of students as well as teacher, than existed before?

These examples have been chosen to represent the extremes of a continuum of issues which would be normal topics for study in a curriculum built upon the pattern we have been discussing. The kindergarten and lower-grade problems represent issues certainly not publicly controversial and certainly intellectually simple. The segregation case is certainly the opposite. In between, the entire gamut will be run. But the basic educational strategy can be the same for all, and this is what our proposal implies. It applies equally for creative art expression and for a class in woodwork or sewing. Creativity is creativity in whatever form it may appear, and it can only be dependably expected when a concerned mind is hard at work upon a perplexing and challenging issue.

Before we stop thinking about this matter, even temporarily, let me hasten to point out another matter which, from discouragingly persistent experience, I know is likely to develop into a source of confused thinking. Please recall that reflective study is possible whether scientific criteria are at work or not. Other criteria may be employed just as well in satisfying the democratic requirement of equality of opportunity to participate in decision-making (see Chapter 11), as well as in promoting independent learning ability or ability to reconstruct outlooks independently. It seems most important that one guard against the high likelihood of concluding that, if one teaches reflectively, one will *ipso facto* promote adequacy and harmony of outlook, and vice versa. *This is a pitfall which should be avoided.*

It is undeniably possible to promote more adequate and more harmonious outlooks without teaching reflectively at all. One can simply set up the conflict or incompatibility and proceed to show how it is to be resolved. This procedure may not achieve as thorough a job as will the reflective process; that I would not only grant, but would insist upon. But it is possible. On the other hand, because adequacy and harmony of outlook are not the only criteria which will make reflective teaching possible, reflection and reflective abilities may be promoted without doing much toward harmonization of outlooks. My heart can be quite all right and my liver go bad; or my liver can be quite all right and my heart go bad. And it certainly behooves me to have a doctor who can diagnose accurately whether it is either one, and, if so, which one it is. The same holds for the educational distinction which I am pointing out. Improved outlook is one thing; improved capacity to reconstruct outlooks independently is quite another. In your thinking, *do not make them one and the same!*

SELECTED REFERENCES

Bayles, Ernest E., *The Theory and Practice of Teaching*, New York: Harper & Brothers, 1950, chaps. 8, 9.

Bode, Boyd H., *Modern Educational Theories*, New York: The Macmillan Company, 1927, Part IV.

Dewey, John, *Democracy and Education*, New York: The Macmillan Company, 1916.

Hunt, Maurice P., and Metcalf, Lawrence E., *Teaching High School Social Studies*, New York: Harper & Brothers, 1955, Part II.

Kilpatrick, W. H., *et al.*, *The Educational Frontier*, New York: The Century Co., 1933, chap. 1.

CHAPTER 14

Appraisal of Pupil Progress

IT is often averred by those in educational measurement that a philosopher is getting pretty far afield when he presumes to set foot in this area. And, to a great extent, educational philosophers seem to honor such limitation, for they do not often devote discussions to matters pertaining strictly thereto.

If, however, it is admitted that before one can tell much about *how* to measure he must first determine *what* to measure, then it seems clear that determination of educational objectives must precede determination of appraisal techniques, and the matter of objectives is certainly within the domain of educational philosophy. Furthermore, the question of suitability of means to ends seems also to be clearly a matter of philosophical concern. Hence, a number of very important aspects in appraisal of pupil progress evidently lie within the domain of educational philosophy. It is to matters of this kind that we shall devote this chapter.[1]

We assume that the purpose of pupil appraisal is instructional rather than merely reportorial; that any classroom examination system should be designed primarily to help youngsters become educated and only secondarily to derive "grades" to be placed on a "report card." We are in no sense decrying the business of making reports to parents, or to other legitimately interested parties, on the

---

[1] This is by no means our first published treatment of problems in educational measurement. Two articles appeared in the *Journal of Educational Research* in 1929 and 1931—"Testing for Comprehension" and "A Study of Comparative Validity as Shown by a Group of Objective Tests"; "The Problem of Testing" in *Science Education* in 1936; "The Philosophical Approach to Educational Measurement" in the *Journal of Educational Administration and Supervision* in 1940; "Suggestions Regarding a Testing Program" in *The Elementary Principal* in 1946; and the concluding chapter in my book, *The Theory and Practice of Teaching,* published by Harper & Brothers in 1950. Occasional paragraphs in the present chapter are, with publisher's permission, taken from the latter.

progress which pupils are making. Indeed, we would be insistent that parents or guardians should be kept informed, with candor and accuracy, as to what Frankie or Susie is doing in school. For a home does have an interest in its own children, and surely in a great majority of cases it is a very wholesome and helpful interest; moreover, one which can be made more so with the aid of accurate and well-handled information. But the major and central function of such information, however used, would surely seem to be the light it will shed on how Frankie and Susie can be helped to do better than he or she has been doing.

There are those who claim to believe, and who advise, that classroom testing be discontinued entirely. Their thought seems to be that testing programs have seldom worked satisfactorily, so perhaps we should get rid of them entirely. Sober professional thought, however, does not seem to have fallen into this line and does not seem likely to do so. For it is a psychologically agreed-upon principle that, except by remote chance, without knowledge of progress toward goal there can be no progress. Thus, a well-designed testing or appraisal program is a necessary part—and perhaps a crucial one —of any instructional program which is likely to give promise of success.

Our experience has been that the main cause for dissatisfaction with testing programs—either on the part of students or of school personnel—has been lack of *validity*. When a measuring instrument fails to measure with accuracy that which it is supposed to measure, what can be expected from its use other than dissatisfaction? When students have been told that they are expected to accomplish one thing and then discover that they are being tested and "graded" on something else entirely, they come out with a feeling—and a legitimate one—that they have been gypped. How can they be other than resentful? To be specific, teachers often are insistent that they expect their students to learn to think, not merely to remember facts. Yet the examinations which they give and on which they base "grades" are made up of items almost exclusively memoriter. How can such practice be anything but unsatisfactory?

It would seem, therefore, that a testing program is highly desirable if not necessary, that it should be primarily instructional, that it should be valid, and that it should be thoroughly compatible with the purposes of instruction. Since one aspect of our recorded educational purpose is to develop an enhanced and more harmonious outlook on the life of which students are a part, we may begin with this.

Enhancement of outlook means increase in scope, breadth and depth, or coverage. How much does one know? If this were all we were interested in, much of current classroom-testing practice would probably be considered more or less satisfactory. As between objective and essay-type tests, the former would perhaps be thought preferable because of the possibility of greater coverage in given time. Between 1920 and 1950, the practice of using objective tests—that is, tests which were *called* objective—grew by leaps and bounds. More recently, however, somewhat of a reversal may be detectable. For, when students are seldom asked to express ideas or answer questions in their own words, they fail to get experience and training in the art of self-expression and also tend to obtain from instruction little more than empty words, the lingo of instructor and textbook. Please note that we have not said that that is all they obtain; we are convinced, however, that the *tendency* is in that direction.

This is also not to say that the only training students get in schools in the art of verbal self-expression is by way of essay-type examinations. But this is a very fruitful way in which such experience may be gained, and it tends to promote transfer of this kind of training because it impresses upon students the value of competent verbal communication outside of English classes as well as within, besides greatly increasing opportunities for supervised practice. It may well be that some of the responsibility for what is thought by many to be the present low state of proficiency in English composition must be assigned to the 1920–1950 growth in the employment of objective tests.

Another consideration in determining *how much* students know is whether it is to be understanding, or mere memory. As we discuss in Chapter 12, understanding represents *using* what one knows, whereas memory requires merely *repeating* what one knows. And, since a wide degree of transferability of what one knows is surely to be sought, then understanding—or ability to apply or use—is certainly to be desired over memory. What is the difference between memory-level and understanding-level testing?

The answer to this question is most simple. It is merely that to test memory we ask for essentially exact repetition of previous experience. But to test understanding we must introduce novelty; to use or apply what one knows, one must be confronted with a situation definitely different from what has been previously experienced. The same generalized relationship has to be applicable, but the details have to be different. If a child has learned to add two and three in terms of fingers and marbles, he has to be tested in terms, say, of toothpicks and pennies. If the exact items used in learning are used also in testing, there is no assurance that the one taking the test is doing other than remembering the items themselves.

It is quite true that one who is meticulous or who possibly is inclined to quibble may reply that memory is also at work in a case of application; the relationship has to be remembered. But this is true only if and when books, notebooks, and other informational sources are not available. Making the test "open-book," wherein all likely relationships are readily available for reference should memory fail, will obviate even this recourse to memory as a necessity.

And why should not such practice be followed in classroom examinations? Is this not comparable to "real-life" situations? How many of us would be happy to trust our lives upon a bridge designed by an architect who relied entirely on memory for the stress-and-strain formulae which he used in drawing up plans and specifications? Or to trust the advice of a physician who we knew never checked his references to keep his memory accurate? Of course, either architect or physician would be slowed tremendously if every time he had to look up every formula which he might have to use. But is it easily possible for us to keep from remembering many or most of the relationships which we commonly use?

Do we have to make such a fetish out of memory-level testing? Can we not "let nature take her course," let our memories do what they will, without benefit of special forcing by teachers? Is it not high time to dispense with memory-level testing entirely? What genuinely educational end does it achieve that perhaps would not be more adequately and economically obtained by a testing program more in keeping with democratic educational objectives? The experimental findings which are presented in our first chapter show that the altered kind of teaching, therein indicated, actually does achieve greater memory-level retention than when memory-level outcomes are sought by forcing, or as ends in themselves.

In a previous work, the writer discussed at considerable length the use of objective-type examinations designed to measure understanding, or the ability to use ideas.[2] Included in an appendix were a number of full examinations exemplifying the various objective types. The plan was that presented by the writer in 1929, somewhat of a modification of that proposed by Morrison in 1926.[3] It seems hardly justifiable to repeat here what is readily obtainable from these other sources. The point of the plan is merely that the test items— verbal statements, questions which require mathematical or other particularized answers, or other suitable items—should be such that an examinee has never seen, heard, or thought about before. They are *novel*.

Of course, novelty is a function of time, place, and person. What is novel for one person may not be so for another, and what is novel for a given person at one time may not be so at another. Hence, novelty *for the greatest number of examinees possible* is what is sought and hoped for; 100 percent novelty is not expected. Therefore, several different opportunities to apply a given idea or principle need to be presented, always using care to avoid what was given or said in class, in the textbook, or may elsewhere have been presented to examinees in an authoritative manner. In as far as possible, opportunity to employ memory to obtain an exact answer must be eliminated.

Incidentally, when it is argued that objective-type tests save a teacher's time, it should be remembered that the making of a high-quality objective test is a time-consuming process. Formulation of a set of 50 test items, a substantial part of which are novel to a large number of alert youngsters, is not something which can be done offhand, while, say, watching television, or in a short time.

Later, we can return to further consideration of objective tests. The point here is that, for identification either of memory-level or understanding-level achievement, objective testing is serviceable and has the advantages of less laborious scoring and greater item coverage, whatever these advantages may be worth. But they certainly give little experience in written self-expression, and, unless memory-level achievement alone is under scrutiny, any saving in overall time and energy is probably at the expense either of validity or of quality

[2] Ernest E. Bayles, *The Theory and Practice of Teaching,* New York: Harper & Brothers, 1950.

[3] Henry Clinton Morrison, *Practice of Teaching in the Secondary School* (rev. ed.), Chicago: The University of Chicago Press, 1931.

and perhaps of both. Moreover, it should be noted that properly designed and constructed essay examinations will probably produce
just as *reliable* results as will objective.

For several pages we have been dealing with testing for enhancement of outlook: coverage, or scope. But harmonization of outlook
is just as important a part of our educational purpose, and on its
achievement little light is thrown by tests designed for coverage
alone. What this aspect of purpose calls for is *an index of consistency,
self-agreement, or compatibility.* This means that we look for something more than mere number of items; we must look for *interre-
latedness among items.* How does acceptance of one item affect, if
it does, acceptance of another?

As I start thinking about this matter, I find myself toying with a
rather intriguing idea. If IQ's (intelligence quotients) and AQ's
(achievement quotients) are good, why not *CQ's* (*consistency quotients*)? The method of computing them would be simple, and the
meaning of the scores would be readily understood. Expressed in
percent, out of a given number of opportunities to demonstrate consistency, in how many was it demonstrated? Suppose eight opportunities were offered and in five of them consistency was indicated.
Five out of eight $(5/8)$ is equal to .625, or 62.5 percent. Regardless
of the number of items taken into account, the quotient is always
on the same scale—the number per hundred, the *per centum,* or
percent. In these days of batting and other averages in the field of
sports, what could be easier?

How might data for these computations be obtained? Recently, I
was examining a set of answers to test questions on an aspect of
American educational history and came across the remark, "Horace
Mann got the idea from visiting Pestalozzi's school in Germany."
In the margin I wrote, "How could Mann in 1842 have visited Pestalozzi's school when Pestalozzi died in 1827 and his school was in
Switzerland?" Unless the writer of the paper could have straightened me out on my question, he evidently had presented two incompatibilities: Pestalozzi could not have been conducting a school
in 1842 and it could not have been in Germany.

Again, not long ago a foreign-language-education expert, after
dwelling at length on how study of foreign languages promotes
proficiency in the grammar of one's own language, said, "All the
teachers are not going to come from urban centers." I wondered why
it was that city-gals would not be teaching; and when. For, if they

are not going to come from urban centers, they must be going to come from nonurban centers; meaning that no city-gals would be teaching. I am quite sure that this is not what was meant, since the expression is very common and is intended to mean essentially the opposite; that is, *not* all are going to come from urban centers. But here is one incompatibility, intended meaning not in agreement with what was said. Another was that here was a person highly trained in foreign languages who was committing the same kind of grammatical error in which one-language persons luxuriate, in spite of a claim which should lead us to expect the contrary.

Again, also recently, I listened to some physicians first opining that group practices in medicine are keeping patients from the advantages of the personal relationship of having one's own doctor when one wants him, then shortly afterward opining that "the public" (their own patients) is so demanding of their time that they develop ulcers and heart conditions trying to keep up. When they then were asked by a nonphysician whether they were really serious about those personal-relationship advantages for patients or were not, they at first did not catch the point of the question.

The moral of all these anecdotes is simply that youngsters, like oldsters, are continually reversing themselves without realizing it. And, in order to obtain data for both class and individual-pupil CQ's, a teacher needs merely to keep eyes and ears open and alert to spot particular cases—in class discussions, on examination papers, outside of class, etc.—make note of them, and later use them both for computing CQ's and also for serving the instructional purpose of sensitizing the pupils to their own inconsistencies and disharmonies, thereby promoting more consistent, more harmonious outlooks. Both class and test questions can be adroitly designed to lay traps for the unwary; the number of traps serving as the divisor, the number of "catches" the dividend, and the quotient the CQ sought. This, of course, is oversimplification for the purpose of indicating the strategy. But it is something which is achievable, and would certainly be educative.

We have now dealt with tests for both enhancement and harmonization of student outlooks, but have said nothing of reflective capacity; self-reliance. It would seem that the obvious procedure in testing for reflection would be to teach reflectively and record observations on the way each student performs. Does he take an active part, contributing without grandstanding, or does he settle back and "let George do it"? Does he think before he speaks, and is his thinking tightly connected and logical? Does he evince an active and fruitful imagination, giving help in formulation of hypotheses? Does he examine each hypothesis sympathetically and fairly, but disinterestedly and stringently? Is he concerned with *who* is right, or with *what* is right? All in all, does he evince a scholarly outlook and attitude, or is he narrowly and emotionally partisan?

The record of such observations may possibly for the most part be carried in a teacher's head. To write them all down could amount to a tremendous job of bookkeeping, could get so mechanical that its very purpose would be defeated, and could constitute a record so intimate and private that it should never be permitted to become public property. To keep the record only in memory tends to avoid these difficulties, and it may not be as devoid of objectivity as is sometimes thought. For, in knowing and sizing up a person, are not these important considerations, and does one forget them easily? Moreover, conscious incorporation of aspects such as these into one's judgments of people may considerably improve such judgments.

What is described in the two preceding paragraphs may be said to constitute an *anecdotal record*. Although not readily amenable to tabulation and statistical treatment, it is a form whose significance and value are receiving increasing recognition. On the other hand, can pencil-and-paper tests be used for measuring reflection? Possibly in no open-or-shut, have-it-or-don't-have-it sense. Reflection is rather will-o'-the-wispish; it comes and it goes; sometimes one practices it, sometimes not; and it seems to be present or absent in degrees, never absolutely. Yet it would seem that pencil-and-paper tests can be designed so as to shed considerable light on reflective capacity and practice.

Since reflection is a way to solve problems, in simplest terms testing for reflection is merely a matter of posing a problem, observing an examinee's procedure in trying to solve it, and arriving at a judgment on the basis of the evidence. Therefore, the first requirement of reflection-level testing is that an examinee must be faced with a problem—an I-don't-know situation. This means that each test item must not only possess novelty for the examinee but must also be sufficiently novel that he cannot at once see how it is to be handled. He has to "stop and think."

It is evident that a given test item will not be reflective for all examinees. Some will catch and handle the point at once, others will have to mull it over. Therefore, several items doubtless will be desirable in order to increase the likelihood that every examinee will be faced with a situation requiring reflection. On the other hand, since reflection requires time, a reflection-level test must include only relatively few items. In this respect it is different from an understanding-level test. Understanding-level items have to be such that, for one who understands the principle in question, the answer is evident almost at once or after a few necessary calculations. Snap judgment handles the item. For upper-grade or college levels, 20, 30, 40, or more items per hour may be indicated. But for a test which is genuinely reflective, 4 or 5 items per hour are probably the limit. And it may well be argued that, if the evidence is to be at all conclusive, whatever time an examinee needs should be available to him.

Whether objective-type examinations can be designed to measure reflective achievement or capacity satisfactorily is a moot question. Under the leadership of Ralph W. Tyler during the 1930's, some headway was made in preparation and publication of standardized tests for reflection, largely of the objective type.[4] But one has only to read a discussion of what must be done to prepare a test of this kind to realize that preparation of an objective-type examination for reflection is hardly something which can be done offhand by a busy teacher. Moreover, published examinations of this kind can deal only with generalized subject matter and therefore cannot be used to cover the particular subject matter of a particular class in a given semester.

Another aspect of the problem of designing objective-type examinations for reflective ability calls for comment. This is the tendency first to analyze the reflective process into constituent elements, then obtain scores on each of the elements, and finally add the scores together in order to obtain a composite score which is supposedly indicative of the nature of the process as a whole. If and when such procedure is adopted, it is tantamount to adoption of the principle that the whole is *equal* to the sum of its parts. Such policy in test construction is entirely out of keeping with the psychological principle of configuration—relativism in psychology—which is that a

---

[4] See, for example, Progressive Education Association, *Science in General Education*, New York: Appleton-Century-Crofts, Inc., 1938, chap. 9. Also Eugene R. Smith and Ralph W. Tyler, *Appraising and Recording Student Progress*, New York: Harper & Brothers, 1942, chap. 2.

given item of experience takes on significantly different qualities in one configuration as compared with another, and still different when dealt with by itself.

For example, one such "element" in the reflective process is taken to be ability to make logical deductions from given hypotheses. In consequence, a test section was prepared which presented a number of hypotheses and, following each, a number of supposed deductions some of which logically followed and some of which did not. The examinee was to indicate which were which. This represented objective form and could be scored by means of a previously prepared key.

This kind of exercise probably would give some sort of indication of whether a given examinee *could* identify logical deductions when they were presented to him. But could he make them himself? And *would* he make them? What dependence could we place upon him to make logical deductions when a situation called for them? Or to know whether and when a situation did make such a call? There seems to be too little recognition in this kind of test design of the second and third aspects of what we have found to be a necessary theory of transfer of training to tell us what we need to know—that is, *whether* an examinee will use deductive ability even if he knows how. Those two aspects (see Chapter 3) are recognition of whether an opportunity exists and disposition to take advantage of it. And when there are half a dozen such "elements" supposedly making up the reflective process and all are will-o'-the-wispish like this, just what does a final, composite score signify, anyway?

Again, some teachers insist that, since a person cannot do a competent job of thinking without facts, all we need is to find whether they "know the facts"; and if they do, we can then be assured that they will be able to think. This proposal for testing reflection impresses me as about as valid as the one of taking the papers for a given class to the foot of a stairway, throwing them all together up the stairway, and giving the heavier ones which have gone furthest the highest grades and the progressively lighter ones landing progressively further down the progressively lower grades. As asked before, is it not about time for us to do away with memory-level examinations entirely?

The problem of "grading" examination papers is a serious one for most, if not all, teachers. How fervently do I wish that we could do without that task. With all due respects to the capabilities of my students who write them, I find no aspect of teaching which is really boring *except* this one. Yet this aspect must be handled well or it vitiates all the rest. I do not want to spend one bit more of energy and time on "grading papers" than is absolutely necessary. Yet I do feel that, if I am to do a good job of teaching, written exam papers are unavoidable and, moreover, that I must read them and judge them myself. Moreover, although recognizing that to make them wholly reflective is beyond my own capacity, I wish to make them as reflective as possible.

During the 1920's I made extensive, almost exclusive, use of objective-type examinations, for both high school and college students. But then I had not come to appreciate the difference between understanding-level and reflection-level thinking. Once I grasped the difference and came to see the democratic necessity for reflective teaching, hence reflective testing, I gave up objective-type examinations. For more than a quarter-century, I have not given objective-type tests. Much as I envy those who can be through with a set of examination papers within an hour or so after they have been handed in, I cannot bring myself to give that kind of examination. Here, I guess, is a case in value-theory wherein the *desired* is not the *desirable*.

For the record, we should perhaps put down the obvious, that "the proof of the pudding is the eating." If it is pudding-making which is to be tested, a pudding should be made and its eatability determined. A pencil-and-paper discussion, to explain why it was prepared as it was, might also have value, but such value would perhaps be peripheral rather than central. But for much of schoolroom instruction beyond the lower grades, pencil-and-paper discussion is so important a proof of the pudding that it deserves concerted attention.

Our experience, continually subjected to reëxamination in light of subsequent experiences, has essentially coerced us into the following examination plan. The essay type is used exclusively, requiring not only an *answer* to a question but also an explanation of its meaning as well as of why it is thought to be a proper one. Ordinarily, from 15 to 25 minutes are allowed for each question, with strict adherence to the stated time limit. Moreover, minimum length is indicated for an answer to qualify for top rating—an "A" if that is top. For all regular classes, examinations are "open-book"; class notes, texts and other reference books, and whatever else may be desired may be referred to as an examinee wishes, except only a classmate's examination paper. These points will be discussed in the order given.

The essay type is used because we are concerned with a student's own thinking, not with whether he can repeat the expressions of instructor or author. We feel that students (and others) are much like Humpty Dumpty, whom Alice met behind the looking glass, when he said, "When *I* use a word, it means just what I choose it to mean —neither more nor less," and, after Alice's query as to whether one could do that with words, added, "The question is which is to be master—that's all." Because a student uses the words of an author does not mean that he is thinking as the author thought. Hence, when an examinee uses words to answer a question, the examiner must ascertain as best he can what the examinee meant by those words; therefore, elaboration, illustration, and explanation are needed. It is at this point that objective tests fall short; there is no opportunity for a given examinee to indicate what the words mean to him. If such an opportunity were given, the test would no longer be "objective." A person has to choose his own words and put them together in his own way if he is to make at all clear what he himself means.

Giving from 15 to 25 minutes to answer a question provides time not only for sufficient elaboration but also for thought. It should be impressed upon examinees that they will probably need to do some thinking; that the questions are devised with that in mind. Also to be emphasized is that parroting the words of instructor or author will not be acceptable. If an exact quotation should be found desirable, it should be enclosed in quotation marks and the examinee should follow it with a statement of what the quoted expression means to him. "Answer each question in your own words" should be a rigorously enforced directive.

Indication of minimum length for an answer to be considered of top quality is at first disconcerting to many students. Hardly ever is an examination given without at least one complaint that there is not enough time to write that much. However, seldom is the complaint repeated by the same person. In the first place, the minimum applies only to a top rating; there is no stated minimum for a lower one. Moreover, the minimum is determined by placing it at about the amount which a person could readily write (say, from memory) in somewhat less than half—perhaps one third—of the allotted time. Taking 30 words per minute as unhurried writing speed, in 20 minutes one could write 600 words. My usual minimum requirement is one-third that number: 200 words in 20 minutes, 150 words in 15 minutes, or 250 words in 25 minutes. This makes the minimum achievable even if one-half to two-thirds of the time were used for thought, a fact readily recognized by students once the explanation is made.

Indication of minimum length for an answer to be considered of top quality seems to be a virtual necessity, particularly nowadays when short-answer tests are so much in vogue. Students must have some way of knowing beforehand that such a vogue is not being followed. This device readily gets the idea across.

Finally, we come to the open-book feature. For either understanding-level or reflection-level thought, accurate information is necessary. If not otherwise available, it has to be remembered. Hence, a question may go unanswered because of faulty memory, not because of faulty understanding. For this reason, we want informational material readily obtainable, should memory start playing tricks. This is the function to be served by textbooks and class notes. Many students, however, fail at first to realize this. They feel that the *answer* to the question is to be found in texts and notes; not the basis for reaching the answer.

Such misapprehensions by students are responsible for either or both of two outcomes. One starts leafing through his book in search of the answer and time gets away from him. Before he knows it, he is asked to begin work on the next question. On the other hand, often a spot in text or notes is discovered which looks like just what is wanted. The student copies it down, then uses remaining time to copy something else or to follow up with his own words. But such appearances are usually misleading; the quoted or copied part rarely is a direct and exact answer to the *question asked;* it therefore tends to slide off the point, and what follows tends to slide further away, so the answer turns out to be highly defective.

Hence, the open-book feature puts the examiner on his toes, and again for either or both of two different reasons. First, he has to devise questions which are somewhat different from any actually confronted previously by the examinees. This represents the novelty of which we have repeatedly spoken. Questions must indeed be chosen which are central to the line of study under examination, but little twists have to be given which throw the principles into somewhat different lights; which require using or applying the principles rather than repeating them or repeating applications which have already been made and may therefore be correctly given from memory alone.

Second, in reading papers the examiner has to keep alert, so as fully to sense what an examinee is saying. Otherwise, he may err in giving either too much credit or not enough. Herein is where the examiner must not be misled by a plethora of words. Students are not averse to using many words to hide lack of insight and often are adept at so doing. That is why the examiner must be insistent that examinees answer the questions which *are* asked, not questions which might have been asked but weren't. On the other hand, the examiner must be alert to catch the full and exact impact of what is on the paper. When it is insisted that each student use his own words, it is those words which must be dealt with; pat phrases and clichés cannot be permitted to pass at face value.

This plan of testing may be thought to be reflective. When questions are such that direct and exact answers are not to be found in readily available sources, examinees have to formulate their own; they have to think. Proof that a genuine difference exists between this kind of examination and the memory-level kind is unmistakable in the altered way in which examinees go about preparation. Customary "boning up" the night before is so ineffectual that students rarely resort to it after a first experience. Those who come to such an examination cocked and primed in the old way are often completely floored by the inappropriateness of their preparation. I find it necessary to give every new class at least one trial examination to help the members get their bearings so that they can turn in performances in keeping with their several capacities. Able students, accustomed to memory-level tests, often do poorly the first time but soon become oriented and become highly delighted with the opportunity to be tested on their capacity to think things through. Students of the docile or submissive type, who enjoy handouts and shrink from being placed "on their own," are upset at the beginning and often remain so for considerable periods of time, sometimes permanently. A large majority of students, however, quickly come greatly to prefer this kind of examination.

To say that the examinations which I give (the kind I have been describing) are wholly reflective would, I am convinced, be a gross misstatement. They seem, rather, to lie somewhere in the twilight zone between understanding and reflection level. Anyone looking over the examinations given over a period of years would probably get the feeling that they are all pretty much the same. Yet, even though every student receives *and retains* a copy of the questions for each test and "test files" probably are available over the campus, I have never been able to detect any "coaching effect" from one class to another. Furthermore, student papers (even for final examinations) are returned with corrections and comments, and even this produces no detectable coaching effect. Class papers do not get gradually better, but have their ups and downs seemingly as class capacities vary (or possibly as the instructor varies). Moreover, papers do not even "read alike," at least not so as to give rise to any feeling of one being copied from another, or even two or more being copied from a single source.

Although I am not averse to going back in my files and occasionally reusing a test previously given, each later test tends to be enough different from previous ones that former answers will not fit; new ones have to be concocted. And, since no two classes ever follow the same pattern (I practically never use class notes and certainly never keep any), even if an old set of questions is used it is always necessary to look them over carefully to see that they fit the class in question. All of this seems to mean that every examination question represents a distinctly novel application of principles developed in class, and at least verges on the problematic, thereby necessitating at least a modicum of reflection.

After the giving of an examination comes the task of evaluating the papers. Here, as well as in making out questions, is where the *examiner* has to achieve a new orientation. If questions are old and answers are preëstablished, evaluation is simple because any and every deviation from an established answer makes the answer wrong. But for questions which are designed to provoke thought, preëstablished answers are wholly unsuited. In fact, requirement of a prefixed answer—fixed ahead of time as in a key—which is taken to be the one-and-only "right" answer is a rather effectual deterrent to reflection by an examinee. He knows from experience that if he tries to "think it out" he frequently gets on the wrong track—at least the one which the "prof" considers wrong—and, even though with opportunity he can demonstrate his answer to be a good one, he gets no credit because his answer is not on the accepted list.

Thought-provoking questions require thoughtful answers, and all such answers should be evaluated on their own merits. How can this be done? This brings us again to the matter of criteria. If no other special criteria are currently in force (such as "What is the author's answer?" or "What is your instructor's answer?"), I employ the overall criteria of *adequacy and harmony of outlook or conclusion in light of obtainable data*. Thus, you see, we have a basis for evaluating a student's own answer. What data has the examinee taken into account in his answer? Has he included all data which can reasonably be expected under the circumstances, ordinarily the facts brought out by the class discussions and the textbook? Such questions deal with the criterion of adequacy.

Next, do his conclusions agree with, or harmonize, the data actually employed? With certain data, certain conclusions are indicated; with other data, other conclusions. No matter how "right" an examinee's answer may otherwise be, if it is not in keeping with the data which he is considering in connection with the question at hand, it is a wrong answer. This is the criterion of harmony, and, if an examiner does not include it in his evaluation, he cannot be said to be discerningly evaluating a thought process.

The criterion of harmony should be applied to relationships among answers to various questions as well as to relationships within answers to single questions. Is there any seeming contradiction between the answer to question one and the answer to question three? In the margin of an answer to question three might then appear the comment, "If you say such-and-such in answering question one, how can you say this now?" Or it might be written, "How can you say this, in light of what was said in class day before yesterday?" One might actually design test-questions to lay traps for the unwary, questions which have likelihood of bringing incompatibles to light. Thereby, not only will data for *CQ's* be obtained, but sensitivity toward inconsistency will also be heightened and more harmonious outlooks promoted.

What we have just said means, first, that reflective test questions must be stated in such way as to require an examinee to give not only his conclusions but also his reasons for reaching them, the latter both in terms of data and of logic. That is to say, the examinee should be asked to indicate the facts he is using and to indicate also *what he considers* those facts to mean, including the whys. What we have said means, second, that the examiner must read carefully and thoughtfully what each examinee has written, because only thereby can he do justice to the paper before him. The examiner should write on the paper his reactions, first, so that the examinee will receive instruction and, second, so that the examinee will have a basis for *evaluating the evaluation.* Here again is democracy—opportunity to appeal a decision or to petition for the redress of grievances.

In the foregoing discussion of what surely leans heavily in the direction of reflection-level testing, we may have made the process seem complicated because we have dealt at some length with certain aspects. Our proposal, however, is really simple in terms of procedure. It is merely to give one, two, or three thought-provoking questions, asking an examinee to give not only his conclusions but also the data and the logic upon which they are based. Sufficient time should be allowed on each question to enable an examinee to consider it thoughtfully and to report his considerations.

In comparison with objective-type examinations on reflection, the type of examination which we propose takes tremendously less time to prepare, less class time to take, but more time to grade or evaluate. However, the papers for a class of 30 students, on a 40-minute examination, can be evaluated in six or seven hours, and that, two or three times a semester, may not be too much to expect—especially when good teaching is at stake. Moreover, the examination which we propose, by giving each examinee opportunity to put down his own data, to write his own conclusions, and to explain his thinking in his own way, makes for a more valid test of the reflective process than when objective-type conditions have to be met.

American teachers need to recognize more clearly than they do that if students are to be taught to think for themselves there is every reason to expect unanticipated answers to appear, each and all of which have to be considered on their own merits as and when they arise. Classes cannot be organized democratically and problems studied scientifically if unanticipated conclusions are not to be given a hearing. And a testing program which is out of keeping with an instructional program is simply intolerable. It is a continual source of insurmountable difficulties, of the kind which always appear when one contradicts one's self.

It has been claimed by many, though critical analysis of such claims has resulted in sharp reduction in the number of claimants, that essay examinations are not reliable. We shall let that pass and consider the more defensible statement that essay examinations are not as reliable as objective examinations. Our first comment is that, even if they were not, for reasons which we have just discussed they appear to be much more valid, and, if we have to choose between validity and reliability, we prefer the former. However, our experience is that, if an examiner knows what he is about, essay examinations can produce evaluations which are almost, if not quite, as reliable as those of objective examinations. Questions must be stated adequately and clearly. An examinee's interpretation of each question must be sensed clearly by the examiner and, if reasonable, should be taken as the question rather than the one originally in the mind of the test maker. Unreasonable, undiscerning, or careless interpretations are, of course, not to be tolerated.

The examiner should have rather clearly in mind what he considers a good answer but should be willing to evaluate each answer on its own merits. In as far as possible, all major criticisms should be written in brief form on the paper. If faults are too extensive to make written comments feasible, the student can be called in for conference. Not only should criticisms be indicated, but for each answer an overall evaluation mark—such as a letter grade—should probably be included. In this way a student is given opportunity to know whether the criticisms are serious or not. Written comments on an answer rated "A" are considerably different from those on an answer rated "D." Both forms of recording an evaluation are useful to a student as he looks over a returned paper. *And papers should be returned.*

Finally, a teacher needs to be insistent that all questions or objections to the way papers have been evaluated be reported to him for further consideration. If the papers have been examined carefully, few changes will result from such reëxamination. But many instructional opportunities will thereby be gained, genuine democracy will be more fully achieved, and student morale will be greatly enhanced. It should be noted that, in the entire scheme of testing which we are proposing, a teacher's attention is concentrated upon what is going on in students' minds and what he can do to improve the product. This we believe is of tremendous importance to teaching. As we said at the beginning of this chapter, we consider the instructional aspect of testing the one of major importance.

In order to keep formal examinations from taking more instructional time than is necessary, we suggest that the testing program be devoted almost exclusively to tests which are as nearly reflective as feasible. To this end we recommend without qualification that memory-level examinations be banished from the program. A reflectively taught class makes so much genuine use of factual information, arranging it always in logical patterns, that a teacher may rest assured of the results without taking the time to demonstrate them. In other words, a teacher can be sure that a reflectively taught class will be able to pass better memory-level examinations over material which has been studied than will a class taught on the memory level, even though the latter is subjected to the most rigorous "drill" for such examinations. This claim is well attested by the experimental findings which are presented in our first chapter.

SELECTED REFERENCES

Bayles, Ernest E., *The Theory and Practice of Teaching,* New York: Harper & Brothers, 1950, chap. 15; appendix.

Cole, Lawrence E., and Bruce, William, *Educational Psychology,* Yonkers-on-Hudson, N.Y.: World Book Company, 1950, chap. 18.

Judd, Charles H., *Education as Cultivation of the Higher Mental Processes,* New York: The Macmillan Company, 1936, chaps. 2, 7.

Morrison, Henry C., *Practice of Teaching in the Secondary School* (rev. ed.), Chicago: The University of Chicago Press, 1931, pp. 313–321, 501–504 (footnote).

Progressive Education Association, *Adventure in American Education,* vol. III, *Appraising and Recording Student Progress,* New York: Harper & Brothers, 1942.

Progressive Education Association, *Science in General Education,* New York: Appleton-Century-Crofts, Inc., 1938, chap. 9.

Saucier, W. A., *Theory and Practice in the Elementary School* (rev. ed.), New York: The Macmillan Company, 1951, chaps. 14, 15.

Wrightstone, J. Wayne, *Appraisal of Experimental High School Practices,* New York: Bureau of Publications, Teachers College, Columbia University, 1936, part 2.

Wrightstone, J. Wayne, *Appraisal of Newer Elementary School Practices,* New York: Bureau of Publications, Teachers College, Columbia University, 1938, pp. 151–205.

Wrinkle, William L., *Improving Marking and Reporting Practice in Elementary and Secondary Schools,* New York: Rinehart and Company, Inc., 1947.

CHAPTER 15

John Dewey and
Progressivism

ALTHOUGH originally not included in the plan for this book, the need for writing a chapter such as this has come to appear really urgent. Long a matter of serious concern on the part of the writer, the identification of Dewey with the educational "Progressivism" of the early twentieth century has become so common, almost so blatant, that it seemingly should be faced squarely and certain facts placed clearly on the record. This should possibly be done in simple fairness to a man who has greatly influenced Western thought, but that need not be our major concern. Since knowing what a thing *is not* is almost as important for genuine understanding as knowing what it *is*, we feel that further clarification of the point of view taken in this book requires elucidation and at least a modicum of documentation on the question of the responsibility of Dewey's philosophy for what has been known as the Progressive movement.

First, let us define Progressivism as we are using the term. Note the capital P, making it a proper name. It is not being used to designate any and every line of thought or action which might be considered forward-looking. It is being used in the time-honored, professional sense of that movement in American education which ran through the first four decades of the twentieth century and was especially identified with the Progressive Education Association. For a time, the term "project method" was one of its banners, as was the expression, "pupil purposing, pupil planning, pupil executing, pupil judging." Later, it became identified as "The Child-Centered School."

Whenever it is possible, we avoid attaching the names of persons to ideas or movements regarding which we find it necessary to register disapproval. But there are occasions when avoidance of so doing seems impossible, and this is one. For in the popular mind, both professional and nonprofessional, Dewey's name and Dewey's philosophy have become so thoroughly identified with and made responsible for Progressivism that no attempt to meet the issue is possible without citing writer, book, and page. It is our contention that the faults which are laid, whether rightly or wrongly, at the door of Progressivism are not justifiably attributable either to Dewey or to his philosophy, but, instead, primarily to lack of clarity on certain crucial matters which has characterized the writings of William Heard Kilpatrick, particularly those which appeared during the high tide of Progressivism. It was Kilpatrick who introduced "project method" into elementary education, even though it may have been borrowed from vocational-agriculture education. It is Kilpatrick whom we seemingly must credit with "pupil purposing, pupil planning, pupil executing, pupil judging," even though one of his most eminent students, Ellsworth Collings, may have been a bit more enthusiastic and a bit less circumspect in its use. And it was Kilpatrick who was dubbed in an authorized biography as "Trail Blazer in Education." And what trail did he blaze if not that of Progressivism?

As background for a study of Kilpatrick, let us refresh our minds regarding two different and rather oppositional sets of assumptions regarding innate, inborn, or original human nature; those of Rousseau and of Dewey. Each set of assumptions is twofold, dealing, on the one hand, with the good-bad aspect of human nature and, on the other, with the active-passive.

First, is a human infant born innately good, or innately bad? Do we assume that we bring with us into this world the soul-searing blot of Adam's sin, or, as Wordsworth phrased it,

> Not in entire forgetfulness
> And not in utter nakedness
> But trailing clouds of glory do we come
> From God, who is our home:

Second, is it inborn human nature to wait inert, like stick or stone, until pushed or pulled about by something outside of itself? Or is a human being a self-starter, "an event going somewhere to happen"? The latter is the active assumption, the former the passive.

With Rousseau, as you well know, it was the good-active pair of assumptions. "Everything is good as it comes from the Hands of the Creator of Nature; everything deteriorates in the hands of man"— so the opening sentence of *Emile* states the "good" position. And his culture-epochs theory exemplifies the "active" position. In other words, we enter this world with the seeds of virtue sown in our souls, ready to come alive, to grow, and to *unfold* into the virtuous life which lies dormant within those seeds. All a teacher needs to do is keep hands off and out of the way, together with making all other "depraved" grownups do likewise. Negative education; save time by losing it; by doing nothing you will indeed produce a prodigy of education; education as *unfoldment*. As Froebel later phrased it, education is permissive, not prescriptive.

With the good-active pair of assumptions, the original wants, wishes, and desires of a child are always right. Just make sure not to spoil him by foisting upon him your own depraved ones. Then unfoldment will proceed naturally and in due time God's glory will floresce. With these assumptions, there is nothing to do other than open class with the question, "Well, children, what shall we do to-day?" The logic is obvious; complete permissivism is the implication.

That you, and I, and "everyone" knows that this cannot, or must not, be done is quite beside the point; as also is the fact that Rousseau never taught a class and, moreover, that every example of what he might do which is given in *Emile* is in violation of this principle. The point is that pupil purposing, pupil planning, pupil executing, pupil judging is a program which is strictly deducible from the good-active premises and the principle of education as unfoldment. If one has any reservations as to the advisability of such a program, one should modify the premises and begin anew. To characterize the above premises and program as the "ideal" but one which can never be realized is to open the gate wide for any and all qualifications which anyone wishes to impose; opportunism is then the order of the day. If such is not to be tolerated, then one must write down the qualifications himself, and that means restating the premises. This is what Rousseau, Froebel, and Kilpatrick did not do; *but what Dewey did.*

As to the good-bad choice, Dewey followed John Locke in adopting neither. That is to say, if man is assumed to be neither innately good nor innately bad, the assumption is that he is born *neutral*.

With Locke, however, the doctrine of "no innate ideas" led to the concept of the *tabula rasa,* a shaven or blank tablet devoid of characters but waiting passively to be written upon by some agency other than itself. But Dewey did not assume passivity. In fact, he avoided both horns of the active-passive dilemma by assuming neither absolute self-determinacy nor absolute outside determinacy. This is where the assumption of *interaction* enters. Man is assumed to be *neutral-interactive.* Since we have discussed interaction (or transaction) elsewhere, we shall not repeat that here. It is seemingly on that point alone that Dewey differs from his predecessors. But this difference has tremendous significance.

On the basis of all genuinely tested human experience, it seems that man is never justified in claiming that what he makes of the sensory stimuli which impinge upon his receiving organs is an exact replica of that which gave rise to the stimulations. He can *hope* that they are, but the final test can never be that of correspondence. How could one apply the correspondence test to an idea when the very thing to which it must correspond is what one is seeking? One might be looking right at it, but how could one know? The only possible *test* is anticipatory accuracy (see Chapters 4 and 5); this is where interaction enters. I agree to call something soft *only* if and when it responds in certain specified ways to certain specified acts of mine. Thus, perception as well as conception is a coöperative matter. Perceiver says, "It will 'give' when I touch it." What is perceived coöperates by doing so. If this does not happen—if the anticipation is inaccurate—then the "deal is off" and a new proposal has to be tried. Thus, we have the rudiments of reflective learning; an inductive-deductive process, the outcome of which is a tested insight.

The assumption of man as neutral-interactive throws a very different light on pupil purposing, planning, executing, and judging. Interaction is a denial of absolute pupil-determinacy; something outside the *self* has to be satisfied also. In a classroom, interaction requires a teacher to become a functioning factor; something more than a mere shield to protect a preciously fragile bud from outside distortion. There is mutual pupil-teacher interplay (interaction) of push-and-pull, out of which "somethin's gotta give"; maybe pupil, maybe teacher, perhaps preferably both. When a teacher reaches the condition wherein he has nothing more to learn in the classes for which he is responsible, it may well be that he should seek other employment; certainly a pupil who has reached it should be promoted.

What now obtains has to be some form of teacher-pupil or pupil-teacher purposing, planning, executing, and judging; else no interaction. Then, however, the whole question of group process arises. What shall be its form—autocratic, democratic, or what? Hence is necessitated our whole discussion of democracy and its meaning for keeping school (see Chapters 10 and 11). If it is to be democracy, then criteria have to be set up so as to avoid status domination, either by teacher or by pupil. For a teacher must repeatedly pass judgments —on curricula, on method, on housing, on equipment, on intra- and intergroup relationships, on thought processes, etc.—hence understandable and workable machinery has to be established and put to work in order that indoctrination and other undemocratic practices may be avoided. The principle of interaction logically calls for such machinery. It places upon a teacher the *obligation* to keep a firm hand on classroom affairs, from time to time a coercive one; a far cry from the easy irresponsibility of permissivism.

Thus, we see that Rousseauism and Deweyism represent two distinctly different thought-and-action patterns. The one logically necessitates anarchistic permissivism, whereas the other not only makes democratic coöperation a logical possibility but also calls attention to the necessity of setting up the machinery needed to realize the possibility. Let us now take a look at the position taken by Kilpatrick, particularly at the time when his influence was strong, widespread, and making a real difference to American education, especially on the elementary level.

(The following analysis of Kilpatrick's writings and, in fact, what appears in this entire chapter have long been an important part of a course taught by the writer, Education 361—Modern Teaching Procedures II. However, much help has been given by a recent study by Dr. Josefa P. Estrada, made while she was on an extended leave from educational work in her native country, the Philippine Islands. The report of the study is cited in the "Selected References" at the close of this chapter.)

We shall now examine Kilpatrick's major work of the 1920's, *Foundations of Method.* And we ask you to keep in mind that at that time, as well as since, he was supposed to be *the* spokesman for Dewey. At the outset we might note that more than half of the book is devoted to development of a connectionist, Thorndikean psychology which, in turn, is dependent upon the reflex-arc concept; in spite of the fact that the latter had been devastatingly analyzed and rejected by Dewey 30 years before in his classic article, "The Reflex Arc Concept in Psychology." It is true, of course, that six years after publication of *Foundations of Method* Kilpatrick did openly acknowledge the failure of connectionism to do what was required by his educational view, and in its stead gave support to an outlook essentially configurational in nature. The only trouble with this rejection is that when, in 1951, Kilpatrick came to "sum up in a statement for others the results of [his] thinking in connection with his life work of teaching philosophy of education,"[1] he was back again with Thorndike, as he himself admitted. "It may be of interest to see how Thorndike's laws of Readiness, Exercise, and Effect are all included (at least in part) in the principle of acceptance counted basic in this book, and how, used in this way, they avoid the logical difficulty that some find in the law of Effect."[2] And again, "In the three places marked above (i), (ii), and (iii) we have, respectively, at work the three Thorndike laws of (i) Readiness, (ii) Exercise, and (iii) Effect."[3]

If, in the foregoing pages of the present book, especially Chapters 2 and 3, we have not succeeded in making clear that the kind of psychological theory supported by Dewey is not fundamentally different from that of Thorndike, then we surely have failed in communication. Yet the above is the record of Kilpatrick, the supposed spokesman for John Dewey. But let us return now to *Foundations of Method,* specifically to Chapter 13, "Purposeful Activity: The Complete Act," in which are presented the four steps—purposing, planning, executing, and judging.[4]

After presenting these steps, Kilpatrick meets squarely the question, presumably stated by a student in one of his classes, "Might one person help another take one or more of the steps? Or might one take one or more of the steps for another person? If so, would this be good or bad?" At the bottom of the page, Kilpatrick's answer is, "If the child is to learn best, the child is to do the purposing."

In response, however, to a student objection that a child can hardly be expected to purpose as wisely as a grownup, Kilpatrick pro-

[1] W. H. Kilpatrick, *Philosophy of Education,* New York: The Macmillan Company, 1951, p. vii.

[2] *Ibid.,* p. 256.

[3] *Ibid.,* p. 257.

[4] W. H. Kilpatrick, *Foundations of Method,* New York: The Macmillan Co., 1926, pp. 203–205.

poses two different meanings of purpose and says, "Do you see any difference between a child's doing what he wishes and a child's wishing what he does?" Then he adds, "Well, our plan is *primarily that a child shall wish what he does,* that he have and put soul and purpose into what he does." The student then counters, "Then the suggestion might come from the teacher, and the child still purpose the matter in the sense *you most wish?"* And Kilpatrick answers, "Quite so."[5]

But the student is persistent, and asks, "And you don't care whether the child purposes in the first sense or not—that is, you don't care whether he does or does not originate the idea, or whether he does or does not choose (that is, decide and determine) what he is to do?" And Kilpatrick immediately replies, "I didn't say I didn't care. I do care." And the student responds, "Now I am completely lost."[6]

At this point, Kilpatrick makes the following explanation which, in light of Progressivist invective of the period against teacher domination, we find to be very revealing, if not downright disconcerting.

Go back to my distinction between doing as he wishes and wishing what he does. Take the first, "do as he wishes." Suppose a child wishes to do wrong; then I wish him stopped, caught, redirected, educated in some way, so that (a) he shall learn that what he had proposed was wrong, (b) he shall learn why it was wrong, (c) he shall so regret wishing this particular wrong that hereafter he will less probably wish it again. In a word when he wishes to do wrong, I wish him to learn the error of his way and so to repent of his wrong inclination that he will hereafter not so wish again. Is this wishing him to do as he pleases?[7]

And the student responds, "No, it is not," then adds, "But who is to say whether he is wrong? That's the rub." And Kilpatrick replies, "The teacher. That's one thing the teacher is there for."

There are eight more pages in the chapter and many more in the remainder of the book. We shall come to those in a moment, but let us now indulge in a bit of analysis. It should be recalled that this was written in the mid-20's, at a time when Progressivism was an active, potent force in American education and quite conscious of its own power. *Moreover, our firm conviction is that, for the time, it*

[5] *Ibid.,* p. 207. Italics added.
[6] *Ibid.,* pp. 207–208.
[7] *Ibid.,* p. 208.

was the greatest single force operating for the improvement of American education and we owe those responsible for it a deep debt of gratitude for a job well done. We needed to be jolted and we were.

The big question of the time was, however, "Do you really mean that we should let pupils do as and what they want to do?" It is this question to which Kilpatrick was addressing himself, frankly, openly, and squarely. We appreciate deeply his candor, his honesty, and his willingness to meet the issue. But we cannot be convinced that he handled the question. In fact, all we can get out of the foregoing and all we could ever get from him, at that time or later, was a case of now you do it, now you don't. When defenders of Kilpatrick insist that he stood for planning and control, we insist that the foregoing was as close as he ever came to forging the machinery necessary for democratic classroom control; and that is not close at all.

The foregoing is a case of dodging back and forth between permissivism on the one hand and dictation on the other. If out of the longest quotation cited above one can make anything short of the most dictatorial attitude that one can imagine, I cannot understand English. Napoleon, Hitler, Mussolini, or Stalin could have asked for nothing more in keeping with their own purposes. It exactly describes the procedure of Goebbels, Hitler's minister for propaganda. The upshot of most of Kilpatrick's thinking, as we have documented it so far, is essentially dictatorial. That is also the pattern of Kilpatrick's rendition of Thorndike's Law of Effect, "Practice with satisfaction; let annoyance attend the wrong."[8]

On the other hand, as we progress through the remaining pages of *Foundations of Method,* we find Kilpatrick gradually, almost imperceptibly, veering to an essentially permissivist pattern. This comes pretty much to a head in his discussion of "extrinsic" and "intrinsic" subject matter.[9] We shall not go into the details of his discussion, but only note that extrinsic subject matter is, for him, what is to be learned to satisfy teacher and intrinsic subject matter is what is to be learned because a pupil wants it.

On page 286, he presents a scale—a horizontal line with an E (for extrinsic) at the left end and an I (for intrinsic) at the right. Then he definitely makes the I-end the ideal and considers conduct of a school at any point short of that a case of compromise, albeit neces-

[8] *Ibid.,* p. 65.
[9] *Ibid.,* pp. 284 ff.

sary, with error. He says, however, "I think Dr. Collings's school was run approximately at I." So, as we anticipated, we come to Collings. But it should be noted that we have first taken *Kilpatrick's own* writings, not those of a "follower." We emphasize this because of repeated practice by writers who seek to make Dewey responsible for the permissive aspects of Progressivism. Over and over again we meet the apology. "Now we know, of course, that Dewey himself did not actually stand for this. But this is *what his followers* have made of it." And it is seldom, if ever, that the particular "followers" which the writer may or may not have in mind are stipulated.

Collings' *Experiment with a Project Curriculum* was a report of his doctoral study, performed under Kilpatrick's direction. But we shall make use of a much less-known book, *Psychology for Teachers,* by Collings and Wilson, the latter a colleague of Collings at the University of Oklahoma, where Collings was Dean of Education. After devoting about 100 pages to discussion and illustration of purposive behavior, explained in consistently connectionist fashion, Collings then devotes Chapters 15 through 18 to the "Nature of Guidance in Successful Purposing," "Planning," "Executing," and "Judging," respectively. In each chapter, the first page-and-a-half is essentially identical to the others except for substitution among the four above words, indicating the four different steps in purposive behavior. This is what is said:

1. Pupil Purposing. Purposive behavior contemplates pupil purposing in every instance. It does for at least two reasons. First, purposive behavior involves, as we have seen, the functioning of a series of interrelated stimulus-response mechanisms along a particular line. Purposing is the functioning of one of these series of stimulus-response mechanisms and, as such, involves the response of boys and girls along their drive in this particular, for stimulus-response mechanisms function in this fashion. Pupil purposing is, in this sense, one of the earmarks of purposive behavior. . . .

Pupil purposing is, in this sense, the key to growth in this particular of conduct. Such growth is desirable for the success of an individual in a democracy depends very largely upon wise purposing. If the teacher does the purposing growth in this particular is thwarted. The resultant change is in the teacher's drive and response since it is her stimulus-response mechanisms that function. Teacher purposing blocks, in this sense, the functioning of the stimulus-response mechanisms of boys and girls along this line and, in so doing, prohibits growth in purposing. Pupil purposing thus is fundamental in purposive behavior and growth. . . .

Purposing includes, as we have seen, three interrelated steps. First, it involves initiation of goal. This includes boys and girls suggesting goals to pursue.[10]

The chapter then continues very much along this line, with insistence even to the point of repetitiousness on pupils themselves doing the purposing, at no place even suggesting that they might purpose wrongly and what to do then. (In fact, Collings' pupils just don't seem to purpose wrongly.) And, as we have said, each subsequent chapter—certainly as far as the above quotation goes, and further—is a replica of the above except only for substitution of planning, executing, or judging, as the case may be, wherever purposing is used above.

Thus, it becomes quite clear that Kilpatrick with caution, and his arch follower with seemingly little caution, fall essentially into Rousseau's good-active pattern, certainly showing little, if any, evidence of neutral-interactive thought. If they had been openly accused of following Rousseau, both would probably have denied it. But the evidence remains; evidence of formal theory supportive of Rousselian permissivism, even though in practice one could be pretty sure (if he knew what to look for) of spotting sufficient dictatorial maneuvering to insure right choices even though particular practitioners may themselves not have been quite conscious that such was going on. However, as a result of occasional talks with several practitioners in the course of many years of professional experience, the writer has found that more than a few of them did know quite well what they had to do and were adept at keeping face straight and fingers crossed.

Our purpose in calling attention to this seemingly clear and significant incompatibility between Dewey and Kilpatrick is certainly not to pin sainthood on one and villainy on the other. It is, instead, to get the record clear on where lies the responsibility for certain schoolroom practices, either imagined or real, which are under attack today and which, if and when they do exist, ought unquestionably to be abolished. Anarchistic permissivism certainly is one of these, as Dewey so well recognized and so persistently opposed during his entire professional life.

But, say the critics, how Dewey felt personally is beside the point; it was his philosophy which counted. On this we agree, and do so

[10] Ellsworth Collings and M. O. Wilson, *Psychology for Teachers*, New York: Charles Scribner's Sons, 1930, pp. 271–272.

with high enthusiasm. In fact, that is exactly the point of this chapter. When anarchistic permissivism is admitted as insupportable, have we necessarily relinquished commitment to relativistic-pragmatic-experimentalist philosophy? The answer is that we have not. For the neutral-interactive assumption on which it is based does not in the slightest degree furnish logical support for anarchism.

Yet, by identifying Dewey with Progressivism, then Progressivism with anarchism, and finally demolishing anarchism, we find writer after writer and speaker after speaker emerging with the triumphant claim, "See how thoroughly I have demolished Dewey and Dewey's philosophy!" To name names and designate publications I never like to do, and do not do if I can reasonably avoid it. I do not believe documentation is needed here. But it does appear necessary to sensitize the profession as well as the public to the fact that this is increasingly being done, and to the fallacious nature of the line of thought which is being employed. For we can well be doing American education the disservice. I think that Dewey's place in history can be left to history itself. But what is being done to American education and will be done in the foreseeable future is a matter which concerns us all. That is why it seems of tremendous importance, before we summarily reject the relativistic-pragmatic-experimentalist educational philosophy, first to achieve an accurate and discerning appreciation of what it is. Otherwise, how can we know but that we are rejecting exactly what we must have if we are to achieve educational salvation?

Not long ago I had some correspondence with the writer of a recent book in educational philosophy in which I felt that the fallacy represented in the thought-line indicated above had been committed. A short excerpt from one of my letters to him seems pertinent here.

. . . aren't you placing reliance on some transcendent absolute which, although early in the book you seem to invoke, as you progress you seem progressively to deny? I am with you in sensing a need for denial, but I do not find your proposals as fruitful of what we both seem to be wanting as are those of relativistic experimentalism which you explicitly decry. Actually, it has long seemed to me that a major difficulty for Kilpatrick has been that he has never really emancipated himself from his pre-1910 absolutistic thinking (whether idealist or realist). You acknowledge what he denies, yet what you find objectionable in him is seemingly what grows out of his agreement with you. Therefore, I cannot see that the remedy for his ills lies in his coming to your orientation but, rather, in both of you coming to a genuinely relativistic orientation.

In the interests of reasonably full analysis, there seem to be two additional aspects of Kilpatrick theory which merit attention. One is the matter of learning. We have already noted his 1926 and 1951 espousals of Thorndike's laws of learning, even though for a time between those two dates he gave some evidence of denial. In Chapter 17 of *Philosophy of Education,* entitled "A Modern Theory of Learning," Kilpatrick presents his theory in a short, italicized statement: *"We learn what we live, we learn each item we live as we accept it, and we learn it in the degree we accept it."* A few lines below, he adds the following also in italics: *"We learn our responses, only our responses, and all our responses; we learn each as we accept it to live by, and we learn it in the degree we accept it."*[11]

In our second and third chapters, we present the insight theory of behavior and of learning, a theory which certainly received Dewey's espousal even though he may not have spelled out all parts of it as explicitly as have others. Convincing documentation of Dewey's espousal and of Thorndike's nonespousal if not clear rejection of the insight theory of learning is, I believe, quite possible but hardly suitable for inclusion here. Our concern at this point is that Kilpatrick's theory of learning, as just quoted, is distinctly "on the fence"; it can be taken either as learning as developing insight or as learning as conditioning, depending on which a reader tries to read into it. But the stronger flavor is that of conditioning, and that is further supported by Kilpatrick's overt statements, already quoted, that Thorndike's laws of learning are still fully acceptable.

That "learning is living" has long been iterated and reiterated by Kilpatrick, and that is exactly what is said above—"we learn our responses." But when *acceptance* is introduced, a question arises. Suppose one *does* something which one does not "accept"? Somewhere Kilpatrick says that "we accept it as we *take it to act* upon it," but that this "taking" may possibly be a "negative" one—taking it to reject it!

What can such statements mean, anyway? Is this not a species of "double talk"; found so objectionable when practiced by representatives of Moscow? The matter is further confused by statements such as, "If labor and management had only learned how to confer

[11] W. H. Kilpatrick, *Philosophy of Education,* New York: The Macmillan Company, 1951, p. 244.

honestly on a basis of getting at the best possible solution of their difficulties, we would have been spared many if not most of our industrial quarrels."[12] Is it really a matter of not having learned; or even, as indicated in the principle, of *degree* of acceptance? Surely one will not seriously claim that failures by labor and management to reach honest agreements are due to failures in *learning* honesty, or even to low acceptance of the principle of honest conferring. Are they not, rather, a matter of each and all "seeing" that their own interests are best served by the steps which they are taking and not by the kind of action which some of the rest of us may feel that they should take? Is not the way to change such behavior one of getting the interested parties to "see" their own interests as better served by altered behavior than by complaining that they haven't learned to "confer honestly"?

The expression, "what we take to act upon," can indeed be reasonably interpreted as "insight." If a person genuinely understands insight as the kind of phenomenon which we indicate in this book, he can easily read that into this expression. But Kilpatrick's uses of the expression do not necessitate such an interpretation, and Kilpatrick certainly does not anywhere indicate that it should be so interpreted. On the other hand, when he says that "we learn our responses" and only those, he certainly is seeming to say that "we learn to do by doing," a principle which is in line with the interpretation of learning as conditioning and not of learning as "doing and undergoing" as Dewey has it.[13]

Just what Kilpatrick would have us make of his so-called "modern theory of learning" seems to be far from clear when one looks at it with care. In this regard, therefore, he cannot seemingly with justification be said to speak for Dewey. In fact, his own statements are that he agrees with Thorndike, and it has long been recognized that, on the nature of learning, Dewey and Thorndike are distinctly apart.

The final aspect of Kilpatrick's educational program with which we shall deal is his principle of *education as growth*.[14] We feel that American experience in the employment of this expression has shown it to be too lacking in precise meaning to serve as an educational directive. The sentiment is certainly to be lauded. But even the following elaboration does not sufficiently clarify: "I should wish to

[12] *Ibid.*, p. 262.
[13] John Dewey, *Democracy and Education*, New York: The Macmillan Company, 1916, p. 163.
[14] Kilpatrick, *Foundations of Method, op. cit.*, pp. 188 ff.

think of education as the process of continuously remaking experience in such way as to give it continually a fuller and richer content and at the same time to give the learner ever increasing control over the process."[15] There is too little discouragement of the "fuller and richer content" being made up merely of additional childhood pranks and foibles—to say nothing of additional ways to break laws and confuse authority—to make clear what is to be included in a curriculum and what is to be excluded.

We do not mean to imply that we feel unable to guess rather accurately what Kilpatrick would wish to include and what to exclude. What we mean is that we would have to be acquainted with Kilpatrick as a person to know that; the principle itself does not afford clear direction. It may vaguely say that socially desirable ends are to be fostered and socially undesirable ones discouraged. But it certainly does not carry within it a definition of what is socially desirable and what is not.

And in this regard, we have one way in which Kilpatrick seems to come close to speaking for Dewey. For Dewey's principle seems to have much the same difficulty. It is true that he specifies *growth which leads to more growth* and shows how he considers such specification as encouraging the social and discouraging the antisocial or asocial. In this context, he explains how antisocial gangs, even of cutthroats and thieves, may find it necessary to practice honor among themselves but violate this principle in their dealings with groups other than their own. Hence, they will not (if they can help it) foster or permit "growth which leads to more growth" within or among groups other than their own or between themselves and other groups.

But American educational experience seems to have shown that this line of thought or reasoning has been somewhat too involved or complicated to constitute a directive clearly understandable even to the run of professors of education. We are aware, of course, that there are many matters—even fairly simple ones—which are not easily made clear to all Americans or even (we shall not say especially) to professors of education. But we do not feel that the principle of "education as growth," whether in the version of Kilpatrick or of Dewey, is clear enough or specific enough to serve its purpose in a democratic educational program.

A clear sense of direction is a vital need for America today, including the educational enterprise. That is why in our thirteenth

[15] *Ibid.*, p. 191.

chapter we have presented a principle different from that of education as growth and that only. That is why we find it needful to specify the educational direction not only as toward an *enhanced* (or broadened and deepened) outlook on the life of which we are a part, but also toward a *more harmonized* outlook and *heightened capacity to reconstruct outlooks independently*. It may be argued that this directive is more complicated than is Dewey's. We do not believe that it is really different from Dewey's, for it seems to catch the very spirit of what Dewey was actually doing every time he took pen in hand and addressed himself to the educational and philosophical world. But we present it in the hope that it may contribute to a clearer sense of educational direction than we have had or do now have; one which is thoroughly in keeping with the democratic aspiration.

In our final chapter, which immediately follows, we shall very sketchily indicate the major movements in educational theory during the first half of the twentieth century which have been designed to improve upon pre-twentieth-century theory and which have been distinctly influential in modifying practice. We close it with the observation that philosophic relativism with its key principle of interaction "still is seemingly a long way from being incorporated in current educational theory and practice," and that "as yet we have not really caught up with Dewey." It may therefore be reasonable to conclude that, although at mid century we may have come to a temporary lull in educational theory, the fruitful way which lies open to us is to go forward *with Dewey* into the atomic era of today and tomorrow by way of a relativistic, philosophical-scientific outlook which he, along with many others, pioneered and which is gaining momentum from day to day, from month to month, and from year to year.

SELECTED REFERENCES

Berkson, I. B., *The Ideal and the Community,* New York: Harper & Brothers, 1958, introduction and chaps. 1, 2.

  Exemplifies the practice of identifying Kilpatrick and Dewey.

Bode, Boyd H., *Modern Educational Theories,* New York: The Macmillan Company, 1927, chap. 7.

  One of the few publications wherein Kilpatrick's identity with pragmatic outlook is questioned.

Bode, Boyd H., *Progressive Education at the Crossroads,* New York: Newson and Company, 1938.

  A pragmatic critique of Progressivism.

Brameld, Theodore, *Patterns of Educational Philosophy*, Yonkers-on-Hudson, N.Y.: World Book Company, 1950, Part Two, Section One.

Exemplifies the practice of identifying Progressivism and Experimentalism.

Collings, Ellsworth, *An Experiment with a Project Curriculum*, New York: The Macmillan Company, 1924.

Collings, Ellsworth, and Wilson, M. O., *Psychology for Teachers*, New York: Charles Scribner's Sons, 1930.

Dewey, John, *Democracy and Education*, New York: The Macmillan Company, 1916, especially chaps. 10, 15.

Dewey, John, *Experience and Education*, New York: The Macmillan Company, 1938.

A critique of Progressivism.

Dewey, John, *Individuality and Experience*, originally in *The Journal of the Barnes Foundation*, January, 1926; later in the Twenty-Sixth Yearbook of the N.S.S.E. (1927), Part II.

An emphatic denial of the principle of refusal to guide pupil development.

Dewey, John, *Interest and Effort in Education*, Boston: Houghton Mifflin Company, 1913 (note the date).

Dewey, John, *The Reflex Arc Concept in Psychology* (1896), reprinted in Wayne Dennis, *Readings in the History of Psychology*, New York, Appleton-Century-Crofts, 1948, No. 41.

A configurational criticism long before the advent of gestalt psychology.

Dewey, John, *The School and Society*, Chicago: The University of Chicago Press, 1900, especially chap. 2.

As the publisher says, "lectures before an audience of parents and others interested in the University Elementary School, in the month of April of the year 1899." Hardly a case of letting "pupil purposing" take over.

Estrada, Josefa P., *A Critical Comparison of the Educational Philosophies of John Dewey and William Heard Kilpatrick*, unpublished doctoral dissertation in the School of Education at the University of Kansas, 1958, 320 pages.

An extensive, careful, and significant study.

Kilpatrick, W. H., *Foundations of Method*, New York: The Macmillan Company, 1926.

Kilpatrick, W. H., *A Reconstructed Theory of the Educative Process*, New York: Bureau of Publications, Teachers College, Columbia University, reprinted 1935 from an earlier article in *Teachers College Record*.

Kilpatrick, William Heard, *Philosophy of Education*, New York: The Macmillan Company, 1951.

Rousseau, Jean Jacques, *Emile* (the Foxley translation), New York: E. P. Dutton & Co., Inc., 1911, 1938.

Tenenbaum, Samuel, *William Heard Kilpatrick*, New York: Harper & Brothers, 1951.

CHAPTER 16

Present Status of Educational Theory in the United States

NOW that we have presented our case, we might indulge in a somewhat sophisticated glance over the course of American educational thought during the first part of the twentieth century, so as to give a bit of perspective to what we have had to say. At mid-century, educational theory in the United States seems to be in a state of suspended animation. Until the early 1940's, the whole twentieth century had witnessed a flood of energetically fostered proposals for improvement of the educational process. Since then, little of note seemingly has been added.

Economic depression, hot war on a global scale, and cold war can very well have served to put a damper on the optimistic, maybe carefree, trying of new ideas, sobering us to the point of thinking things over more carefully before putting them into experimental form, even giving encouragement to what educational personnel feel to be unwarranted and irresponsible "attacks" on an educational system which has grown to be a mammoth enterprise. Consequently, running somewhat of an inventory and indicating a bit of appraisal, even though without benefit of much detail, may provide a sort of background to highlight what has already been discussed.

At the turn of the century, Dewey was already on stage and Thorndike was standing, trained and ready, in the wings. But Dewey's relativistic field-theory was too innovational for that time. It was Thorndike's psychological connectionism and pedagogical specific-objectivism which caught the fancy of American educators and became the central attraction for the next quarter-century. Even though as early as 1896 Dewey had published a devastatingly derog-

atory criticism of the reflex-arc theory,[1] the connectionism of Thorndike and the behaviorism of Watson were yet to come and, in their
wake, the curricula based on Bobbitt's (or similar) activity analyses,[2] the work-sheet and workbook methodologies of Washburne[3] and
Morrison,[4] and the real nail-clincher, objective-type examinations.

It is small wonder, of course, that Thorndike should have gained
the upper hand, for his was an absolutistic pattern of thought
thoroughly in line with the science, philosophy, psychology, and
pedagogy of Newton and Locke. Even cursory examination of
Locke's "Some Thoughts Concerning Education" will reveal how
strikingly similar to his proposals was the specific-objectivist pattern of American education in the 1910's and 1920's. Locke did
not have the reflex-arc theory, provided later by Pavlov, but stra-
tegically and tactically his "ideas" worked in the same manner and
to the same ends as Thorndike's S-R bonds. Even William James, as
late as 1900 in his "Talks to Teachers," warmly espoused a strictly
reflex-arc explanation of, and program for, habit formation, in spite
of his copioneering with Dewey in the promulgation of pragmatic
philosophy.

Perhaps we should supply a bit more elaboration of what we have
seen fit to call "the specific-objectivist program" in American education. A human personality represents the functioning of the various S-R bonds which have been established in his nervous system.
Bonds become established through lowered synaptic resistances
caused by repeated passage of neural impulses over given pathways.
Learning is bond formation, evoked by repetitive drill. Learning
transfers when a later stimulative "situation" includes an "S" which
has already been bonded to a given "R" (the identical-elements
theory).

In order to determine what bonds should be established (curriculum), we must determine a child's "needs"—what he needs to learn
in order to "do better what he is going to do anyway" (Bobbitt,

[1] J. Dewey, "The Reflex Arc Concept in Psychology," in W. Dennis, *Readings in the History of Psychology*, New York: Appleton-Century-Crofts, 1948, pp. 355–365.

[2] F. Bobbitt, *How to Make a Curriculum*, Boston: Houghton Mifflin, 1924, chaps. 2, 7.

[3] C. Washburne, "A Program of Individualization," Twenty-Fourth Yearbook, National Society for the Study of Education, Part II, pp. 77–83, 257–272. Also Twenty-Sixth Yearbook, Part I, pp. 219–228.

[4] H. C. Morrison, "The Practice of Teaching in the Secondary School" (rev. ed.) Chicago: The University of Chicago Press, 1931, pp. 304–312.

Briggs). This was known as *activity analysis*—finding what people do in order to find what children should be taught. Clusters of suitably similar bonds could then be gathered together into "units," and "worksheets" or "guide-sheets" could be prepared so that each pupil could determine for himself what was expected of him and proceed, individually if that was the plan, to accomplish it. Finally, an easily administered and examined objective test was given the pupil, and, if performance was satisfactory, he would be credited with the unit and ready for the next one. In essence, this was the pattern of both Washburne's Winnetka plan and Morrison's unit plan.

Needless to say, this represented a neat program. Once materials were prepared, classes could proceed like clockwork and a teacher might well be able by 5 P.M. to lock the door on the job and be done with it until next morning. Of course, preparation of materials presented problems, but between 1925 and 1935 publishing houses helped materially and school mimeographs were kept busy. But the program was perhaps too neat. Pupils did not enjoy being handled that way and school personnel became sympathetic. The protestations of Progressivism against mental regimentation by teachers may also have played a part. Moreover, there are those nowadays who claim that the foregoing description does not do justice to the point of view, that it was never intended to be so narrowing in process or effect. To these we can only reply that a theory has to be taken for what it is, not for what we would like it to be. If it does not turn out to be satisfactory, then reject it and work out something better. This is what, with very few exceptions, such claimants have failed signally to do.

Almost exactly contemporaneous with connectionistic specific-objectivism has been the educational program popularly known as Progressivism or Progressive Education. Under leadership centered in the Progressive Education Association, this movement stressed emancipation of child life and child minds from the blighting effect of overly solicitous domination by adults. Freedom, creativity, self-realization were much-used words. Pupil purposing, pupil planning, pupil executing, and pupil judging was the recognized classroom pattern, as was also the expression, "project method."

Although it may seem that in the minds of American educators Progressivism is much more clearly identified than is specific-objectivism, further investigation may show that the Progressivist thought pattern is the less clearly defined or delineated of the two.

Ever since the middle 1910's when Kilpatrick first familiarized the American public with the term, "project method," the question has been asked and reasked, "Do you really mean to let pupils do what they want to do?" When the spokesmen for Progressivism were hard pushed, the answer was almost universally in the negative.[5] But the spring-back with the removal of pressure was usually prompt and dependable, so the question remained a bone of contention for a quarter-century. Even today the feeling persists that Progressivism means letting children do what they want to do.

It is not our purpose here to settle this question. We are trying to identify significant movements in the United States (since 1900) having to do with changes in educational theory. Although Progressivism never has enjoyed anywhere near so widespread adoption of its tenets and procedures by American schools as has specific-objectivism, its generalized impact on elementary education has surely been the greater, and this may even be true for secondary education. Even college and university practice has not come through unaffected. And, even though many of the real and imagined ills of American elementary and secondary education have been popularly attributed to the malign and debilitating influence of Progressivism, the informed and sober thought of today is probably agreed that the Progressive influence has been the most potent single force for betterment of American education that was exerted during the first half of the twentieth century.

During the early 1930's an attempt was made to counter the heavily individualistic emphasis of Progressivism. This was the build-a-new-social-order movement, championed by George S. Counts[6] and that doughty protagonist until then of "the child-centered school," Harold Rugg. Wishing to deal with "man thinking" as well as "man feeling," Rugg proposed the derivation of a curriculum by analyzing the ideas of "frontier thinkers"[7] and in this way he arrived at the content included in his hotly controversial series of social-studies textbooks for the intermediate grades. Support for these ideas was, seemingly, to be elicited through classroom instruction. With minor variations, this appears to be essentially

---

[5] W. H., Kilpatrick, "Foundations of Method," New York: The Macmillan Company, 1926, chap. 13.

[6] G. S. Counts, "Dare the Schools Build a New Social Order?" New York: John Day Company, 1932.

[7] H. O. Rugg, "Culture and Education in America," New York: Harcourt, Brace and Company, 1931, pp. 269–282.

what is today being proposed in Brameld's Reconstructionism.[8]

Brameld has indeed added facets of his own. "Social concensus" is to be the determinant of curriculum content, even of truth itself. Although he recognizes both the "problem method" and the "concensus method" of teaching, it is the latter on which he tends mainly to rely. The idea that education should constitute preparation for participation in politics but should not itself be promotive of one particular political view over another seems to be distinctly unsatisfactory to him. It seems to be at this point that he repudiates the Bode, and perhaps the Dewey, position.

A proposal which, if it meant anything, definitely tended to throw the weight of the schools on the side of building a *new* social order was bound to incur the active opposition of all forces in favor of the old. By them it was immediately branded as indoctrinative and opposed on such grounds, even though, as long as it was tending their way (as it long had and, for that matter, still does), they were very happy to use the schools indoctrinatively. It was at this point that Bode entered the controversy, opposing indoctrination whether for the old social order or for the new.[9] His reason for opposition was the democratic commitment that *all* views were to be equally heard but were equally obligated to stand the test of classroom study and criticism. His stand was not well understood at the time—even Dewey almost failed him once[10]—but, as time goes on, the thinking of American public-school educators may be rather surely and steadily, though slowly, coming to his position.

The last major development which we find as bearing upon fundamental educational theory—even though it should itself be classed perhaps merely as a device—is the core-curriculum movement, including its somewhat watered-down form which today carries the caption, "common learnings." Although almost exactly like Herbart's century-old principle of correlation and concentration and strikingly similar to Charles A. McMurry's consumer-type projects, the proposal was forcefully brought to the fore during the later 1930's by

---

[8] T. Brameld, "Patterns of Educational Philosophy" (Yonkers, N.Y.: World Book Co., 1950), Part 3, Sec. 2; "Ends and Means in Education: A Mid-Century Appraisal" New York: Harper & Brothers, 1950, chaps. 10, 13.

[9] B. H. Bode, *Social Frontier*, 5:38–40, Nov., 1938. This article was merely one in a series (not even the first) and, though addressed to Childs, was on the movement in general.

[10] J. Dewey, *Social Frontier*, 5:71–72, Dec., 1938. Bode replied to this article in the following issue of the journal.

Hollis L. Caswell.[11] The curriculum was to be integrated; subject-matter lines were to be ignored. Take problems where you find them; teach children, not subjects.

Since the last expression, "teach children, not subjects," somewhat antedated Caswell and was rather an offshoot of Progressivism, it serves to point up the ease with which Progressivism, after 1940, could fall into the core-curriculum movement, shifting emphasis as it did from child *interests* to child *needs*.[12] Moreover, specific-objectivist-trained personnel had matters essentially delivered into their hands because their "activity analyses" had long since pointed out the presumed "needs" of children. Thus, via core curriculum and common learnings, two streams merged into one, a Washburne could become twice president of the PEA, and even the name could be changed to the American Education Fellowship.

And this, except for final demise of the AEF, is about where matters stand today. But I am not sure that it represents an entirely satisfactory resolution of forces which are at work. The boat may not possess sufficient depth below waterline, nor sufficient ballast in terms of fundamental theory, to withstand much rocking. Points of vulnerability possibly are becoming highlighted as a result of today's "attacks on the schools," even though the base positions from which many of the attacks are made may themselves be yet more vulnerable.

If we are to make progress toward improved educational theory, we must first come clear on our assumptions regarding the social context in which education is to take place. In other words, in this country we must clarify our thinking about democracy and of what it means for keeping school. A seeming difficulty of our past thinking about democracy is that we have defined it in terms of product, not of process. This always involves a self-contradiction, because, if a people is to be sovereign, then whatever decisions it makes must stand (until changed by it) regardless of whether they be good, bad, or indifferent. It is the *process of reaching* decisions, rather than the decisions themselves (the product), which makes it democratic. This requires, in consequence, that classroom training must be such as always to give the process of reaching decisions preced-

[11] H. L. Caswell and D. Campbell, "Curriculum Development" (New York: American Book Co., 1935).

[12] B. H. Bode, "Progressive Education at the Crossroads" (New York: Newson, 1938), chap. 4.

ence over any given decision reached at any given time. This, of course, is the essence also of scientific procedure and of the scientific attitude.

Progress toward improved educational theory requires, second, that we come clear on our assumptions regarding the nature of learners and of learning. This requires open questioning of the outworn theory of connectionism and serious consideration of the various forms of field theory. It is high time that educational psychologists face up to the facts of life, especially to the fundamentally unscientific impact of the excuse, "Well, that's my theory, but you must not take it too seriously." Moreover, to define learning as "a change in behavior," as educational psychologists so frequently do, is to ignore what is more or less obvious to most—namely, that when a confronting situation changes or when a personal goal changes, a person's behavior will change and in neither case is learning involved. These and other psychological follies are part and parcel of commonly adopted educational theory today, and it is time to get our thinking straightened out. (See Chapters 2 and 3.)

This writer's experience has been that, once we get the foregoing assumptions clarified, the way tends to smooth out and the remainder of a thoroughgoing educational program is pretty much a matter of logical deduction. From preceding assumptions even an overall educational purpose can be deduced, as well as the further corollaries of the criteria for choice of subject matter and the criteria for choice of method. (See Chapter 13.)

In this résumé nothing has been said about religious education. The reason is simply that in the United States the pattern for religious education was established long ago and in it the twentieth century has witnessed no basic change. Even though efforts at evangelism have become less emphasized, perhaps, and buildings, equipment, and teaching procedures have undergone modernization, the fundamental purpose for maintaining a parochial or other sectarian school—promotion of the faith—still remains what it has been throughout our national and prenational life.

Finally, it may be asked why, except for our opening statement, Dewey has not been mentioned. The reason seems to be that as yet we have not really caught up with Dewey, and thus there is not much to report. It was Lockean realism which underlay the connectionistic, specific-objectivist movement spearheaded by Thorndike. In the heyday of Progressivism, it was Rousselian-

Froebelian thought which was mainly at work. In Froebel, as in William T. Harris, this was idealistic, and Dewey's repeated proddings were never successful in causing twentieth-century Progressives to sever themselves cleanly from the old moorings, from making of the child an absolute with which there was to be no tampering. In contrast, the build-a-new-social-order movement tended to treat the new social order as an absolute. The machinery for "continuous reconstruction" was not clearly written into the program, and this was the ground for Bode's rejection. Core curriculum appears to be a device rather than a philosophy and, like the lecture method, can equally well serve diverse faiths.

It seems defensible to say that Dewey's principle of "interaction" (later called transaction) is what differentiates pragmatic-relativistic thought from what has gone before. It is the key which unlocks most, if not all, of the either-or dilemmas in man's thinking: mind-body, determinism-free will, individual-social, labor-leisure, interest-discipline, etc.[13] My design for living is based not on what is "really out there," but on *what I take to be* out there. What comes to me— light rays, sound waves, tactile impressions—may be one thing; what I make of them may be quite another. But it is the latter on which I design by behavior, for good or for ill. This is relativism: in physical science, in psychology, in morals, in politics, in philosophy. And it still is seemingly a long way from being incorporated in currently adopted educational theory and practice.

[13] J. Dewey, "Democracy and Education," New York: The Macmillan Company, 1916. A majority of the book's chapters are devoted to resolutions of this kind.

Index

Absolutism, 65, 66–70, 71, 74, 183
  and appreciation, 126
  defined, 76–77, 132–133
  and perceptual interaction, 132
  in religion, 133, 137–138
  and values, 103–104, 109–110, 112, 115
Abstraction as insightful, 42
Activity analysis, 254, 257
Adequacy, as a scientific criterion, 87–88, 193, 207–208
  in life outlook, 208–209, 215–216, 250
Affective, the, 41, 124, 127
Agnosticism, 112, 134, 181
American Association of University Professors, 175
American Education Fellowship, 257
American Historical Association, 179
Anarchy, 112, 145, 149–150, 159, 240, 245 ff.
Anticipatory accuracy as a test of truth, 34, 42–43, 80, 100–101, 113, 114–115, 134, 194, 239
Appraisal, 217 ff.
Appreciation, dictionary definitions, 121–122
  as evaluation, 123 ff.
  meaning of, 120 ff.
  related to criticism, 126
  teaching, 121, 128 ff.
  -type subjects, 131
  without respect or approval, 126, 128–129
Aquinas, Thomas, 74
Archimedes, 52–53
Aristotle, 74
Art, defined, 64–65
Assumptions regarding human nature, 237
  good-active, 238, 245
  needed in educational theory, 257–258
  neutral-interactive, 239 ff.
Atheism, 134
Autocracy defined, 159
Avery, Torry C., 6, 7, 8

Axiology, 76
  absolutistic, 103–104, 109–110, 112
  relativistic, 103 ff.

Bacon, Francis, 85
"Bad indoctrination," 179
Bayles, Lewis A., 167
Behavior, as configurational, 38, 59, 197
  design of, 100
  prediction of, 34 ff.
  as purposive, 43
Belief, in God, 134–135
  vs. knowledge, 134–135
Bergmann, Gustave, 95
Bernard, Claud, 81
Bias in scientific truth-getting, 81
Boards of Education, powers of, 169
Bobbitt, Franklin, 253
Bode, Boyd H., 42, 49, 85, 156, 182, 184, 210, 211–212, 256, 259
Both-and outlook, the, 66
"Brain storming," 54
Brameld, Theodore, 182, 256
Breed, Frederick S., 181
Bridgeman, P. W., 85
"Build a new social order" movement, 179–180, 255–256, 259

Caswell, Hollis L., 257
Character education, absolutistic, 111–112
  democratic, 110 ff., 140 ff.
Child-centered school, the, 236
Cognitive, the, 41, 50, 124, 127
Collings, Ellsworth, 237, 244 ff.
Commandments as absolutes, the, 66–69
Commitment, 125, 129, 139
Common learnings, 256–257
Complete act of thought, the, 1, 85
Conant, James B., 88, 90
Configurational psychology, 65, 225
  See also Behavior; Insight
Confronting situation, defined, 38
  a factor in prediction of behavior, 38 ff.
  in transfer theory, 58–59

Consistency, index of, 222–223
quotient, 222–223, 232
Contextualism, 75
Control groups in educational experimentation, 5–6
Controversial issues, 212, 215
Core curriculum, 256–257, 259
Correspondence, test of, 239
Counts, George S., 179, 255
Creativity, development of, in schools, 54–55, 215
Criteria for, choice of method, 209
choice of subject matter, 206 ff.
criticism, 112
definitions, 148–149
democratic guidance, 130, 183–185, 206, 209, 215–216, 240
grading examination papers, 232
scientific conclusions, 87, 193, 207–208
Cromwell, Oliver, 135
Culture-epochs theory, 238
Curies, the, 213
Curriculum making, lay participation in, 172
Cybernetic "feedback," 51, 178

Deduction, 84
in scientific investigations, 86
Deductive reasoning, 81
Deism, 73
Democracy, 77, 138
amount of education required by, 185–187
and control of student attitudes or beliefs, 177–187
and control of student behavior, 168–171
defined, 110, 157, 183, 204
derivation of the definition, 147 ff.
educational purpose and program in, 204 ff.
and keeping school, 166 ff., 240, 257
power structure in, 167
process vs. product in, 152–153, 257
and relationships between the educational profession and the body politic, 171–177
religious instruction and character education in, 140 ff.
and teaching, 188
and teaching of appreciation, 129–131

Democracy—(*Continued*)
in test evaluation, 233, 234
as a way of life, 156
Determinacy, 97
Dewey, John, 37, 42, 47, 54, 75, 85, 104, 107 ff., 109, 136 ff., 156, 184, 199, 200, 201, 207, 209, 210, 213, 236 ff., 252, 253, 256, 258–259
Discipline, 104–105, 139, 168 ff.
Disharmonies in outlook, 209
Divinity, 138–139
Drill to be avoided, 51–52
Droll, Helen Andres, 2 ff.

Edison, Thomas A., 55
"Educating the whole child," 125
Educational philosophy defined, 63–64
Educational theory, present status of, 252 ff.
Einstein, Albert, 53, 66, 84, 85, 88, 91
Emotion in appreciation, 124 ff.
Emotional balance and stability, 125
Ends-means continuum, 108, 138
Enhancement of life outlook, testing for, 219 ff.
Enlightened self-interest, and democratic commitment, 105
as opposed to selfishness, 104–105
Epistemology, 75, 99
Equalitarianism, 154–155
Equality of opportunity in democracy, 163
Essay-type tests, 219, 227–231
reliability of, 233–235
Essence, 93
Eternal verity, 67, 180
Ethos, 116
Euclid, 66
Existence, assumption of independent, 78
Existents, ontological, axiological, and epistemological, 99
Experimentation, 80, 81, 85, 192
Experimentalism, 75–76

Fact, 195, 200
Feedback, 51, 178
Feeling tone, 127
contrasted with insight, 41
Field theory, 74
Finite mind, 70
Fixed-habit theory, 49
Flexible-habit theory, 49

Frame of reference, 180
Free invention, Einstein's principle of, 53
Freedom, democracy as, 149
  of the press, 168
Froebel, J. F., 238
Frontier thinkers, 180, 255

Galileo, 71
Generalization, 194
  in transfer, 58, 60
Gestalt psychology, 46
Ghandi, 133
Goal, defined, 38
  a factor in appreciation, 123
  a factor in prediction of behavior, 38 ff.
  a factor in transfer, 57–58, 59
Goal-insight theory, defined, 45
Grading examination papers, 226–230, 231–232
Greene, Theodore W., 180–181
Group process or group dynamics in teaching, 144–145
"Growth which leads to more growth," 210, 248–249

Habit in relation to repetition, 38 ff.
Habit-level behavior, 35 ff., 60, 188
  as a creative process, 49
Harmony, in life outlook, 208–209, 210 ff., 215–216, 250
  testing for, 222–223, 232
  as a scientific criterion, 87–88, 193, 201, 207–208
Harris, William T., 259
Herbart, J. F., 256
Historical development in curriculum planning, 201
History, place of, in development of insight, 53–54
Horne, Herman H., 181
Hullfish, H. Gordon, 49
Hypotheses, 71–72, 80, 86, 88, 90–91, 191–192

Idea, 69
Idealism, 65, 73–74, 93
  defined, 69–70
Identical-elements theory, 253
Inadequacies in outlook, 209–210
Inalienable rights, 157
Indeterminacy, 97
Individual differences, teaching designed to care for, 16–17, 19, 21

Individuality, respect for, in democracy, 150–152
Indoctrination, 121, 129, 141 ff., 178 ff., 188, 205, 206, 215, 240, 256
Induction, defined, 85
  not characteristic of modern science, 83 ff.
  in teaching, 88–89
Infinite mind, 70
Insight, as configurational, 78
  defined, 40–43, 78–79
  factor in prediction of behavior, a, 38 ff.
  formation of, 48 ff., 52–54, 201
  as intuitive, 53, 59
  learning as development of, 46 ff., 61, 248
  place of, in appreciation, 123 ff., 127, 128
  in transfer, 59–60
  as unitary, 47–48
Instrumentalism, 75
Intellectual creation, 48
Intellectual independence, 205–206
Intelligence defined, 101
Interaction, 42–43, 47, 100, 115, 132, 139, 239 ff., 250, 259
Interest, 200
Intra-personal conflict, 212, 213–214
Intuition, 70, 81
Intuitive, the, 53, 59
Issues (controversial), 212, 215

James, William, 37, 47, 75, 78, 253
Jent, H. Clay, 163
Johnston, Laura C., 6–11
Jurisdiction, 110, 156, 162, 163–164, 168 ff., 183, 185

Kekule, 53
Kelley, Earl C., 43, 47
Kilpatrick, William H., 182, 237 ff., 255
Kinesthetic insight, 42
Koehler, Wolfgang, 48
Koffka, Kurt, 48

Law, natural, 97
  as universal, 71, 93
Laws of learning, 241, 247
"Learn to do by doing," 248
  and Dewey, 37, 52
Learning, as "change in behavior," 45, 258

Learning—(*Continued*)
  as change in or development of insight, 46 ff.
  as conditioning, 49–50
  as gradual, 49–51
  Kilpatrick's theory of, 247–248
  nature of, 45 ff.
Least Action, principle of, discussed, 39 ff.
  stated, 38, 43, 59–60
Lieberman, Myron J., 167, 172
Lincoln, 163
Line-of-command principle, 173–177
Lobatshevski, 66
Locke, John, 74, 132, 238–239, 253, 258
Logical vs. psychological, 198–201
Logical break-point, 206, 209
Logical positivism, 95
Lying, 67–68

McMurry, Charles A., 256
Majority rule in democracy, 154
Meaning, 194
Means-ends justifications, 117
Memory-level teaching, 55
Memory-level examinations, 60, 205, 219–221, 235
Mental health, 212–213
Minority rights in democracy, 158, 162–163, 177, 184
Moral and spiritual values, 141 ff.
Mores, 116
Morrison, Henry C., 55–56, 195, 221, 253–254

Negative education, 238
Newlon, Jesse, 179, 181–182
Newton, Isaac, 52–53, 71–73, 85, 88, 90, 132, 213, 253
Newtonian conception, 66, 71
Non-theism, 136 ff.

Objective relativism, 76, 94
Objective-type tests, 219–221, 225–227, 228
Observation, truth by, 71, 81
Ontology, 76, 93 ff., 113
Open-book testing, 220, 227–229
Order, independent natural, 96–99, 113
Outlook on life, 206–216, 250

Paine, Thomas, 73
Parochial-school pattern for religious instruction, 141

Pasteur, 53
Pavlov, J. P., 253
Peirce, Charles Sanders, 75, 149
Permissivism, 181, 236 ff.
Philosophy defined, 63–64
Pittenger, B. F., 180
Plato, 73, 74
Politics vs. education, 182
Practice in learning, nature of, 51–52
Pragmatism, 65 ff., 69, 75
  on truth getting, 78–81
  and absolutes, 77–78
Problem, defined, 53, 86, 188–189, 191, 197
  solving, 189 ff., 200–201
Professional autonomy, 171 ff.
Professional incompetence, criteria for judging, 173, 176
Program, American Educational, 209 ff.
  stated, 209
Progressive Education Association, 236, 254
Progressivism (Progressive Education), 236 ff., 254 ff.
Project method, 236, 237, 254
Propaganda, 181–182
Psychological vs. the logical, the, 198–201
Pupil purposing, 236–245, 254
Pupil-teacher planning, 200
Purpose, American Educational, 203–209
  stated, 208

Reader, Edna C. L., 22–29
Realism, 65, 73–74, 85, 93–94, 97, 99
  defined, 70
Reality, relativistic definition of, 94–95, 99
Reasonable doubt, 208
Recitation, 194
"Reconstruction of experience," 209
Reflection-level testing, 223–235
Reflective behavior as creative, 49
Reflective teaching, 188 ff.
  and adequacy and harmony of outlook, 215–216
  comparative gains by pupils of varying capacities, 18–19, 21
  defined or described, 1, 2, 28, 30, 52, 189–193
  employed with spelling and arithmetic, 19–20

Reflective teaching—(*Continued*)
  experiments with, 1–33
    conclusions about, 28–33
    in a conventional school, 31–32
  holding power of achievements gained
    through, 27
  in kindergarten, 110–111
  logically required by democracy, 205,
    209
  Morrison plan not, 55–56
  promotion of creativity, 54
  year-to-year improvement in, 22, 31
Reflex-arc concept, 241, 253
Relationalism, 75
Relative absolute, 77
Relative fixity, 77
Relativism, 74, 76, 94, 112, 113, 213,
  225, 246–247, 250, 259
Relativistic axiology and humility, 113–
  114
Relativistic religion, 132 ff.
Relativistic thought, 68, 213
Relativistic value theory, 103 ff.
Relativity, 65, 66
Religion, non-theistic, 136 ff.
  relativistic, 132 ff.
Religious education, 258
Religious instruction in the schools,
  139 ff.
Revelation, truth by, 70, 73, 133
Riemannian geometry, 66
Roberts, Lawson M., 6–7
Rousseau, J. J., 238, 245
Rugg, Harold, 178–179, 255

Sailer, Roy L., 6–7, 11–14
School discipline, 168 ff.
Science, Baconian-Newtonian, 97
  defined, 64
  as inductive, 83 ff.
  as inductive-deductive, 92
  kinship with morality, 114 ff.
  laboratory work as inductive, 88–89
    as inductive-deductive, 90
  Newtonian method of, 85
Scientific method, criteria employed in,
  87, 93, 207–208
Scientific-reflective thinking, 189
  contrasted with nonscientific reflective
    studies, 87, 192–193, 209
  described, 86 ff.
Self and non-self, 35, 59, 239
Sheer contemplation, 70

Solipsism, 42, 47, 74, 94, 100, 139
Specific-objectivist program, 253–254,
  257, 258
Spelling, teaching of, 195–197
S-R bonds, 253
Student wishes, democratic approach to,
  169–171
Superhumanity, 138–139

Tabula rasa, 239
Teaching, democratic, *see* Democracy and
  teaching
  for development of insight, reflective
    or nonreflective, 55–56
  memory-level, 193–194
  non-reflective, 193–198
  reflective, *see* Reflective teaching
  understanding-level, 194–198
Testing, open-book, 220, 227–229
Testing program, functions of a, 218–
  219
Theism, 134
Theoretical as practical, the, 194–195
Thinking, non-reflective, 188
  reflective, 188 ff.
Thomism, 74
Thorndike, Edward L., 48–49, 240–241,
  243, 247, 252–253, 258
Thought, the complete act of, 1, 85
Thought guidance without thought con-
  trol, 145, 177 ff.
Transaction, 42–43, 47, 115
Transfer of training, 195, 219, 226
  meaning for teaching, 60–61
  a theory of, 56 ff.
  the theory stated, 58, 59
Transmutation of elements, 135
Trefz, Ida R., 14–22
Truth, defined pragmatically, 80, 113
  nature of, 69 ff.
Tyler, Ralph W., 225

Ultimate reality, 64, 69, 79, 93, 94–95,
  97
Understanding-level teaching, 55–56,
  194–198
Understanding-level testing, 194, 219–
  221, 225
Unfoldment, education as, 238
Unit method of teaching, 55–56
U.S. Chamber of Commerce, 178–179
Universal order, 96–99

Validity, 218, 233
Valuation vs. value, 106 ff.
Value(s), arbitrariness of, 106 ff., 109
    cosmic, 103–104, 109–110, 112, 115
    hierarchy of, 103
    instrumental vs. intrinsic or consum-
        matory, 106 ff., 115–118, 203–204
    relativistic character of intrinsic, 108–
        109
    verifiability of, 107 ff., 115 ff.
Value theory, 75, 103 ff., 203–204
    desired vs. the desirable, the, 105–
        106, 109, 227
    "end in view," 109
Value system(s), 41, 123–124
    development of, 116–117, 141 ff.,
        203–204

Voltaire, 179
Voting as democratic necessity, 157–158

Walsh, J. L., 88, 91
Washburne, Carleton W., 253–254, 257
Watson, John B., 253
Wertheimer, Max, 46, 88
Wheeler, Raymond H., 38, 39, 197
Wild, John, 180
Wilson, M. O., 244–245
Wordsworth, 237
"Workshop way of learning," 144–145
World of effect, 47, 210
World of insight, 47, 210
Wrightstone, J. Wayne, 13–14